CONTENTS

Cruising
through
CAREGIVING

Reducing *the* Stress *of*
Caring *for* Your Loved One

Jennifer L. FitzPatrick, MSW, CSP

GREENLEAF
BOOK GROUP PRESS

This book is intended as a reference volume only, not as a medical manual. The information provided here is intended to help you make informed decisions about you and your loved one's health. It is not intended as a substitute for any treatment your doctor has provided. If you suspect you or someone you are caring for has a medical problem, you should seek competent medical help. You should not begin any new health regimen without first consulting a medical professional.

Published by Greenleaf Book Group Press
Austin, Texas
www.gbgpress.com

Copyright ©2016 Jennifer L. FitzPatrick

Distributed by Greenleaf Book Group

For ordering information or special discounts for bulk purchases, please contact Greenleaf Book Group at PO Box 91869, Austin, TX 78709, 512.891.6100.

Design and composition by Greenleaf Book Group
Cover design by Greenleaf Book Group
Cover images © Flat_Enot and © Sundra. Used under license from Shutterstock.com.

Cataloging-in-Publication Data is available.

Print ISBN: 978-1-62634-319-1

eBook ISBN: 978-1-62634-320-7

Part of the Tree Neutral® program, which offsets the number of trees consumed in the production and printing of this book by taking proactive steps, such as planting trees in direct proportion to the number of trees used: www.treeneutral.com

Printed in the United States of America on acid-free paper

20 21 22 23 24 25   12 11 10 9 8 7 6 5 4 3

First Edition

"Caregiving is truly the most difficult job you will ever take on. Whether you are new to caregiving or an exhausted caregiver wondering what you got yourself into, read this book. *Cruising through Caregiving* is written as an extended conversation between a caregiver and a wise and experienced senior care expert. Ms. FitzPatrick guides you through a discussion of concerns common to all caregivers while encouraging you to take *care of yourself*. She takes a unique approach as she suggests that caregivers consider their role as a choice and not a mandate. This perspective allows the reader to reframe or rethink their caregiving role in a way that reduces guilt and anxiety and focuses on what is best for their loved one and how that can be accomplished. This book encourages you to identify your caregiving style, whether you live with a loved one, live across the country, or somewhere in-between, and then, identify community services and persons who can join with you in providing care for your loved one. Ms. FitzPatrick describes the challenges faced by many caregivers negotiating unfamiliar senior services, financial resources, difficult parent-adult-child relationships, absent family members, and health care services. She enlists a crew of experienced professionals in senior care to help her provide a down-to-earth exploration of how to be a caregiver without losing yourself in the process. The narrative is written in such a way that it feels like you are sitting in the room, talking through the concerns that every caregiver faces."

—**Sandra S. Swantek**, MD, FAPA, Chief, Geriatric Psychiatry, Rush University Medical Center, Chicago, Illinois

"I *love* this book as it speaks directly to my current situation of caring for my eighty-six-year-old mother, whom I adore. Jennifer let me laugh at myself (for my martyrdom), yet she also gave me concrete suggestions on how to set boundaries without feeling guilty (something I struggle with every day). I highly recommend this book for any adult child caring for an aging parent (while also trying to care for yourself). The book is divided into easy-to-digest chapters that can be read one at a time, as needed. I found this approach very helpful, as things seem to change rapidly with my mom (and I need to adjust my approach). *Cruising through Caregiving* is easy to navigate and gets you great information quickly and efficiently."

—**Valerie M. Grubb**, Operations Consultant and Trainer, Val Grubb & Associates, Ltd., Author of *Planes, Canes, and Automobiles: Connecting with Your Aging Parents through Travel* (Greenleaf Book Group, October 2015)

"In my life care planning law practice, my elder care coordinator and I work with many families struggling with the challenges of caregiving. As we focus on the elders who need care, we work hard to ensure that their families have access to the tools and resources they need. But until *Cruising through Caregiving*, we have not had a framework for helping the caregivers understand that they have a right to include their own needs in the choices that are made. Now, I find it natural to use Ms. FitzPatrick's terminology when I discuss those options with our clients and their families. I strongly recommend this book not only to families dealing with the stress of caregiving, but also to the professionals who seek to help them."

—**Marsha Goodman**, CELA, President,
Life Care Planning Law Firms Association

"When I first saw the book title, I mistakenly thought that 'cruising' meant 'easy' as in coasting or drifting! Instead, the author creatively draws parallels to a boat cruising through waves of ups and downs—sometimes through calm waters, at other times in turbulent ones, and occasionally anchored in periods of relative stability. She ingeniously utilizes boating symbols—such as lifejackets for tips and resources, or the life ring for vital information—throughout the book. It is an engaging and informative read for caregivers where they can pick and choose chapters relevant to them, and return to a specific chapter when they hit a stormy period and need to strengthen their cruising techniques."

—**Nancy R. Hooyman**, PhD, Professor of Gerontology, University of
Washington School of Social Work, and author of *Social Gerontology*

"Quite often, caregivers are just putting one foot in front of the other, doing the best they can. But they can easily find themselves off-balance in their lives, and this can affect their physical and mental health. Jennifer FitzPatrick's book encourages caregivers to assess their own strengths and weaknesses. Am I doing too much? Do I have enough support on my team? Should I have Mother move into my house? The author provides caregivers with excellent perspectives, tips, and resources to help them regain their footing. I highly recommend this insightful book to all caregivers as this is one of the most difficult jobs to traverse."

—**Barbara Kane**, MSW, LCSW-C, Co-Author, *Coping with Your Difficult Older Parent: A Guide for Stressed-Out Children*; Founder, Aging Network Services

"What makes this book invaluable is Jen's expertise on caregiver stress. It's one thing to get a handle on the obvious—Will the money run out? Who helps me? Is aging-in-place a good idea?—and another to be open-minded about the emotional challenges we face in the eldercare process. There are many ways to be a good caregiver; but perhaps the greatest skill of all is the willingness to change course and correct mistakes. This book shows you how."

—**Joy Loverde,** Author of *The Complete Eldercare Planner*
and *Who Will Take Care of Me When I Am Old?*

"Caring for a loved one is a challenge—and most people are unprepared for the myriad of complex issues they will face. *Cruising through Caregiving* is a must-read for any caregiver. This informative book not only offers advice for handling the tough emotions, but also provides solid guidance for medical, financial, housing and dementia care. Caregivers who read this book will be empowered to better manage the pressures that are common to all caregivers."

—**Dianne C. McGraw,** LCSW, CMC, President,
Aging Life Care Association (ACLA)

"*Cruising through Caregiving: Reducing the Stress of Caring for Your Loved One* is a thoughtfully-written 'user's guide' for an ever-growing phenomenon in our developed society: caregiving for our frail elders. As a palliative and geriatric provider, I envision this book filling a need for many of our patients and their loved ones. Thoroughly researched and referenced, *Cruising* addresses many of the questions that go unanswered during the journey through advanced age and function and memory loss, from how to best utilize one's providers to knowing when hospice is appropriate. By linking the metaphor of a ship's journey with carefully crafted key points or 'life rings,' section summaries, and real-life examples, the author empowers caregivers and patients to safely navigate their course together."

—**Miguel Paniagua,** MD, FACP, Adjunct Associate Professor, Palliative Care,
the Perelman School of Medicine, University of Pennsylvania

"In all my years working with caregivers, I have never met a 'non-stressed' caregiver. Ms. FitzPatrick adeptly illustrates the varying roles and responsibilities of a caregiver. She provides practical strategies and valuable resources that can potentially reduce stress while maximizing quality care for your loved one."

—**Mary Belanich,** MA, Senior Health Manager, Virginia Hospital Center

"Raising children that you prepared for and loved more than anything in this world is a walk in the park compared to caring for an adult loved one that may get dropped in your lap without any warning. This book offers tools to assess your role and your environment, and is a great guide that helps you understand that your doubt and questions about your abilities, anger, frustration and sense of guilt, are all normal."

—**Pany Nazari,** PT, BCB-PMD,
Senior Physical Therapist, Virginia Hospital Center

"This book would be very helpful to any family trying to deal with disability and death of a loved one. Many of the topics I discuss with clients every day are thoroughly discussed with appropriate resources provided. The emphasis on pre-planning is excellent!"

—**Kelly A. Thompson, Esq.,** Thompson Wildhack PLC; Chair,
Virginia Bar Association, Elder Law & Special Needs Section

This book is dedicated to the memory of my grandparents, Hank Lubaczewski Sr. and Helen Lubaczewski. I hit the jackpot when it came to grandparents. Their love and support influenced (and continue to influence) every aspect of my life and work.

A WORD TO HELP YOU CHART YOUR COURSE

The world's most supportive grandparents, along with a high school job in a nursing home, inspired me to focus my life on working with and on behalf of older adults. Because I experienced a powerful, enduring bond with my grandparents, I grew up expecting to enjoy older people. As a teenager, the job and the time I spent at the nursing home reinforced the belief that I would continue to enjoy the company of the majority of older people. But what I also discovered was that many of the older people receiving nursing home services were not enjoying their lives, and their family members didn't always look forward to visiting them. Eventually, after those early experiences, I knew my life's goal was going to be to help older adults and the families who were helping to care for them live happier lives.

In over twenty years of managing senior service programs and coaching and educating older adults and their families, I saw that caregiving often impacted families in powerful ways; sometimes for the better and sometimes not. Some families grew closer; others became estranged. Some families stepped up to the challenge but created healthy boundaries with their older loved ones; some martyred themselves and became angry and bitter toward their older loved one and the rest of the family. Some caregivers tried to do everything themselves and literally made themselves sick; others embraced help and were able to still find humor during the darkest, most stressful days. The way we handle the stress associated with caring for an older loved one influences our health, finances, careers, and perhaps most importantly—our relationships with family and friends.

Currently, I am a speaker and consultant on caregiving and generational issues, and an adjunct instructor of gerontology at two colleges (including

Johns Hopkins University). In addition to my professional experience, I have also personally served at different times as a caregiver for both my grandparents and my grandmother-in-law. Those personal caregiving experiences further increased my commitment to helping other caregivers. After all, even though I knew better, I found myself making many of the mistakes I caution families about and have helped them fix. Over the years, I have observed other well-respected leaders in the senior care field talking similarly about their personal caregiving experiences. They knew what to do but didn't always do it. If it's that hard for those of us who live and breathe this industry, I can only imagine how hard it is for everyone else.

When we feel like we have control, we feel less stress. My goal in writing this book is to make you feel more powerful and to let you know you have lots of options. You have power as a caregiver—you don't have to just let things happen to you. In recognizing and harnessing this power, you are going to experience less stress, suffer fewer negative consequences of that stress, and in turn, your older loved one is going to have a better quality of life.

There are so many ways to be a responsible, loving caregiver for an older loved one. The landscape for senior care options has changed so much since I was a sixteen-year-old working in the nursing home. During that time, many people seemed to think there were two options: put your mother in a nursing home and be a bad daughter; or take care of her at home for the next ten years and be a martyr. A lot of people still think there are only two choices, but in reality there are so many options that fall somewhere in the middle. There are resources for all budgets that can help caregivers of older loved ones. It's just a matter of knowing how to find them and when to figure out how to apply them to your caregiving situation.

It is possible to be a loving, responsible caregiver and not give up your entire life. Of the thousands of caregivers I have worked with, I have witnessed firsthand many who are doing a great job but still work, go on vacation, and spend time with friends. Caregivers don't have to always be exhausted, harried, or suffering psychological and physical symptoms of caregiver burnout.

Personal caregiving for an older loved one is
challenging for every single caregiver.

So many times I have heard caregivers try to dismiss the suggestion that they can have a less stressful caregiving experience. They say things like "I don't have a lot of money" or "I don't have a big family; it's just me" to explain why they can't have a life outside of caregiving. But it doesn't matter. While plenty of money and a big family can be advantages for caregivers, I have seen plenty of caregivers with those so-called advantages who are burned out and have no life outside of caregiving. I have also observed caregivers who have very little family helping and very few financial resources, and they still manage to have a life outside of caregiving. It really is all about opening your mind to the possibility that there are many ways to be a good caregiver. There are dozens, possibly even hundreds of ways to accomplish caregiving while minimizing your stress level.

Personal caregiving for an older loved one is challenging for every single caregiver. It doesn't matter if you already have experience like the longtime geriatric nurse now taking care of her own mother or if you're someone who knows nothing about senior care—an accountant, an engineer, or a cashier at the grocery store. Like it or not, caregiving will pretty much impact everyone at some point.

I wrote this book because I want the more than forty million American caregivers of older and disabled adults to know that they have power over how their caregiving experience goes. Caregiving is not a one-size-fits-all approach. I want them to know that however it's going so far, if they want to, they can reduce their stress, improve their life, and the life of their older loved one while saving money, energy, and time.

I also wrote this book because I wanted caregivers to understand the insider perspective. While not even an insider is a perfect caregiver, it is possible to be an effective caregiver and a less stressed-out one for sure. If you apply the strategies discussed in this book, caregiving for your older loved one can be less stressful and maybe even a little more enjoyable.

As a gerontologist and educator, I have had plenty of experience with pointing caregivers in the right direction and even seeing them through the entire process. But I didn't want to write this book from only my perspective. I wanted to find some of the most thoughtful opinions in the senior care field and offer them to you for your consideration and use. Drawing from a compilation of different professional perspectives, this book will provide caregivers with a variety of strategies to apply to their individual situations.

I knew this would be an interesting project for me, because I would be spending time with professionals I really respected and learning more about their beliefs and philosophies about successful caregiving. But I was not expecting how much my views would be influenced by these extraordinary interviewees. I personally have learned so much from conducting the interviews, and I know the advice that I now give families has been significantly enhanced. I knew some of the professionals featured in this book personally prior to the interviews; others I had met only a few times. But even people I know intimately surprised me with some of their insights. I know their views will help you. (For more information about the interviewees, please see the "Meet the Experts" appendix at the back of the book.)

You don't have to read the chapters in order. If money is no object, you probably can skip chapter 10. If you come from a most rare family where everyone equally pitches in, maybe you don't need to read chapter 8. But you may want to read the book from cover to cover if you are very stressed-out, feeling powerless, or are just starting out on your caregiving journey.

I have long believed that the caregiving experience shares parallels with boating. There are beautiful days on the water, and there are rough ones. Living on the Chesapeake Bay as I do, I also know that weather can change on a dime. There are *always* issues with maintaining and operating a boat: little hassles and—of course—big emergencies. Boating also comes more naturally to some people than to others—as does caregiving.

Throughout *Cruising through Caregiving*, I use boating imagery to illustrate different points in caregiving. For example, every captain dreads and wants to prevent a crew member or passenger going overboard. I discuss caregiving mistakes (going overboard) and how to avoid and fix them by making a course correction. You will also see an icon for Life Jackets, which points you to tips and resources. The Life Ring icon calls your attention to especially important information. Please also note that I use both the pronouns he and she throughout the book when referring to caregivers, older loved ones, and professionals.

The first chapter helps you identify what type of caregiver you are. After that, each chapter focuses on a theme that helps you reduce stress over the course of your caregiving journey.

Family and friend caregivers have one of the most important and stressful unpaid jobs in the world. You deserve to have a life outside of caregiving for your older loved one. You also deserve to come out of the caregiving experience emotionally, physically, and financially healthy. With more than four hundred years of collective senior care advice, this book helps you save money, energy, and time, so you can have an improved caregiving experience. In addition to the tips and best practices you'll read, I include vignettes of caregivers who may resemble you and your situation. These stories are composites of many families I have worked with, and I offer them in the hope that they will help you resolve stressful situations so you can cruise through caregiving. Turn the page to begin reducing the stress of your caregiving voyage today by first understanding why you're a caregiver and what type you are.

One

CAREGIVING 101

I f you picked up this book, it's likely you are a caregiver, even if you don't already think of yourself as one. After all, most people don't read books like this for fun. And unfortunately, most people don't read books like this ahead of time. (If you are reading this book just to plan ahead for if or when you become a caregiver, that's great, and you will be better prepared when the time comes.) This chapter explores the role of a caregiver and helps you better understand the answers to the following questions:

- What do the terms *caregiving* and *caregiver* mean?

- What are the three different types of caregivers?

- What type of caregiver are you?

- Why is a caregiving team, or "crew," better than a solo caregiver?

- Why do we become caregivers?

- Why do some of us have a more natural aptitude for caregiving than others do?

What Exactly Is Caregiving?

Before we go any further, we need to define caregiving and clear up why there is sometimes confusion as to whether someone is a caregiver or not. I've talked with countless people, for example, who clearly fit the caregiver profile but don't identify themselves as such.

When many people hear the term *caregiving*, they frequently think of basic practical tasks like bathing or feeding an older loved one. But this term is very broad and encompasses so many different types of responsibilities. In addition to helping with activities of daily living (also known as ADLs) like bathing or eating, caregiving actually encompasses all kinds of duties. Here are some examples:

- Helping with instrumental activities of daily living (also known as IADLs), such as grocery shopping and paying bills or getting your older loved one to a doctor's appointment or church/synagogue

- Helping the older loved one with decision-making tasks

- Coordinating and supervising services brought into the home like home care aides, professional organizers, house cleaners, repair persons, and life alert programs

- Interviewing and hiring professional services such as money managers and elder law attorneys

- Arranging and participating in tours of nursing homes and/or assisted living communities and making decisions about them

- Managing finances, insurance, and benefits applications

- Paying out-of-pocket for necessities or luxuries for the older loved one that enhance quality of life (but that the older loved one can't afford or does not want to pay for)

- Providing social or emotional support opportunities for the older loved one

Many times people don't consider themselves a caregiver unless they live with their older loved one. While many caregivers do live in the same residence with the persons they are caring for, many more do not. Some caregivers live across the country from their older loved one, so geography is not the determining factor. It doesn't matter where you live; if you are helping out with one of the tasks mentioned previously, you likely can call yourself a caregiver. Further, if you are providing support to someone who is doing the tasks mentioned previously, you are also a caregiver, just a different type.

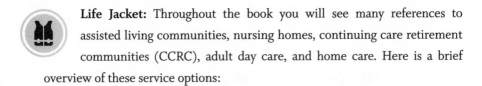 **Life Jacket:** Throughout the book you will see many references to assisted living communities, nursing homes, continuing care retirement communities (CCRC), adult day care, and home care. Here is a brief overview of these service options:

- **Adult day care** is a supervised place where older loved ones socialize and have meals (often with medical support) while their caregiving crews work (or just take a break).

- **Assisted living** offers residential services to people who are more independent than those who need nursing home care.

- **CCRCs** are generally communities you pay an entrance fee to move into, and they offer an independent living section, assisted living, and nursing home—the major benefit is typically that you are guaranteed care for the rest of your life at that location.

- **Home care** commonly offers help with ADLs and IADLs to keep older loved ones in the private home. Home care is frequently confused with *home health care* services. Home care is typically a long- or short-term private pay service provided by non-degreed professionals like home care aides.

- **Home health care** is typically a short-term service that is provided by degreed professionals like physical therapists and nurses. Medicare and other insurance often cover home health care while home care is almost exclusively private pay.

- **Nursing homes** typically provide short-term rehab (e.g., for a broken hip) and also offer long-term residential services for people who can't manage their activities of daily living (ADL) like bathing and dressing and instrumental activities of daily living (IADL) like grocery shopping and preparing meals.

What Type of Caregiver Are You?

So, if you aren't sure whether you are a caregiver or not, let's figure that out right now. It's highly likely that most readers will fall into one of three categories: primary, secondary, or tertiary. What caregiver role type best describes you?

Primary Caregiver

A *primary* caregiver is the main person coordinating, planning, and/or providing care for the senior. In other words, the primary caregiver is the person in charge, the organizer, who also often does the bulk of the caregiving tasks. Think of the primary caregiver as the captain of a ship.

As I mentioned previously, many people have the idea that if someone is the primary caregiver it means the elderly loved one has moved in with her or she has moved in with the older loved one. Primary caregiving can involve living with the older loved one, but living with someone does not necessarily mean you are a primary caregiver. A primary caregiver may be the key person handling things from some distance (from a single mile to thousands of miles).

There is almost always one individual who functions as the primary caregiver. Seldom are there multiple primary caregivers; it does happen, but very rarely. Perhaps two sisters live close to their father and truly split the duties equally. But even then, in almost all cases one does a little more and is the true primary caregiver. As boaters will tell you, there can only be one captain, and it is mostly the same in caregiving situations.

During the course of this chapter, I will use the Brady family to illustrate the different types of caregivers and their possible duties. Let's meet Susan, the primary caregiver.

At seventy-three years old, Susan Brady is the primary caregiver for her seventy-four-year-old husband, Bill Brady, who had a stroke. She hires the home care aides, coordinates his doctor's appointments, and manages all the bills. She also provides a great deal of hands-on care like helping Bill dress and shave.

It is not surprising that Susan, being the wife of a disabled older man with whom she lives, is the primary caregiver. Statistically and historically speaking, women are most often in the primary caregiving role. Daughters, daughters-in-law, wives, nieces, granddaughters, female friends, and neighbors are primary caregivers far more often than their male counterparts are. But many male spouses, sons, and grandsons do take on this role as well. Often it is pretty obvious who in the family will take on the primary caregiving role when the need arises, but sometimes it's surprising to see who rises to the occasion to assume this important role.

While a primary caregiver like Susan often performs many of the direct personal care tasks like helping Bill bathe and dress, ideally she would delegate many of those responsibilities. To avoid the risk of making you seasick by using another boating reference, let's use a few different analogies in this chapter. Let's think of a primary caregiver as the general manager of a hotel. She is ultimately in charge of everything but arranges or delegates much of the work.

A hotel's general manager is typically capable of doing many of the functions that keep a hotel running successfully. But does the hotel manager typically make the coffee you are drinking at breakfast? Does the manager clean your room? Does the manager provide your wake-up call in the morning? Hopefully not. While a general manager may pitch in sometimes with these duties, the hotel is running best when these duties are assigned to others. Typically, the restaurant staff prepare the coffee. Most likely, the housekeeping staff clean your room. Often your wake-up call comes courtesy of an automated wake-up call system that the manager has arranged for hotel guests. An efficient hotel general manager focuses on the big picture, recruits the best people to oversee and work in the different hotel departments, and pitches in during overly busy or emergency situations.

Think about it for a minute. Would you have confidence staying at a hotel where the general manager was doing everything? Or would you feel better if there were lots of hands on deck pulling together as a team to make your stay at the hotel as comfortable as possible? Most of us prefer a competent team working at the hotel rather than relying solely on the general manager. Actually, if we saw a general manager cleaning our rooms, serving coffee, and personally providing the wake-up call, we would think something was very wrong.

The primary caregiver should consider herself the general manager of the older loved one's care. That's why she needs secondary and tertiary caregivers to back her up. Just as we would prefer a general manager *not* to be doing all the tasks at a hotel, senior healthcare experts recommend that no primary caregiver should try to be the one and only caregiver in an older loved one's life.

Secondary Caregiver

A *secondary* caregiver is a person invested in the older loved one's care but who is not able or willing to be on the front lines as often or as closely. If we consider the primary caregiver the captain of the ship, the secondary caregiver is the first mate. The secondary caregivers may perform some of the direct caregiving duties to help the older loved one, but additionally, they may do things to support the primary caregiver.

Let's use a different analogy—Hollywood films—to explain this a little further. If the primary caregiver is the lead actor in a movie, then a secondary caregiver is in a supporting role.

Films are seldom made featuring only one actor. Sure, we have the lead actor—often a famous leading man or leading lady like George Clooney or Meryl Streep. But supporting actors are necessary to help the lead actor move the storyline along. The film industry recognizes this and knows that a good supporting actor is invaluable.

> *Having a team of support by way of secondary caregivers should be the goal of the primary caregiver.*

Families must recognize that good secondary caregivers are invaluable. Ideally, multiple secondary caregivers will support the primary caregiver. Unfortunately, this does not always happen, especially in a new caregiving situation. But having a team of support by way of secondary caregivers should be the goal of the primary caregiver.

Back to the Brady family. Susan and Bill's daughter Kara comes over one afternoon a week to help Bill eat lunch. Susan goes to her book club at this time. Kara is not only providing direct care to her father, but she is also supporting her mother. Kara is a secondary caregiver.

The Bradys' other daughter Kim does the grocery shopping each week for her parents. This benefits both Susan and Bill. Kim is also a secondary caregiver.

Believe it or not, teens and children can be fantastic secondary caregivers. Families often dismiss the idea that young people can be of much help in caregiving situations. But the Brady family has embraced the concept fully. Bill and Susan's six-year-old grandson, John, loves football. So does Bill. So every Sunday during football season, John comes over and watches the game with Bill. This visit enhances Bill's quality of life because he loves spending time with John and also gives Susan a much-needed break.

While good secondary caregivers are invaluable, it's important for them to resist stepping out of their supporting roles. Secondary caregivers have to be very careful about stepping on the toes of the primary caregiver. They should be respectful and defer to the primary unless there is true imminent danger to either the older loved one or the primary caregiver. For example, if a secondary caregiver sees that the older loved one is not getting her medications, it may be appropriate to step in. But if the secondary caregiver merely notices that the older loved one is not getting her dinner at exactly 6:00 p.m. every evening, it is probably wise to back off. To use a film analogy, the supporting actor should not steal the show from the lead.

Tertiary Caregiver

Tertiary caregivers provide support to and take stress off the primary caregiver. A tertiary caregiver is similar to the dockhand at the marina. Any captain will tell you that docking can be stressful, even under decent weather conditions. And, even with the help of your first mate, docking can go awry because of unpredictable winds, mechanical malfunctions, or the angle at which the vessel next to your slip is tied up. When there is a dockhand at the marina, it is much easier to dock the boat.

Typically the tertiary caregiver does not have much direct contact or impact on the older loved one. But the tertiary caregiver can have a significant impact on the primary and/or secondary caregivers. Let's take a look at how tertiary caregivers are making the caregiving process less stressful for the Brady family.

Susan has three tertiary caregivers providing support to her. Bill's sister Janet lives in a different state. Once or twice each year, she sends a gift card to a local spa for Susan to get a massage or have her nails done, which makes for a nice respite for Susan.

> *Typically the tertiary caregiver does not have much direct contact or impact on the older loved one. But the tertiary caregiver can have a significant impact on the primary and/or secondary caregivers.*

The Bradys' longtime friend and neighbor Graham mows the lawn during the summer. This takes a huge burden off of Susan. Her sister Laura, a kindergarten teacher, makes an effort to check in via phone once a week to see how she's feeling. Her call provides Susan an opportunity to vent if she is feeling overwhelmed and frustrated, or just provides a welcome distraction when Laura has funny stories to tell about her students.

EVERY CAREGIVING CREWMATE ROLE IS CRUCIAL

Let's look at the 2011 film *Moneyball*. Clearly Brad Pitt playing the Oakland A's general manager Billy Beane was the lead actor (primary caregiver), while Jonah Hill was the supporting actor playing the assistant general manager Peter Brand (secondary caregiver). Think of all the fans in the baseball stadium (uncredited extras) like tertiary caregivers. Pitt, Hill, and the extras all play important roles. While many would say Pitt is clearly most important, Hill's performance enhanced the film so much he was nominated for an Oscar.

Some might say the extras weren't critical to the film's success, but wouldn't it be odd to watch a film about baseball without stands filled with cheering fans? While the fans play much smaller parts than Pitt and Hill, they are an integral part of the film's landscape. So just as *Moneyball* needed the uncredited extras to play the cheering fans, tertiary caregivers add tremendous value to a caregiving situation. While many families might not think they need tertiary caregivers, having them makes the caregiving experience significantly less stressful for both the primary and secondary caregivers.

When caregivers are truly comfortable in their respective roles, they tend to suffer less stress.

Your relationship with your older loved one need not necessarily dictate if you are primary, secondary, or tertiary. Every caregiving situation and every relationship is unique. What's more important is that you are comfortable in your role. If you are not, you should consider whether a role switch is possible. When caregivers are truly comfortable in their respective roles, they tend to suffer less stress.

Why Are You a Caregiver?

People's stories vary about how they began caring for a friend or family member who is elderly, sick, or disabled. Maybe you got a phone call in the middle of the night that your mother-in-law broke her hip. Perhaps your husband was just diagnosed with Parkinson's disease. Or you've witnessed over the past decade the slow and steady decline as your favorite childless uncle became increasingly less independent. Many people become caregivers by default; caregiving sneaks up on them when an older loved one begins declining or has a health crisis. Because of this, most people caring for older parents, spouses, and family members don't research or read ahead of time about best practices in caregiving. Most caregivers wait until they are thrust into caregiving before seeking help.

Nobody looks forward to being a caregiver. We all want and hope our older spouses, parents, and other family members will remain independent and healthy. And many people do live to old age completely and totally independently, never needing any type of caregiving assistance. But more commonly, older adults need at least some type of help. It may be a little bit of assistance or complete care; it may be long term or just for a brief period. So why do people become caregivers? The answers can be surprisingly complex. Many people feel like they have no choice, but they do—after all, there are very few things in life that we truly don't have a choice about. I discuss this idea further in chapter 13.

> *Many people feel like they have no choice, but they do—after all, there are very few things in life that we truly don't have a choice about.*

Many caregivers cite love as their reason for becoming a caregiver. They love their spouse, parent, grandparent, or dear friend. Others become caregivers out of obligation or a sense of honor or duty. They are caregivers, because they would feel bad if they weren't or they think it would be morally or religiously wrong for them to not be involved in their older loved one's care.

Some caregivers say they want to give back. When Amy was twelve, her mother died. That's when Sarah, Amy's godmother, stepped in to fill the space and provide support for Amy. Now that Sarah needs assistance, Amy wants to repay Sarah for all the ways she's been there for her.

Other caregivers explain, "There's nobody else." They had to step up and manage their older loved one's care because nobody else would or nobody else was local. Or maybe there really is nobody else. While this can happen, it is actually extremely rare—even the most eccentric and prickly among us usually have *some* friends and family.

In other situations, caregiving fulfills a need for the *caregiver*. This is actually very common and often something the caregiver may not be consciously aware of. Maybe you feel like you have unfinished business with the older loved one you are caring for. Were you the problem child Mom always had to worry about and this is your way of making up for the mistakes of your younger years? Maybe you have always been Uncle Lou's favorite niece, and you haven't really made time for him since you had your own children. Now he is sick, and you feel like you owe it to him to be his caregiver.

Perhaps you are facing an empty nest, and you still feel the need to nurture someone. Maybe you don't work and your kids and even grandkids are grown and you don't feel very useful right now. Caregiving can make someone feel needed and important. Maybe you are just good at caregiving, and you know it. You genuinely enjoy being a caregiver. Perhaps you have professional experience doing it and believe you are the best person for the job.

You may be the type of person who thrives on chaos. Do you get an adrenaline rush from running around at one hundred miles per hour with an overstuffed schedule? Maybe you're worried about what other people would think of you if you were not a caregiver for the person who needs help. Would people judge you? Would that embarrass you?

But if you are honest with yourself about why you are a caregiver, it helps you figure out what strategies you need to apply to make caregiving less stressful for you.

Just as every caregiver's story about how they began is different, everyone's reason for doing it is different too. Dig deep and ask yourself honestly, "Why am I doing this?" It's possible it might be more than one of these reasons. No reason is right or wrong. But if you are honest with yourself about why you are a caregiver, it helps you figure out what strategies you need to apply to make caregiving less stressful for you.

Are You Comfortable Functioning as a Caregiver?

In over twenty years of working with older adults and their caregivers, I have seen almost all primary caregivers struggle with at least some aspect of the role. Perhaps you are that rare caregiver: confident, calm, and feeling under control all the time. But most caregivers struggle at some point emotionally and/or physically, particularly at first.

Perhaps you feel like you are never doing any of it quite right. This feeling of apprehension is pretty common for people taking care of their older loved ones. If you are not entirely comfortable in your role, you are not alone.

If you are the typical caregiver, you probably do struggle at times, feeling lost or overwhelmed about some aspect of your older loved one's care. Maybe you feel uncomfortable about *all* aspects of the care. Caring for your older loved one can be downright daunting. Perhaps you feel like you are never doing any of it quite right. This feeling of apprehension is pretty common for people taking care of their older loved ones. If you are not entirely comfortable in your role, you are not alone.

WHAT IS A CAREGIVING INSTINCT AND WHO HAS IT?

Picture this scenario. Someone hands you a broken computer and asks you to fix it, not knowing that you are not mechanically inclined. How would you feel? You may feel inept. You may feel frustrated. Maybe you're nervous. What if that person is really *counting on you* to fix that computer, though? Might you be overwhelmed, resentful, angry? Perhaps. You may be asking yourself, "Why on earth is someone relying on me to do something *I can't do*?"

Lots of family members feel this way when caregiving does not come naturally to them; they simply do not have a natural caregiving instinct.

It has been demonstrated repeatedly that the role of caretaking in most cultures (for children, sick family members) and caregiving (for older adults) falls to the women. Usually we expect women in the family to step up, especially for the primary caregiving roles. But some women do not have a natural caregiving instinct for older adult caregiving, even if they are mothers.

While most people do not look forward to caring for or even helping out with care for an older loved one, there are people who do have more natural caregiving instincts. It's hard for people less mechanically inclined to realize that there actually are people who confidently look forward to the challenge of fixing a broken computer. This analogy applies to caregiving as well. There are some people who see caregiving as challenging, but they feel much more confident and equipped than others to handle it.

~~~~~~

Caregiving is like a muscle that can be developed and strengthened. This book helps you strengthen that caregiving muscle.

While managing an older loved one's care is a skill, some family members have more of that skill than their other family members do. People with more empathic and nurturing personalities often have an easier time cultivating the caregiving skill. That certainly doesn't mean that family members with less nurturing temperaments won't be able to develop the skill. Caregiving is like a muscle that can be developed and strengthened. This book helps you strengthen that caregiving muscle.

You've already taken the first two steps toward stress-free caregiving by identifying what type of caregiver you are—primary, secondary, or tertiary—and by asking yourself why you are committed to caregiving. Now it's time to honestly consider how comfortable you are with your role. When you are comfortable with the caregiving role you have taken on, it is easier to reduce the stress that may be associated with that role. Let's look at two couples to illustrate what I mean.

Melissa is the primary caregiver for her husband, Gary, who has Alzheimer's disease. Melissa and Gary have been happily married for forty-two years. Melissa wants to be the primary caregiver for Gary; she wouldn't have it any other way.

She's obviously clear about what type of caregiver she is, why she cares for her husband, and how comfortable she is with her role.

The situation where Michael is the primary caregiver for his wife, Jean, is quite different. He and Jean had an unhappy marriage for thirty-eight years and were seriously discussing divorce right before her stroke.

Their daughter Valerie offered to assume the primary caregiving role and allow Michael to move into the secondary position, because he complained about how much he hated the role. Valerie felt that ultimately it would be better for everyone if she managed her mother's care. Although she was a secondary caregiver, she genuinely would prefer to be the primary caregiver. But Michael refused Valerie's offer. He was the only person who really knew how bad their marital problems were before the stroke. But how would it look to their family and friends if Michael turned things over to their daughter?

While Melissa is well suited to be the primary caregiver for Gary, Michael clearly should be the secondary caregiver for Jean. Why? First of all, Michael is totally uncomfortable as primary caregiver; he hates doing it. Second, Valerie is willing to do it and wants to. Ultimately Jean is more likely to have better quality of life if the person functioning as primary caregiver does not resent her.

~~~~~~

WHEN YOU WANT TO CHANGE ROLES

If you are a secondary caregiver who would like to become the primary, tread carefully. Even in the case of Michael and Jean, where the primary caregiver has been open about his dissatisfaction, it may take a while for him to get used to the idea of letting go of the primary caregiver role. Just because a primary caregiver does not want the role, it does not mean he is ready to turn it over to someone else. If Valerie speaks directly to her father about switching roles and he refuses, she may want to consider slowly taking on more and more responsibility with his blessing. Sometimes hanging on to the primary caregiver role is about a sense of responsibility and concern about what others would think rather than a true desire to perform the role. Valerie should also look out for any natural opportunities to make the switch more palatable for Michael. When more personal care is needed for Jean, Valerie might make the case that it would be more comfortable if a female were in charge. Or if Jean goes to the hospital, Valerie could suggest that Jean be discharged to her home instead of Michael's, at least on a temporary basis. Strategies like this may give Michael a graceful exit from the primary caregiving role if he is truly looking for that.

~~~~~~

But I Didn't Plan to Be a Caregiver

Many couples consciously plan for having children, and if not, they at least have some advance warning of their arrival! In contrast, caregivers of older loved ones are often unprepared because it seems that the caregiving responsibility sneaks up on them. Caregivers often report being taken by surprise by their older loved one's needs. Some families deny the changes taking place with their older loved ones.

Most people feel this way because they don't "get" aging; that is, they don't understand what normal aging really looks like. They've never been educated on the aging process, diseases that frequently occur in the senior years, the normal changes that happen to the older brain, or the unique challenges of caregiving. They don't have any experience coordinating or providing hands-on care for an older person. Additionally, it's hard to comprehend how little Medicare, Medicaid, or private insurance may be paying when help is needed for the older loved one.

> *But why would you expect to feel confident*
> *taking on the care of your older loved one*
> *unless you have had experience?*

Most of us expect a learning curve when we're faced with a new responsibility. When you are inexperienced and less than adequately prepared for elder care, it is normal to feel apprehension. Typically, people understand this intellectually but many expect an awful lot from themselves in such a personal situation. But why *would* you expect to feel confident taking on the care of your older loved one unless you have had experience?

> *Also, remember that it takes a caregiving*
> *crew—no captain should ever go it alone!*

To reduce caregiving stress, be patient with yourself and try to educate yourself as much as possible about your older loved one's conditions. Also, remember that it takes a caregiving crew—no captain should ever go it alone!

 Life Jacket: Go to www.jenerationshealth.com to download a worksheet on determining whether your role as primary, secondary, or tertiary caregiver is the best match for your caregiving situation.

Now that you have identified your role in the caregiving crew—that is, whether you are the primary caregiver (captain), secondary caregiver (first mate), or tertiary caregiver (dockhand)—it's time to look at what you can do to make the caregiving experience as low stress as possible. In the following chapters, I offer you best practices and advice (navigational tips) from my own experience and wise words from many other caregiving experts. But, because caregiving is an imperfect endeavor, we also cover areas where it is common to make mistakes such as falling overboard or running aground on a sandbar. And, as all seaworthy captains do, I show you how to avoid obstacles or course-correct when you must encounter them.

Two

LET YOURSELF OFF THE HOOK

Gone Overboard: Making "The Promise"

Most people don't make promises with the intention of ever breaking them. But in the world of caregiving, promises often are made (and broken) every day by the caregiver. While it can be very upsetting to both the caregiver and the older loved one, sometimes breaking promises is absolutely necessary—especially if that promise is "The Promise."

> *Loving caregivers often don't realize how many*
> *others have been in their shoes. You are not alone.*

If you have not made any promises to your older loved one about how you will care for her, and you think you would never make any promises you couldn't keep, you may be tempted to skip this chapter. But I recommend that you continue reading. Even people who think they would never make a caregiving promise that would be difficult to keep sometimes do so in an emotional moment. Sometimes requests from an older loved one you care about can tug at your heartstrings. Sometimes pleas from your older loved one don't seem so unreasonable at the time, and you don't yet understand the gravity of what you are agreeing to. Almost every caregiver is at risk for making a promise that he can't keep.

Whether or not you've made a caregiving promise, it's important to remember why you signed on as a caregiver in the first place: You wanted to make sure your loved one is taken care of. Like all aspects of caregiving, you need to constantly monitor how things are going and change course when necessary. Let's figure out when it makes sense to keep The Promise and when it is in everyone's best interest to chart a different course.

This chapter helps you with the following concepts:

- What is "The Promise," and why should you avoid making specific promises in caregiving?

- How can you become comfortable with the idea that not all caregiving promises should be honored?

- What are some strategies for modifying promises that have already been made?

Just What *Is* The Promise?

Every healthcare provider has heard countless family caregivers say some version of the following at one point or another, "You don't understand. I *promised* my mother/wife/friend I would *never*—

- Put her in a nursing home;

- Bring strangers into our house to care for her;

- Sell her house; and/or

- Spend her money on care that was supposed to be an inheritance for her kids."

Ah, The Promise. I imagine you're now familiar with this expression and could fill in the blank with other variations of your own. Loving caregivers often don't realize how many others have been in their shoes. You are not alone. Caregivers frequently see themselves as being in a unique position, having made a promise with the best of intentions and being unable to find their way out of it—even though the special promise they made becomes a major source of stress.

The origins of The Promise seem to have several sources. For instance, many older adults cite the sickness and health part of their wedding vows. But those vows don't get into specifics about caregiving or about making unrealistic, superhuman promises later in life.

These caregivers assume that the only options are a rundown nursing home or caring for their loved one at home, when actually there are many, many varied options in between.

Some senior care professionals believe The Promise originated because older adults (especially those born before 1940) saw their parents and grandparents in nursing homes and were horrified. While nursing homes are still very much a last resort in most cases, they really are much nicer and better regulated than many older adults remember them being. Others have read or heard sensationalized media reports about abuse, neglect, and exploitation at the hands of nursing assistants or aides who help out in private homes. These caregivers assume that the only options are a rundown nursing home or caring for their loved one at home, when actually there are many, many varied options in between.

While some nursing homes are not clean, and exploitation and abuse can happen at the hands of in-home home care aides, these are exceptions rather than the norm. But it is this type of fear that often motivates an older person to insist that a family member make The Promise. When an older loved one asks for something, we want to try to honor the request out of love, obligation, or simply just respect for her wishes. Making The Promise is certainly understandable.

While The Promise is most frequently made between a caregiver and an older loved one, there are variations of it. Sometimes a primary caregiver makes The Promise to herself and never even verbally relays it to the older loved one. When Karen's eighty-year-old father started suffering from dementia symptoms, she moved him into her own home without even discussing other living arrangement possibilities. She felt he could not receive enough personal attention at an assisted living community and made The Promise to always make sure he had someone in his family to watch over him for the rest of his life. The primary caregiver just made up her mind about how care *should* be delivered and moved ahead. Did Karen know that her father might prefer the social interaction he would get at an assisted living community? Did she consider how having her father live in her house would restrict aspects of her life? Probably not.

THE PROMISE FROM OTHER CAREGIVERS

Ironically it's not just primary caregivers who make The Promise. Sometimes secondary caregivers will make The Promise and expect the primary to keep it! Ideally, all caregivers will be on the same page, but no caregiver is responsible for promises made by another caregiver.

When secondary caregiver Sal was in town visiting his mother, Robin, who has congestive heart failure and limited mobility, he reassured her that she would never have to move out of her home. When he repeated this sentiment to his sister Trish, who was the primary caregiver, she was taken aback. While Sal was a wonderful secondary caregiver, offering Trish emotional and even some financial support for their mother when needed, Trish was dumbfounded that he thought he was in the position to make that kind of promise to their mother. Sal flew into town a few times a year for a couple of days while Trish was doing all the day-to-day caregiving. But because Trish didn't want to be the bad guy, she felt she needed to keep Sal's promise.

After a few frustrating months went by, it occurred to Trish that she needed to talk to her brother about his promise. While Sal was defensive at first, he eventually realized how much he had stepped over the line. He understood that if he was not able to step into the primary caregiving role, he did not have the authority to make such promises.

It's great that Sal and Trish were able to eventually have a reasonable discussion about this. But if Sal were not able to understand Trish's position on the promise he had made to their mother, Trish would have had to consider other solutions. She could continue keeping the promise her brother had made even if it was very difficult. Or, she could set some boundaries with her mother and discuss alternatives. Many caregivers resist the second option because they want to avoid confrontation or disappointing the older loved one. At this point, it's important to weigh the pros and cons of a confrontation and disappointing the older loved one. Would you rather keep a promise you didn't make or face a difficult conversation?

~~~~~~

Another variation of The Promise is the one made to someone on his or her deathbed. Jin's father, Haing, died when Jin was only sixteen years old. Just before Haing died, they had a long talk about the future. Haing asked Jin to always take care of his mother, Ming, in his absence. Fast-forward forty years. Jin still carries this vow around but has never discussed it with anyone else, including his wife or mother, who is now facing a Parkinson's disease diagnosis. To Jin, the conversation he had with his dying father meant that nobody but family will ever care for Ming. Is this what his father meant? Would Haing have asked the same of his son if he understood Ming's condition and the burden it could create?

Healthcare providers frequently hear about a caregiver's particular promise for the first time in response to a suggestion the caregiver is rejecting. Do you see yourself in either of the following examples?

Example 1

> **Social worker:** Your husband doesn't seem safe at home anymore because of his dementia. He's wandered out of the house three separate times. I think you need to consider an assisted living home.

> **Primary caregiver:** No, that's not an option. I promised him I'd *never* move him out of this house.

Example 2

> **Doctor:** Maybe you should think about getting some help in your home so you can get more sleep.

> **Primary caregiver:** No, I can't—you don't understand. I *promised* my husband I would take care of him myself.

Healthcare providers are sometimes not the only ones in the dark about promises a caregiver has made. Maybe a friend or another family member offers a suggestion, particularly someone functioning as a secondary or tertiary caregiver. Have you ever responded in one of these ways?

Example 3

> **Secondary caregiver:** I was thinking we should at least go tour some nursing homes in case we need to place Mom there at some point down the road.

> **Primary caregiver:** She's *never* going to a nursing home; they won't look after her the way we do. Anyway, I promised her she would live at home for the rest of her life.

Example 4

> **Tertiary caregiver:** You never want to leave the house anymore because of all your mom's needs. You won't even let me take you out to lunch. Maybe it's time to see what that adult day care is all about.

> **Primary caregiver:** That would be great if I could, but I promised her I would *never* make her go to one of *those places*. I really don't have a choice.

Listening to suggestions from others can help
you navigate through unforeseen challenges.
Often they have the objectivity to see before you
do that your promise is not necessarily in the
best interest of your older loved one, you, or the
rest of the family and/or caregiving crew.

When a healthcare provider, friend, or another family member you trust challenges you about The Promise you've made, you may be surprised. You think they should just take it at face value that you gave your word. Don't they see that you are doing the right thing, the selfless thing? You may want everyone to leave you alone about it. Once a promise is made, that's it. Subject closed. But well-meaning healthcare providers, friends, and family *should* be challenging you on some caregiving promises. When you signed on as a caregiver, you began a voyage that can sometimes lead into rough waters. Listening to suggestions from others can help you navigate through unforeseen challenges. Often they have the objectivity to see before you do that your promise is not necessarily in the best interest of your older loved one, you, *or* the rest of the family and/or caregiving crew.

As a caregiver, it is vital to understand how The Promise is affecting your life and the people around you. It's important to take a step back to determine whether keeping your promise is healthy, safe, and an overall good decision for your older loved one, you, and the rest of the family/caregiving team.

Should You Ever Keep The Promise?

Sometimes making The Promise works out just fine, and the caregiver never has to worry about letting herself off the hook. I hope that will be the case for your caregiving crew, just as it was for the family members in the following example.

Many years ago, Megan, a fifty-year-old server at a restaurant, promised her mother, eighty-five-year-old Wanda, that she would never put her in a nursing home. As a child, Wanda hated visiting her grandmother in a nursing home and thought it was just about the worst thing she'd ever experienced. She remembered the nursing home as dirty and scary and was terrified at the thought of ever having to live in one. As Wanda got older and her health declined, she struggled with a number of health issues. Megan and her two sisters, Donna and Colleen, who both lived nearby, were able to pull together for the ten months Wanda was dependent at the end of her life. Splitting shifts between the three of them, one of the sisters was always at Wanda's home until she passed away. One of the ways they all were able to keep Wanda at home was by taking time off (under the terms of the Family and Medical Leave Act, or FMLA) from their paid jobs at different points. Ultimately, they kept their promise and felt really proud of that.

~~~~~~

FMLA

The Family Medical Leave Act was established in 1993. Its purpose is to ensure that most organizations allow employees to take up to twelve weeks of unpaid time to provide caregiving to a loved one when needed. While not every organization or every employee qualifies for this benefit, most American workers in most private and public organizations do. To determine your eligibility, ask your human resources department or check out the United States Department of Labor regulations on FMLA at www.dol.gov/whd/fmla/.

~~~~~~

Why Avoid The Promise?

The situation for Wanda and her daughters worked out just fine, and that is what we all hope for. Sometimes, however, keeping The Promise under certain circumstances can be downright unhealthy or even dangerous. Let's take another look at Wanda's story if her dependency had lasted ten years rather than ten months.

Things that can be put on hold for ten months can't necessarily be put on hold for ten years. Sacrifices that we are able to happily make short term can become untenable when they become long term. What if, during the additional nine years and two months Wanda lived, she needed round-the-clock care?

Perhaps Megan's chronic sciatica pain worsened because of the physical toll hands-on care was taking on her. What if Donna, a stay-at-home wife and mother, started struggling with a bout of depression during this time? What if Colleen, a pharmaceutical sales representative, and her husband moved out of town because of a big promotion Colleen was offered? Colleen's departure would leave only two sisters to divide the care. The consequences of keeping The Promise in this case could be much more far-reaching than if it were a temporary ten-month commitment. Its reach is akin to the thunderous wake that a boat speeding past a tranquil marina leaves in the middle of the night.

Before deciding to break or keep The Promise, it is critical to look at who is being helped or hurt by keeping this promise. Caregivers may feel better for keeping their word, but are their loved ones receiving the best care possible? Your loved one may be grateful that she can stay in her home, but is her lack of social interaction with others causing depression? Could you or one of your crewmates accidently give your mother the wrong dosage of a medication in an exhausted effort to keep The Promise? It is a gray area, and all caregivers need to consider how their choices ultimately affect their loved ones and themselves.

Knowing what you do about the three sisters in our updated scenario, what are the potential consequences of keeping Wanda out of a nursing home during these ten years? Just as an exercise, write down as many potential problems that could result for the caregiving crew and for people beyond the caregiving crew if they insisted on keeping The Promise to Wanda.

How many did you come up with?

Here are just some of the potential problems that could arise:

- Megan's back problems get worse, making it difficult for her to continue working at the restaurant.

- Donna's depression gets worse, straining her ability to care for her children and husband.

- None of the sisters are spending much time with their children and/or spouses.

- Colleen becomes a very bossy secondary long-distance caregiver, second-guessing everything her sisters are doing, because she feels guilty she's not local.

- They decide to hire home health aides to help them keep Wanda at home, but the costs are very high and this is putting financial strain on all of them.

- There is tension in all their households.

- The sisters begin to pick at each other, accusing each other of not doing as much or contributing as much as they should financially.

- All the daughters' relationships with Wanda become only about caregiving and they miss their mother. They now view her more as a patient than their mom.

- Megan and Donna become estranged from Colleen because they feel she abandoned Wanda and them.

- Donna's kids may be struggling in school as a result of the tension between Donna and their father.

- Megan goes on disability because of the worsening sciatica problem, and her sisters expect her to do the bulk of the caregiving now because she doesn't "have to work."

- Colleen and her husband are fighting about money all the time, because she is constantly sending her sisters extra funds now that she lives out of town.

> *The real irony—and one that many caregivers*
> *never see—is that keeping The Promise may*
> *be the worst thing for the older loved one.*

These are simply examples of the unintended consequences of making The Promise. The tragedy that I often see play out is that caregivers make themselves sick trying to keep The Promise. The real irony—and one that many caregivers never see—is that keeping The Promise may be the worst thing for the older loved one.

When a promise is kept without evaluating whether it makes sense, the older loved one's care is often compromised. In Wanda's situation, what could *she* be missing as a result of her daughters' pledge to keep her at home indefinitely? Again, just as an experiment, write down as many possibilities as you can think of.

Did any of these make your list?

- Without outside help, such as home care aides, Wanda only sees Donna, Megan, their kids, and spouses and doesn't have much other social interaction besides the television.

- If home care aides are hired to assist, Wanda is still isolated in her home (even though she has a little more human interaction besides family). The money that is being spent on home care may be better spent on assisted living or adult day care where Wanda would interact with many more healthcare providers and other older adults, and have a change of scenery as well.

- Wanda is heartbroken over the tension between her three daughters.

- Wanda is suffering from depression, because she feels so isolated.

- Donna and Megan and the rest of the family are getting on *Wanda's* nerves!

- Wanda hates that she never has any privacy.

- Wanda misses the mother-daughter relationship she used to have with her daughters; now she feels like their patient.

Keeping The Promise under any circumstances often leads caregivers like Megan, Colleen, and Donna to make superhuman sacrifices to honor a vow that very well may not even be in the older adult's best interest—and frequently doesn't work well for the rest of the caregiving crew either. It can lead to tremendous guilt for the caregivers when they have to break The Promise, which often happens.

*Keeping The Promise under any circumstances
often leads caregivers. . . to make superhuman
sacrifices to honor a vow that very well may not
even be in the older adult's best interest . . .*

There are countless problems that could potentially arise over a decade of caregiving in the home and many more potential negative outcomes that this family could encounter if they put The Promise ahead of everything else and never consider letting themselves off the hook.

Shannon, a dental hygienist, promised her mother, Lucy, that she would never bring strangers into the home to take care of her after her stroke. Lucy made it clear that she didn't really want anyone around besides Shannon and her husband, Bryan. Lucy also insisted that Shannon never bring up the idea of a nursing home or assisted living. After all, Lucy had taken care of her mother (Shannon's grandmother) when she had health problems later in life, so she expected Shannon to step up for her. Shannon always had a hard time saying no to her mother because she was an only child, and she and Lucy had always been close. Shannon admits that at times her mother is controlling.

Shannon and Bryan, a general contractor, began providing direct care to Lucy. By making The Promise to her mother, Shannon guaranteed that two people with no experience or education in post-stroke care would be handling everything! To make matters worse, most of the bathing, dressing, and toileting became Shannon's responsibility almost exclusively because Lucy did not feel very comfortable with Bryan providing that kind of help.

As much as Bryan loves Shannon and is fond of Lucy, he is becoming very resentful of the situation. He doesn't want to be at Lucy's beck and call. At times, despite Lucy's protests, he has had to help her with personal care like toileting because Shannon was at work, and he finds this extremely uncomfortable.

Fast-forward three months. Lucy is more dependent on Shannon and Bryan than ever. Even when Lucy's health improved, she refused to do certain things for herself. She recently became short tempered with Bryan when he didn't want to get her a glass of water. Following doctor's orders, Bryan suggested to Lucy that she get up more often and do things for herself. It got to a point where all Bryan and Shannon discussed were Lucy's needs. But when Bryan talked to Shannon about setting some limits with Lucy, she rebuffed him saying, "My mother needs us."

Are Shannon and Bryan's actions really in the best interests of Lucy? Their choice to cater to all of Lucy's needs, some legitimate and some not, may actually be hindering her recovery. The stress of taking care of Lucy created tension between Shannon and Bryan. What if Shannon and Bryan wind up separated because of this tension? Then, Lucy might even be reliant on only Shannon. Maybe it's time Shannon took another look at The Promise she made.

Why It Is Okay to Reconsider The Promise

There are times in life when we may have made a promise and didn't quite understand what we were agreeing to. For those of you who are married, did you know what you were agreeing to when you said, "I do?" Really and truly? How about those of you with children? Were you truly prepared for what was ahead? Most people laugh when I ask these questions. Most married people or those raising children agree that before making the commitment and actually being married or becoming a parent, they really didn't understand what they were saying yes to.

Take Melanie, for instance. Prior to having children, she said she didn't believe any child should ever take any psychiatric medication, under any circumstances. It was a very black-and-white issue for her. She remembers criticizing a friend whose teenage daughter was taking medication for depression and telling her that there were so many other options, like counseling and yoga. But after Melanie's eight-year-old son, Drew, was diagnosed with ADHD, she now believes differently.

For years, Melanie sent Drew to a counselor and tried many different types of holistic strategies in an effort to control his impulsive behavior and his inability to concentrate on homework and at school. Nothing worked. Desperate, Melanie finally accepted the advice of both Drew's psychotherapist and pediatrician to give medication a try. Drew's symptoms have now significantly improved. He is doing much better in school, listening to his parents, and fighting less with his siblings. While Melanie still is not thrilled about the medicine, she realizes that it is the best option right now.

Melanie and Drew's situation is quite similar to The Promise made frequently in senior care. Even with the best intentions, Melanie had made an uninformed, inflexible parenting decision about a situation involving her son before she experienced it firsthand. Before Drew was born, she never could have predicted he would have ADHD; or that he wouldn't respond to non-pharmaceutical interventions; or the impact the ADHD symptoms would have on his and the rest of the family's quality of life. Once she had experienced the facts, she was able to see the situation as gray, rather than black-and-white. She recognized her plotted course in parenting was facing rough waters so she course-corrected, which resulted in much smoother sailing. Her decision to revisit her position and finally let her son try medication was the best thing for him.

> *These feelings are all reasonable and natural, but there is no way a caregiver can see everything ahead and make any kind of guarantee.*

Caregivers of older loved ones who have made The Promise are in a similar boat. Often we look at how much we love our older loved one or how obligated we feel toward them or how we would want someone to treat us if we were the one needing care. These feelings are all reasonable and natural, but there is no way a caregiver can see everything ahead and make any kind of guarantee.

Connie witnessed her friend Beth hiring home care aides to help out with her mother a few days each week. At the time, Connie thought, *I can't believe Beth would do that! Beth's mother probably hates those strangers in her home. What if they steal from her? How does Beth really know that her mother is in good hands? I would never do that if my mother needed care. I would do it myself.* She thought of Beth as really selfish.

Now that Connie is taking care of her father-in-law, however, she understands exactly why Beth needed to hire help. Because her father-in-law is six foot four and weighs 250 pounds, Connie cannot help him out of bed if he soils the sheets while her husband is away on a work trip. After spending all day at her full-time job, she is often too tired to clean her house and make dinner. She and her husband end up spending a lot more money than they used to on take-out food, which is not so healthy. Caregiving can affect so many aspects of a person's life physically, emotionally, and financially that it is impossible to predict them all.

When most people sign on to caregiving, they have absolutely no idea what they are getting into (much like marriage and childrearing). But at least with marriage and childrearing we have some advance notice and most of us are looking forward to the new roles (at least in the beginning!).

If you are trying to keep The Promise, it needs to be revisited frequently. In long-term caregiving situations (a year or more), it is critical to reevaluate the overall caregiving plan at least quarterly. In assisted living and nursing homes, most state regulations require this! You constantly need to evaluate the course of your caregiving journey. This includes The Promise.

~~~~~~

REEVALUATING THE PROMISE

If even one member of the caregiving crew answers yes to even one of the following questions, it is time to revisit The Promise:

1. Do you feel at risk of losing your job since committing to The Promise?

2. Is the partner/spouse of the caregiver struggling with the demands of the caregiver keeping The Promise?

3. Do you find yourself struggling with a new or worsening physical health concern since committing to The Promise?

4. Do you find yourself struggling with new symptoms or worsening symptoms of a mental health concern, like depression and/or anxiety, since committing to The Promise?

5. Is your child/grandchild struggling with grades since caregiving began?

6. Is your child/grandchild struggling with behavioral problems at school since caregiving began?

7. Are you experiencing more frequent or more volatile arguments with the other caregivers in the caregiving crew since committing to The Promise?

8. Are other members of the caregiving crew suggesting you should reconsider The Promise?

~~~~~~

Caregivers must understand and appreciate their own limitations, especially when it comes to older adults with chronic illnesses or advanced dementia diagnoses, such as Alzheimer's disease.

Throughout this chapter, we discussed numerous unforeseen effects on the lives of both the caregiver and the older adult when The Promise is made. Caregivers must understand and appreciate their own limitations, especially when it comes to older adults with chronic illnesses or advanced dementia diagnoses, such as Alzheimer's disease. In cases like these, the condition and prognosis of the older adult is paramount to your decision about whether to revisit The Promise.

Gail Sheehy is a best-selling author, reporter, and biographer. Several of her books focus on issues related to aging and getting older. In *Passages in Caregiving*, she shares her personal journey caring for her husband, who had cancer and was chronically ill for seventeen years. In this book she addresses the challenges of caregiving when you don't know how long you will be a caregiver. She says, "It's one thing to take on primary responsibility for someone with an acute illness. It's a sprint, and most of us can do a sprint for some months." She goes on to say,

"A chronically ill person's future is inherently unpredictable." Because many of the conditions afflicting older loved ones are chronic, caregivers must be able to adapt to changing circumstances. I believe revisiting any promises made is part of this adaptation.

For the past two years, Ross has been struggling with managing the care of his mother, Ruth, who has Alzheimer's disease. Ross moved her into his home and monitored her care himself. Recently, while he was at the drugstore picking up her medication, Ruth wandered out of the house in the rain and fell. The accident landed her in the hospital. When Steve, the nurse discharge planner, approached Ross about whether Ruth was going back home with him, Ross looked incredulous. Ever so earnestly he said, "Actually you don't understand. I promised I would *never* place her in a nursing home."

Like many people taking care of loved ones with Alzheimer's disease, Ross believes he can handle all aspects of his mother's care. Her fall was simply an accident, and he will be more careful and make sure she cannot wander outside when he is not around to watch her. He would feel like he failed her if he placed her in a nursing home or an assisted living community. But is it really practical for Ross to believe that he can monitor his mother all the time?

Alzheimer's disease is a chronic degenerative terminal condition that lasts an average of eight years from the time symptoms begin until the patient passes away. Not only is short-term memory, judgment, and the ability to communicate impacted, but the patient also gradually loses the ability to do things for herself such as activities of daily living (ADL) and instrumental activities of daily living (IADL). For example, the patient with Alzheimer's disease may no longer be able to feed or dress herself (ADLs) or grocery shop (IADL). According to the Alzheimer's Association website, approximately sixty percent of patients with Alzheimer's disease wander out of their homes. Eventually most people with Alzheimer's disease become incontinent. Caregivers of people with Alzheimer's disease have much more to deal with than just their older loved one not remembering what day it is. They also have to manage issues such as losing sleep due to worry that the older loved one will walk out the front door in the middle of the night or that they will have to change a disposable incontinence undergarment.

In cases where the older adult suffers from a degenerative disease like Alzheimer's, professional outside care may be necessary. Many residential communities are specifically designed to accommodate patients with Alzheimer's disease. Despite making The Promise to never put Ruth in a nursing home, Ross is not equipped to deal with the degenerative health problems that come with his mother's diagnosis. Keeping The Promise is actually doing her a disservice.

Peter Rabins, MD, MPH, is one of the foremost experts on Alzheimer's disease. The coauthor of one of the most popular books on dementia care, *The 36-Hour Day*, Dr. Rabins recently retired from his long-held post as professor and director of the Division of Geriatric Psychiatry at the Johns Hopkins University School of Medicine. When I interviewed him about patients with irreversible dementia for this book, he stated that it's "unfortunately often not possible to keep them at home," particularly when the spouse or caregiver is also older or frail or both. He also said that when a caregiver has to make the hard decision to place someone with dementia outside the home, "that's not a failure . . . it's really meeting the person's care needs." For many caregiving crews (even those comprised of a primary caregiver and numerous secondary and tertiary caregivers), it is next to impossible to keep someone who has irreversible dementia at home indefinitely.

Because this disease is constantly changing, you could have made The Promise while your older loved one was in the early stages of Alzheimer's disease. But as the disease progresses, keeping The Promise most likely will not be feasible. (We will get into much more detail about dementia caregiving in chapter 12.)

Why Caregivers Struggle with Undoing The Promise

Just don't make any promises at all.

If you are a new caregiver and have never made any specific promises to your older loved one about how you will care for him or about things you will or would never do, good! You may have dodged one of the biggest stressors in all of caregiving. Just don't make any promises at all.

But for many of you, The Promise is already out there. Let's be honest. For most people, breaking The Promise is not easy. Despite all logic and reason telling you what needs to be done, some caregivers continue to hide behind The Promise. Why do these well-meaning people continue to try to keep The Promise? Look in the mirror. Do any of these scenarios seem familiar?

- Like Jin, whose father died when he was a teenager, you remember a loved one when you think of The Promise.

- Like Shannon, whose mother is very demanding, you revert to a subordinate role and let the person receiving care call the shots.

- Like Ross, whose mother has Alzheimer's disease, you are in denial about the level of caregiving that is necessary to ensure the safety of the older adult.

- Like many other caregivers, you think you can "stick to it" even though you may not yet really appreciate the time and energy caregiving takes.

It's important to take some time to think about why you are so resolute. If you can get to the bottom of that, you often can make peace with breaking The Promise. Remember that your goal is to provide the best care you can for the older adult. Putting your ego or emotions to the side can help reduce the stress of caregiving.

Journalist Virginia Morris is a best-selling author who provided care to her own parents during their older years. In *How to Care for Aging Parents,* now in its third edition, she suggests that "most people in a nursing home have a spouse or child who swore he or she would never, ever put this person in a nursing home. Forgive yourself utterly and completely, from head to toe." Easier said than done, right? Not necessarily.

Maybe you did promise your mother several years ago that you would never sell your childhood home because she wanted it to stay in the family. But circumstances have made selling the home the best option: Your mother is incapacitated and needs more care than you can afford to provide in her home, and you simply need the funds from the house sale to pay for your mother's assisted living. Have you spoken with the other members of the caregiving crew? What about professionals involved in your older loved one's care? How about your friends who aren't involved in the caregiving?

> *Sometimes we just need someone we trust and*
> *respect to tell us that we are doing the best we can.*

Speaking with others and explaining the idea of breaking The Promise, despite not knowing how they will react, can be beneficial. Explaining your thoughts and reasons for breaking The Promise to other people can reinforce your decision. When others can hear about the physical, emotional, or financial burdens you are experiencing, you may be surprised at how many of these people will agree with you. By gaining permission to rescind The Promise from someone you trust, the feelings of guilt and insecurity can be alleviated. Sometimes we just need someone we trust and respect to tell us that we are doing the best we can.

If you don't have someone in your caregiving crew or other friends or family who will support you in amending your promise, it's very important to seek professional help. Getting support from a good psychotherapist or spiritual advisor familiar with caregiver stress may help you feel stronger about your decision.

Make a Course Correction: Steer Clear of The Promise

If you haven't already made The Promise, think carefully about how you will respond if your older loved one asks how you'll provide care. If your older loved one says something like, "I don't ever want to leave this house; promise me you will never let that happen," take a breath before you answer and choose your response carefully. Try saying something like, "I will do what I can to keep you home as long as it is safe"; or "I don't want you to have to leave home either, and I will do my best so you can stay home as long as you want." Better yet, offer to table the discussion so that you can take some time to think about the entire caregiving plan. While it might be difficult to resist promising your older loved one what he is asking for, it is easier to word your response carefully now rather than have to go back and let yourself off the hook later if you do have to rescind The Promise.

TAP INTO RELIEF

Because of my hands-on experience with caregiving, I have insisted my husband, Sean, make me what I call the Tandem Anchor Promise (TAP). If my health were ever compromised, he promises that he will be sure to get as much help as necessary so we *both* would have the best quality of life possible. While, like most people, I would prefer to be at home for the rest of my life, I trust that Sean would arrange for the best possible care for me if I could no longer live at home. Mary Faith Ferretto, LCSW-C, an aging life care expert and the owner of Ferretto Elder Care Consulting, has a similar deal with her husband. She has told him that she wants to be sent to adult day care if she is ever diagnosed with dementia. Ferretto's reasoning: "I'll have a nice day and he gets a break!"

The one constant in life is change: our physical condition changes, our emotional health changes, and our financial condition changes as well. Medical treatments and technology will change. Given the medical problems many older adults encounter later in life, it is important for caregivers to have some flexibility regarding the caregiving plan and to constantly reevaluate that plan. Acknowledging there are options helps reduce the stress of caregiving. If you are currently a caregiver, consider initiating such a promise with your spouse or children. If more of us agree to a Tandem Anchor Promise, perhaps we as a society can minimize the number of promises in caregiving that need to be broken.

*Your goal in caregiving should be getting
the best possible care for your older loved
one while respecting the boundaries and
limits of all caregiving crew members.*

The decision to keep or rescind The Promise is ultimately yours. However, caregiving is an ongoing dependent relationship between you and your older loved one. You take on the responsibility for aspects of your older loved one's life that he or she has difficulty handling, and the older loved one must recognize and respect your role. Your goal in caregiving should be getting the best possible care for your older loved one while respecting the boundaries and limits of all caregiving crew members. Understanding that The Promise can be detrimental to the ultimate goal of caregiving is important for both parties to understand. As I discuss in the next chapter, even though The Promise can't always be honored, the wishes of the older adult can't be totally ignored either.

Three

AN OLDER ADULT IS STILL AN ADULT

Gone Overboard: Helicopter Caregiving

One of the best things about living in the United States is that we have a lot of rights. We can make our own decisions—good or bad. Competent adults don't need everyone they know agreeing with their decisions or even liking them. Another great thing about living in the United States is that it is very difficult to take away our right to make our own decisions. At least most of us think this is a great thing until we are caring for an older loved one. Then many of us start forgetting that competent adults, especially older adults who need care, do not have to justify their decisions, good or bad.

This chapter helps you with the following concepts and tasks:

- Understand why sometimes you forget your older loved one is an adult.

- Recognize whether you are treating your older loved one like a child.

- Appreciate the potential consequences of treating your older loved one like a child.

- Accept that in most cases your older loved one has the right to make decisions you don't agree with.

- Have more respectful conversations with your older loved one about your concerns.

Why We Forget the Older Loved One Is a Grown-Up

When you think about older adults, what image comes to mind? Most of us associate certain physical characteristics with an older man or woman. Take a minute and write down what you envision when you are asked to describe an older adult.

What did you come up with? If you are like most people, you probably envisioned some version of the "elderly person uniform" consisting of gray or white hair, a bald or balding head, and wrinkled skin.

But wait. Those physical characteristics apply to many of us. Plenty of people who have gray hair, are going bald, or have wrinkles would *not* qualify as an older adult. Here are some *other* characteristics that more narrowly describe older adults. They may—

- Wear accessories such as a hearing aid or glasses

- Use a walker, cane, or wheelchair

- Speak a bit slower than other people

- Ask to have things repeated

- Have slower reflexes

- Walk with an awkward gait

- Have a stooped back and shoulders

- Wear a hospital gown

- Sit in a hospital bed

These stereotypes and preconceived notions regarding the elderly lead much of our society to view older adults as helpless and dependent. Simply wearing the elderly person uniform is reason enough for people to treat older adults like dependent children. Add in some other factors, like physical or mental health problems or cognitive impairment, and you've got the impetus for caregivers to begin treating these people more like babies, rather than people who have seventy, eighty, or ninety-plus years of life experience.

Many adult children caregivers really feel the
need to just simply take over for their parent. Most
often, there is an emotional component to this.

So why do so many caregivers treat their elders as children rather than adults? If you are an adult child caring for an older loved one, you've no doubt heard the phrase "parenting your parent." Many adult children caregivers really feel the need to just simply take over for their parent. Most often, there is an emotional component to this.

Dr. Linda Rhodes is a former Pennsylvania Secretary of Aging and current director of the Hirtzel Institute on Health Education and Aging. In her book *The Essential Guide to Caring for Aging Parents*, Rhodes identified four motivators that influence emotional responses from caregivers: They want to save the older loved one from herself; they believe "someone has to take charge"; they need to be a "good son or daughter"; or they feel like nobody is listening to them. I believe these motivators also illustrate why some adult children often wind up treating their older parents more like kids than adults.

Each of these motivators specifically delves into an emotional response that occurs when an adult child cares for a parent. Do any of Rhodes' motivators resonate with you?

If you find yourself wanting to save your older loved one from herself, could it be that she has always made poor decisions? If you feel like you need to be a good son or daughter, are you seeking approval from the older loved one, others, or yourself? If you feel like nobody is listening to you, or believe "someone has to take charge," are you trying to take over to assert control? If you can see yourself in any of these, you may gain some insight as to why you are treating your older loved one less like an adult and more like a child.

Another reason a caregiver may treat an older adult like a child is much more basic. It could be that it just makes things easier or more efficient for the caregiver. The thought pattern behind it certainly seems rational. The caregiver thinks, *It takes my older loved one a long time to walk to the mailbox so I'll just go ahead and mail her letters for her.* Now, in many ways this is efficient thinking, and even considerate, but in the long run it is not always good for the older loved one or the caregiver.

Signs You Are Treating Your Older Loved One Like a Child

Treating an older adult like a child can add additional stress to caregivers and be detrimental to the wellness of the person under care. Taking over responsibilities for tasks of an older adult, even basic ones, just adds another item to the often-long list of things already being handled by a caregiver. This also can hamper the recovery of the older adult, thereby lengthening the caregiving process and adding even more stress to the caregiver. But how do you know if you may be treating the older adult under your care like a child? As you read the following situations, ask yourself whether you've ever experienced any of them.

Talking Down to Them

"H-i-i-i-i, M-o-m-m-m. How are you tod-a-a-a-y? Did you eat everything on your plate at lunch today? It's cold in here. You should be under that blanket." Caregivers sometimes begin talking to their loved one in a way that sounds like they are speaking with a small child. This seems to occur more frequently when the older person suffers from a dementia diagnosis or a hearing loss. The thought or sight of an older adult in a vulnerable position, such as in a hospital bed, can also elicit this behavior. A good litmus test is to ask yourself these questions:

- Would you talk to a peer the way you are talking to your mom/dad now?

- Would you want to be spoken to the way you are speaking to your older loved one?

If you are not sure whether your tone of voice involves "talking down" to your older loved one, ask someone you trust to tell you if you are doing this.

You Find Yourself Speaking for Them

"The lady will have the spaghetti and meatballs, with a side salad and iced tea." Seems pretty harmless, right? Just being courteous, right? Not necessarily when you are a caregiver for an older adult. Despite your mother being perfectly capable of reading a menu and placing an order, you tell the server, "My mother can't eat salt." Your mother has heard her doctors and knows they have encouraged her to restrict her salt intake. Think about it: Would you want someone else assuming you couldn't make your own choices at a restaurant when you still were capable?

Other People Bring It to Your Attention

Caregiving requires a crew of people, each participating in various roles. When someone is a primary caregiver, it is common for her to accompany an older adult to appointments, such as doctor visits. You may know as much about your older adult's health as she does, and it is common to insert yourself into the process. But, despite your assistance, a healthcare provider is there to help the older adult and address his or her problems. Has a healthcare provider ever interrupted you during a visit to speak with your older loved one saying, "I want to hear what she thinks"? Other members of the caregiving crew will also notice how you interact with the older adult. Has a friend or family member joked or made light of the fact that you are doing too much for an older adult? Your brother, who visits with your mom twice a week, says, "You know, the last time I checked, Mom knew how to turn on the TV." When there are others helping with the care of an older adult, it is important to acknowledge their observations.

They Accuse You of Babying or Disrespecting Them

Despite all your efforts to take care of your older loved one, has he ever done or said anything that seems unappreciative? For instance, after your own busy day at the office followed by preparing dinner for yourself and your father, does he tell you, "I'm perfectly capable of heating up a bowl of soup, you know"? After your mother's hip surgery, she had trouble bending over, and you had to help her dress. While helping her put on shoes, your mother tells you that she was the one who taught *you* how to tie the laces. Are these people being ungrateful? Perhaps—but maybe they think you are not giving them the respect they deserve when they are in a vulnerable state. Sometimes our actions, as well intentioned as they may be, infantilize the older loved one.

Fallout from Treating Your Older Loved One Like a Child

Even when an older loved one is still able to do many things for herself, a caregiver may begin to physically do things like preparing meals and paying bills. The old adage of "use it or lose it" is very real during the aging process. When the older loved one "loses it," more problems can occur for you *and* for your older loved one.

Doing Too Much for Them

Many caregivers start doing tasks, especially routine ones, for their older loved one because they are trying to be helpful. It may begin when the older loved one returns from the hospital after a minor surgery. For example, to be helpful, a secondary caregiver stops by the day after the procedure and does the laundry. The primary caregiver and the older loved one both tell the secondary caregiver how much they appreciated that gesture. Feeling appreciated and useful, the secondary caregiver keeps doing the laundry every time she visits. Soon, it's expected that the secondary caregiver will always do the laundry. The older loved one could still do her laundry but she gets out of the habit of doing it because her secondary caregiver took over.

Lifting a laundry basket or sorting a load of laundry may provide some much-needed exercise to an older adult recovering from a minor surgical procedure. In this case, getting back into the habit of doing the laundry benefits the older loved one. Then the secondary caregiver can turn her attention to another task the older loved one is really not capable of doing yet—grocery shopping, perhaps. The primary caregiver is relieved, because when the secondary caregiver took over the grocery shopping it was one less thing she had to deal with. Allowing the older loved one to do her laundry was good for the older loved one *and* for the caregiving crew.

It's very tempting to take over these routine tasks because, by themselves, they don't seem like a terrible inconvenience. "Dad has been taking a long time getting dressed so I'll just help him button up his shirt," says the primary caregiver to herself. But maybe the practice of buttoning a shirt or tying shoelaces will help with his arthritic fingers. While a caregiver has every intention of making this assistance temporary, it can develop into a routine pattern.

Eventually, when crew members do too much for the older loved one, she becomes more and more dependent on the caregiving crew. It can be hard to break these habits once they are formed because sometimes rather than feeling infantilized, your older loved one enjoys being pampered or taken care of. Or maybe today she enjoys not having to walk to the mailbox, but in a year she will resent that she is no longer able to.

Making All the Decisions for Them

Quite often, once caregivers get involved with helping out their older loved ones with things like physical activities, they begin to think they need to take over everything. If my dad can't even mow his lawn, how on earth can he take care of everything else in his life? To some people, that question sounds crazy. To a caregiver of an older adult, it often makes complete sense. Making—or attempting to make—all the decisions for the older loved one is perhaps the most damaging and common way caregivers forget their older loved one is an adult.

You may have heard the term helicopter parents. This expression describes the phenomenon of overzealous moms and dads who want to do way too much for their kids, even sometimes when those children are teens and young adults. Examples of this include parents who do their child's homework, go with them on job interviews, or handle all their finances. Helicopter parents tend to forget that the child is an adult, or in the case of older teens, nearing and preparing for adulthood.

Most teen and young adult experts agree that a healthy parent–child relationship involves input from the parent while it allows the child to experiment with decision-making and taking responsibility for mistakes. Helicopter parenting creates dependency and hinders the maturation of teens and young adults.

Helicopter caregivers tend toward this same takeover approach, and it can be equally unhealthy. Instead of respecting that the older adult has decades of life experience, the caregiver bulldozes the older loved one. Although this is often done with loving intentions, it most often leads to discord—even estrangement—between the older loved one and the caregiving crew. It can also lead the older adult to lose some of her abilities to do things for herself. Just as helicopter parenting does not allow a child to mature and move forward, helicopter caregiving frequently leads to the regression of older adults' skills.

ARE YOU A HELICOPTER CAREGIVER?

You may risk making the mistake of becoming a hovering and domineering caregiver. Check items in the following list to determine whether your behavior falls into this pattern:

- You recognize the signs of helicopter *parenting* in yourself.

- You don't think there is anything wrong with helicopter parenting.

- You want to force your older loved one into decisions.

- You think you are the only one who knows what is best for your older loved one.

- You don't believe that your older loved one should weigh in on decisions.

- You don't believe that your older loved one is capable of weighing in on decisions even if she does not have symptoms of advanced dementia.

- You have a take-charge personality.

Now, there are certainly times when a caregiver truly does have to jump in and force a situation (typically in cases where there is advanced dementia, which is covered in chapter 12). If an older adult is competent and has capacity, it is important for the caregiver to respect her decisions. The concepts of *competency* and *capacity* relate to medical and legal conclusions that are reached about an older adult's abilities. According to Amy Tao, MD, and Jeffrey S. Janofsky, MD, who authored the chapter "Capacity, Competency, and Guardianship" in the *Johns Hopkins Psychiatry Guide*, competency can really only be determined officially by a judge. On one hand, competency "denotes a person's legal ability or inability" to make healthcare decisions and to sign a will or a contract.

If an older adult is competent and has capacity, it is important for the caregiver to respect her decisions.

Most of the time a judge will not become involved in determining the competence of your older loved one unless there is the rare situation where the caregiving crew is attempting to have that person declared incompetent. More often, a trusted attorney can help you understand if your older loved one is capable of making certain decisions. Evan Farr, certified elder law attorney (CELA), and best-selling author of *The Nursing Home Survival Guide*, explains, "There's all kinds of different levels of competence." He says, "It differs from document to document."

On the other hand, capacity is determined by a doctor and refers to a person's ability to make healthcare decisions.

Best practices for caregiving recommend considering an older adult's opinions even if that person does not have competence or capacity. But when adults *do* have competence and capacity, it becomes even more important to respect their decisions as adults. It is okay to question decisions and express opinions if you think major mistakes are happening. But it is not reasonable to force an older person to do things in the same manner or use the tone of voice we use when we insist a small child brush his teeth.

Forgetting your older loved one is a grown-up and taking over responsibilities for her is a major caregiving mistake because it negatively impacts your relationship with that person. When an older adult senses she is being talked down to or treated like a child, the original relationship she has with the caregiver, whether it is parent–child or husband–wife, suffers. Many people fear getting older and will not acknowledge some of the limitations that aging creates. Add to that the perception that their liberties are being taken away, and an older adult can withdraw from, even resent, the people who are trying to care for him.

Adult children of an older parent are typically the worst offenders at treating an older adult like a child. As functioning adults themselves, adult children caregiving for a parent are used to making decisions and feel empowered and confident in doing so. After all, they are currently making many important decisions every day regarding their jobs, finances, and raising their own children. Spouse–partner caregivers make this mistake less often, unless there was a history of infantilizing the care recipient during the course of the relationship. There may be a variety of reasons for this. A spouse or partner has a history with the care recipient as a peer and can recall numerous instances during their relationship when the care recipient didn't need assistance. A spouse or partner is quite often in the same age bracket and has empathy for the care recipient's ailments. Sometimes a spouse or partner simply refuses to accept the limitations of the loved one's condition.

Fifty-year-old secondary caregiver Jeff was very worried about his eighty-year-old mother, Lillian, who was diagnosed recently with Alzheimer's disease. Jeff explained that his father, primary caregiver David, was very much in denial about his wife's diagnosis. Jeff was filled with anxiety and stress, waiting for David to accept the diagnosis and for the two of them to begin taking action steps to plan for Lillian's future. Jeff began pressuring his father to seek the counsel of an elder law attorney, look into Alzheimer's Association support groups, and consider touring some assisted living communities "just in case."

When Jeff's father failed to make any appointments or read any of the research materials he printed for him, Jeff became frustrated and began taking these steps on his own. He began scheduling appointments at assisted living communities without consulting his father. He met with an elder law attorney and had a power of attorney drafted for his mother. Jeff was overzealous and began to alienate his father. David was making the conscious decision to spend time with his wife rather than going to a support group or meeting with a lawyer. In Lillian's lucid moments, Jeff was agitating her by pushing her into looking at the future.

Jeff should be applauded for taking the situation so seriously and wanting to help his mother. But he needed to be reined in a bit. David and Lillian are still grown-ups. Jeff *is* right on target with his suggestions. It *would* be ideal for David to talk to an elder law attorney, consider support groups, and look into some housing options in case Lillian's living at home gets to be too difficult for him to handle. But David is the primary caregiver in this case. David is the husband who should be making the decisions on behalf of himself and Lillian. Actually, Lillian might be able to make some decisions still, depending on how advanced her Alzheimer's disease diagnosis is.

IS POWER OF ATTORNEY (POA) A GOOD THING?

Power of attorney is a legal role in which an individual is given legal authority (health or financial) to make decisions on behalf of someone else when that person does not have capacity. Power of attorney documents can be very useful when it comes to caregiving, especially when an older loved one has a degenerative diagnosis. But sometimes individuals with power of attorney fall overboard.

Frequently when a caregiver says, "I have power of attorney," with emphasis on the word power, it is a sign that a caregiver has forgotten that the older loved one is a grown-up. Many caregivers assume if they are the designated healthcare or financial agent that they can simply begin making decisions on behalf of the older loved one. Often the type of power of attorney (immediate or springing) that the caregiver actually has does not go into effect unless the older adult is deemed incapacitated.

No matter the health, mental health, or cognitive diagnoses older adults face, they are still grown-ups. The older adult is not a child that a caregiver can ever truly have complete control over, even if a power of attorney or guardianship is in place. This means that the caregiver's instinct to do what's best for that person has to constantly be tempered with treating that person with dignity and making sure her opinions and choices are honored.

~~~~~~

Make a Course Correction: Treat Your Older Loved One Like a Grown-Up

How do you course-correct if you have been treating your older parent like a child? How do you stop making unilateral decisions for your older parent? How do you prevent yourself from becoming a helicopter caregiver in the first place if you are new to caregiving?

If you recognize yourself in this chapter, take a step back and look at your intentions. Intellectually, many caregivers do recognize that their loved one is an adult, but ultimately they fall into treating her like a child because some of her habits or behaviors are—or appear to be—extremely dangerous or scary. If your older loved one has exhibited any type of self-neglecting behavior, this may have been the catalyst for your overzealous approach. According to the US Department of Health and Human Services' National Center on Elder Abuse website, "Self-neglect is categorized as the behavior of an elderly person that threatens his/her own health or safety."

Caregivers, both new and experienced, read this definition and feel justified in taking over the older loved one's life and decision-making. After all, countless behaviors may fall into the category of self-neglect, depending on the views of certain caregivers. This list includes items that caregivers may consider as self-neglect:

- Not preparing/planning for important health, safety, and financial needs

- Unsafe smoking

- Living in a dirty home

- Putting needs of others ahead of own health

- Not paying bills on time

- Hoarding

- Not going to the doctor or following doctor's orders

Although getting out of bed and leaving your house could theoretically threaten the health or safety for *any* person, a caregiver looks at the loved one in the "elderly person uniform" and panics. My mother doesn't take a shower every day. My husband drank two glasses of wine last night, and his medication label says not to. My father is still smoking, and surely that is a threat to his health! Not paying bills on time, not keeping the house clean, not following doctor's orders, the list goes on and on. What about the older person who spends too much money for holiday gifts for the grandkids and then skimps on healthy food at the grocery store? Again, these are examples of behaviors persons of all ages may exhibit. So why should older adults be held to a different standard? The short answer is they really shouldn't be.

The National Center on Elder Abuse website further explains, "The definition of self-neglect *excludes* a situation in which a mentally competent older person, who understands the consequences of his/her decisions, makes a conscious and voluntary decision to engage in acts that threaten his/her health or safety as a matter of personal choice." You may not agree with some of the decisions an older adult under your care makes, but to determine whether you are treating that person like a child, you should try to look at the situation through a different lens.

As an experiment, ask yourself the following three questions to help you determine whether you are treating your older loved one as less than an adult due to your concerns about alleged self-neglecting behavior:

"Would I interfere if Dad or Mom were thirty years younger?"
In other words, if your mother were fifty rather than eighty, would you be asking her about getting her aching shoulder examined? Maybe you would . . . but you would likely be much more

amenable to the idea that it is Mom's decision, and she ultimately has to make the appointment with the doctor. Granted, normal aging really does make nearly everything in the human body a bit more vulnerable. So issues that may not be as serious when we are younger (e.g., the flu) can be life-threatening to an older adult. But it is still a thought-provoking question to pose to yourself when you are trying to determine whether you are being too pushy.

"Would I want someone to interfere if I were exhibiting this behavior?" Now, certainly there are going to be many cases where you will say absolutely! For example, if you had emphysema and were connected to an oxygen tank, yet chose to continue smoking, you should want somebody to intervene and do everything in their power to get in your way, to persuade you to stop. But what if you are drinking too much coffee? Most caregivers would probably say, "No. If I am doing something as benign as that I wouldn't want anyone to interfere." But when it comes to the older loved one, some caregivers become fixated on small issues.

"How would I feel about one of my kids or younger relatives jumping in and trying to take over if I were exhibiting this behavior?" For instance, suppose you are a fifty-five-year-old woman caring for your eighty-five-year-old mother. Would you want your twenty-five-year-old son or nephew treating you the way you are treating Mom? Many caregivers balk when they consider this possibility because most don't believe a twenty-five-year-old possesses the life experience and maturity to be a caregiver. After all, you've had another thirty years to grow and learn. There is a big difference in attitude and behavior between a fifty-five-year-old and a twenty-five-year-old. There may be some merit to that belief, but if that is the case, think about how you would feel as an eighty-five-year-old and the life experience you'd collect by then.

The responses to these three questions can be eye-opening for caregivers. Maybe your responses genuinely reinforced your decisions as a caregiver. But if you answered honestly, did your responses make you pause and reevaluate the way you have been treating the older loved one? Could you be unfairly treating an older adult like a child? Could you be a helicopter caregiver? If so, you can change that course too.

Your main objective as a caregiver is to ensure the well-being of your loved one. Whether it is because of pride, stubbornness, ignorance, or denial, some older adults are reluctant to listen to the younger generation when it comes to their care. There are many effective ways to encourage or persuade older loved ones to consider the perspective of the caregiver, but treating them with dignity and respect that an adult deserves is the best way.

Create an Agenda

When you talk to your older loved one about concerns or suggestions you have on how to improve her health or quality of life, decide what you'd like to get out of the discussion. Do you want to just plant the seed of an idea? Do you want her to agree to see a specialist by the end of the conversation?

If you want your older loved one to create a will or trust, and your goal is to just plant the seed, subtly bring up the topic. You could discuss a situation about a friend of yours whose older loved one passed away without creating a will or trust and how that caused discord within that family.

But if you are looking for immediate action, such as you want your older loved one to book an appointment with an elder law attorney today, decide that ahead of time. Consider what motivates your older loved one. Would knowing that you were concerned about the lack of an estate or incapacity plan motivate her? Would the idea that there could be family discord inspire her to take action? Would having control over where her assets would go provoke her? Would letting her know that she could always cancel the appointment make her feel better about agreeing to set it up in the first place?

Don't Make Assumptions

Sometimes caregivers think they know everything going on in an older loved one's mind, but often that's not the case. You may be a wife married to a husband for fifty-three years, wanting to discuss the possibility of him looking into getting a hearing aid. You may be expecting him to explode with anger when you suggest this, so you delay bringing up the topic and have your defenses up. But maybe he is tired of missing out on all the conversations lately. Maybe he had been thinking about getting a hearing aid but didn't want to bother you, or he had no idea where to go to get one. If you go into the conversation assuming he won't ever consider a hearing aid, and he is actually open to it, your discussion might lead you away from the desired outcome.

Pick the Right Place

Or better yet, don't pick the wrong place. If you are an adult child who wants to discuss Mom moving in with your family, don't have this conversation at Mom's kitchen table where she's fed you for the past forty years. Automatically you are in a setting where you are still the child. It is hard enough for the older loved one to take advice or suggestions from an adult child sometimes (you are still her baby); why make it harder? Consider a neutral setting like when you are out for lunch, out shopping, or even while you are driving together.

~~~~~~

SAMPLE CONVERSATION STARTERS

Example: You want your older loved one to move in with you.

1. What's the most difficult part of living alone for you right now?

2. How much longer do you see yourself in your house now that you have trouble with the stairs?

3. What challenges have you had at home since you got out of the hospital?

4. What would the possible advantages be if you ever decided to live with us?

5. What do you like most about living in your house? What do you like least?

6. What do you find most comforting about your home?

These questions are open-ended. It can be effective to start the discussion by asking for her opinion on what's working or not working with the status quo. Then you can follow her lead by asking relevant follow-up questions or weighing in with your decisions. While many older loved ones will do better with a direct approach like "Would you consider moving in with us?" some may need a gentle, subtler approach to warm up to an idea.

Expect Denial

According to *The Social Work Dictionary* (Barker 2003), denial is "the defense mechanism that protects the personality from anxiety or guilt by disavowing or ignoring unacceptable thoughts, emotions or wishes." If you are trying to convince your older loved one to consider assisted living, he may find that to be an unacceptable thought. Perhaps denial is not always such a bad thing for an older adult. Denial allows the person to slowly consider the reality of changing circumstances. As older adults begin to experience the difficulties in taking care of themselves, concepts like assisted living communities become more palatable. Frequently the caregiver is going to see the bigger picture much sooner than the older loved one does. But, just because someone initially says no, it does not mean he won't change his mind at some later point.

Choose Your Battles

As a caregiver, you become involved in many sensitive areas of an older adult's life. Things like health, finances, and appearance are topics that many people don't feel comfortable sharing with others. Even with time, the walls around discussions on these topics may not come down. You may need to accept alternative ways to deal with these situations to honor your loved one's wishes and reduce your stress.

For example, you have recommended that your older loved one hire someone for lawn care. Your older loved one can afford the service, but he or she does not agree with spending money on such a *luxury*. Sometimes when a caregiver believes the service is necessary and can afford it, it's better to just pay for it if it will keep the peace. You could offer the service as a gift or thank you for the older adult. In respecting that your older loved one is a grown-up, you may have to choose your battles, especially in sensitive areas.

Practice Patience

Some caregivers are control freaks and therefore naturally impatient. Do whatever you can to reduce the stress this is causing you so you can practice more patience with your older loved one. Counseling, meditation, exercise, and consulting with senior care experts are some good places to start.

Some caregivers are going to be impatient because they are genuinely scared that the older loved one is in danger. If that is the case, consider contacting your local Adult Protective Services office to make a referral. By explaining your concerns and providing examples, they can help determine whether your loved one is appropriate for investigation. The individuals who work at these organizations are trained to identify serious risks and have methods of dealing with older adults in danger.

*Caring for an older adult is often a long
voyage, and stepping away, even for a brief
time, can help you stay on course.*

The majority of caregivers grow impatient with older loved ones simply because they have a lot of other things going on. Many caregivers are working, still have kids at home, grandkids they want to see, volunteer work they are enjoying, or travel they want to get to. Enlisting the help of other caregivers, whether in a secondary or tertiary role, gives the primary caregiver necessary breaks. Caring for an older adult is often a long voyage, and stepping away, even for a brief time, can help you stay on course.

Be Persistent

Maybe your older loved one isn't ready to hear your idea today, but try again. Circumstances change. Maybe your mother will move out of denial or change her mind about an earlier suggestion on how to improve health, safety, or quality of life. If you keep treating her with dignity and respect, recognizing that the choice is ultimately hers, she will be more likely to keep hearing what you have to say.

For the past two years, Jack has discussed the topic of bringing home care services in for his mother, Lydia. When he made the suggestion, he always kept the ball in her court, reminding her that it was her life, her decision. He kept track of the number of times he discussed it with Lydia—nine times. Finally, when Lydia's best friend went into a nursing home after a bad fall while she was in the shower, Lydia relented. The catalyst was Lydia's best friend's predicament, but Jack had been warming her up to the idea for two years. Change does not always happen as quickly as we'd like, but gentle persistence can sometimes do wonders.

Be Their Advocate

There are many healthcare providers who will call you out if you are not allowing your older loved one to speak for herself. But, some healthcare providers themselves are the worst offenders. If a healthcare provider is directing questions only to you, doesn't look at your older loved one, or talks about your loved one as if she isn't there, it's important to deal with it.

When you are caring for an older loved one, especially if this person has diminished cognition, a private conversation may be necessary. Otherwise, healthcare professionals should direct their opinions to their patient. If you find a healthcare professional bypassing the older adult in conversations about his care, speak up. Don't be afraid to have a direct conversation with the healthcare provider. Doing so in the presence of the older adult can also reinforce your recognition of his own role in his care.

It is very easy to fall into the trap of treating an older adult like a child. Making a few minor changes in the ways you treat your older loved one can reduce stress and lead to better overall care. If you aren't sure whether you are treating your older loved one like an adult or not, ask a trusted friend, a family member, or a healthcare professional. Their perspectives may sometimes surprise you. Enlisting the help of others can almost always help reduce the stress of caregiving.

Clearly, treating your older loved one like a child, which means you're doing some helicopter caregiving, is not good for the older loved one or for you the caregiver. If you have a tendency toward helicopter caregiving, you might succumb to making the older loved one the center of your world. The next chapter helps you avoid going overboard in this way.

Four

THE WHOLE CAREGIVING CREW IS AS IMPORTANT AS YOUR OLDER LOVED ONE

Gone Overboard: Making Your Older Loved One Your Only Priority

When a caregiver prioritizes only the older loved one, stress intensifies dramatically.

While it's never a good idea to have only one priority in life for an extended period of time, it is necessary sometimes to make one goal or person a priority for a short period of time. For example, writing this book was a temporary top priority for me. But if one thing is the only priority in your life indefinitely, you wind up out of balance and with tunnel vision. It is unhealthy for your older loved one to be the only priority in your life indefinitely. When a caregiver prioritizes *only* the older loved one, stress intensifies dramatically.

This chapter helps you with the following concepts and actions:

- Understand how your older loved one might become your only priority.

- Consider what the potential consequences are of making your older loved one your only priority.

- Create nonnegotiables for the caregiving crew (which prevent you from making your older loved one your only priority).

- Recognize the signs that you've gone overboard by making your older loved one your only priority.

- Course-correct if you've made the older loved one your only priority.

Who Is Impacted by the Caregiving Voyage?

Sometimes caregivers don't consider the far-reaching consequences of caregiving and just how many people's lives are impacted.

 Life Ring: Take a moment to write down everyone you believe is currently being impacted by the fact that your older loved one needs care. Keep this list, because at the end of the chapter I will ask you to do this again to see if your list has changed.

⚓

There are often many persons important to the primary and secondary caregivers who never actually become members of the caregiving crew, but who are still very much impacted by the caregiving voyage.

As I discussed in chapter 1, the ideal caregiving crew consists of a team of primary, secondary, and tertiary caregivers. It's probably obvious by now that being a primary or secondary caregiver is going to have a big impact on your life in many ways. What may not be so obvious is that the caregiving duties can also have a major impact on *those people who are important* to the primary and secondary caregivers. Frequently these persons include spouses, romantic partners, children, grandchildren, or even friends of primary or secondary caregivers. Sometimes these persons, because they are so important to the primary or secondary caregiver, eventually become secondary or tertiary caregivers themselves. There are often many persons important to the primary and secondary caregivers who never actually become members of the caregiving crew, but who are still very much impacted by the caregiving voyage. Often when speaking to audiences of executives at corporations, I hear stories about how caregiving duties have impacted the executives' bosses, subordinates, customers, and even board members!

All members of the caregiving crew, and those people important to the caregiving crew, have needs. Unfortunately, when you are taking care of an older loved one who is vulnerable, frail, sick, or memory-impaired, the caregiving crew often begins to focus almost exclusively on the needs of that older loved one. All too often the happiness, health, safety, and financial well-being of the caregiving crew members gets overlooked in favor of "the greater good" for the older loved one. But when caregiving crew members focus only on the health, safety, mental health, and financial well-being of the older loved one, it is not good for the crew, and it is often not the best thing for the older loved one.

Your Older Loved One Might Become Your Only Priority

But in many caregiving situations, the voyage is much longer than the caregiver expects. Whether the time period is short or long, however, caregiving must become a part of the caregivers' life, not their entire life.

Often, rather than integrating caregiving into the caregiving crew's routine, a complete focus on caregiving becomes the new routine. Sometimes this happens because caregivers tend to think of the caregiving situation as temporary, though it often winds up being long term. The mind-set can be like this: "Once I take care of everything going on with Aunt Susan, we can get back to normal"—normal being the typical routine for eating well, exercising, working, socializing, and having fun. But in many caregiving situations, the voyage is much longer than the caregiver expects. Whether the time period is short or long, however, caregiving must become *a part of* the caregivers' life, not *their entire life*. Sometimes the caregiving crew also is waiting to go back to their typical routine until the older loved one dies, thinking that will be sooner rather than later. And often, as I will discuss in chapter 14, even when an older loved one has a terminal condition she may live longer than anyone expects.

Consequences of Overprioritizing Your Older Loved One

Let's use the analogy of parenting to illustrate the point of overprioritizing one person. Forty-seven-year-old Kristen and forty-eight-year-old Ray just welcomed a brand-new baby girl, Bailey. In addition to being a later-in-life surprise for her parents, Bailey was also born premature at only four pounds, three ounces. Even under normal circumstances, families have a tendency to focus all the activities and conversations around the new baby. But because Bailey was a surprise and born prematurely, she became the center of the family immediately.

But Kristen and Ray have two older children who are ten and twelve. Those kids also deserve the attention and love of their parents. It would be completely irresponsible for Kristen and Ray to only consider the needs of the newborn from now on. Sure—at first—Bailey, who is completely dependent and so small, will get lots of attention, visitors, and gifts. There's certainly an adjustment period where the parents will direct significant time and energy toward Bailey, especially until she gains some weight and attains some developmental milestones. But within the first year or so things settle down and everyone gets into a new routine that includes the new baby. Time, energy, attention, and love will be more evenly distributed. Healthy families understand that the newborn will not be shiny and new for long and that this little one needs to be integrated into the family's routine.

But if Kristen and Ray continue to overprioritize Bailey, never making the transition back to their normal family routine, what are the potential consequences for everyone? This list includes some of the possibilities:

- Bailey could become spoiled, overly attached to the parents, and unable to stay with a sitter.

- The older kids could become resentful of their youngest sister and their parents.

- Because the youngest daughter refuses to stay with a sitter, Kristen and Ray never get any time to connect as a couple.

- Kristen and Ray's couple friends don't reach out to them anymore to get together, because they won't get a babysitter.

- Kristen and Ray's jobs could be negatively impacted because of Bailey's unhealthy attachment (as Bailey gets older she may have trouble in school with teachers and classmates, etc.).

- Kristen's relationship with her mother could become strained, because her mother is critical of the way Kristen and Ray favor Bailey over the other children.

- Bailey could lack confidence as she grows because she is always reminded that she was premature.

Bailey has become the center of this family's world. Ray and Kristen talk about her being a "miracle baby" and the consequences of this impact not just Ray, Kristen, and Bailey. The two older children, Kristen's mother, Kristen and Ray's friends, and Bailey's teacher and schoolmates are also impacted. It's doubtful that Ray and Kristen intended to make Bailey the center of their world, and they may not even see that they are doing it. But many people do see it and, more importantly, other people are being impacted.

How does this scenario translate to caregiving? Caregiving often sneaks up on us like a surprise, midlife baby. Can you think of some special need an older loved one might require for a period of time only, after which you can go back to treating her as you normally do? Write down at least five such special needs.

Did the examples you wrote down include any of these temporary special care situations?

- After breaking a bone

- During a bad cold or flu

- While recovering from a surgery

- While dealing with a bad infection like a urinary tract infection (UTI)

- Following discharge from the hospital after treatment for a minor problem

Sometimes caregivers adjust their routines to accommodate these short-term problems of their older loved one but they never get back to their normal schedules because they begin doing too much.

There are more serious issues, of course, that result in the older loved one's needs immediately becoming justly prioritized. For instance, the older adult has had a major stroke or is diagnosed with Alzheimer's disease, in which case the caregiver crew is thrust into major changes and never pulls back.

Whenever we are taking significant money, energy, and time and directing them mostly at our older loved one, rather than at other people or pursuits, we risk overprioritizing the older loved one. Obviously, this is neither healthy for the older loved one nor for the caregiving crew.

Life Ring: Answer this question honestly: "Since I began caregiving, what people and pursuits have I had less money, energy, and time for?" Make a list of the people and activities you have put on the back burner. Review the list and figure out how to integrate those most important people and activities back into your life.

For years, studies have suggested that the stress from caring for an older loved one puts caregivers at an increased risk for mental health problems, for physical health problems, and for mortality. These studies include Berglund, Lytsy, and Westerling (2015); Perkins et al. (2013); and Thomas, G. et al. (2015) just to name a few. But a study published in the *American Journal of Epidemiology* suggested that there is *no increased mortality rate* among caregivers; actually, caregivers of aging loved ones *live longer* than do their non-caregiver counterparts (Roth et al. 2013). But despite some research poking holes into our long-standing belief that caregivers deal with increased health risks, many healthcare providers believe that it is how caregivers approach the situation that determines if and to what degree they will experience health risks. For instance, a study published in *Quality of Life Research* (Litzelman et al. 2014) determined that global stress, not caregiving specifically, was the true risk factor. Global stress means your overall stress, coming at you from different angles. Global stress includes not just your perceived stress from caregiving, but also stress from anything else in your life: taking care of your kids; dealing with your own medical, financial, or legal problems; realizing you aren't doing anything just for fun or relaxation anymore. Significant global stress, in my opinion, indicates you are just completely burned out on a variety of fronts.

Global stress includes not just your perceived stress from caregiving, but also stress from anything else in your life.

So, you guessed it: The point here is that it's likely your global stress is going to be higher if you are making your older loved one the center of your world. When you have a lot of global stress, you are probably not taking very good care of yourself as a primary or a secondary caregiver. I believe global stress is most likely to affect the primary and/or secondary caregivers, but at times, global stress can affect tertiary caregivers and people close to anyone in the caregiving crew. Let's take a look at a real-life example of a caregiving situation where global stress is in play because the primary caregiver is making the older loved one the center of the world.

Ed is a textbook example of a caregiver who has made the loved one he cares for the center of the world. For the past six years, Ed has been the primary caregiver for his wife, Hannah, who has emphysema and a number of other health issues. Hannah's brother Wade and Hannah's best friend, Natalie, are the secondary caregivers.

Ed is extremely protective of Hannah, and for the first two years he did nearly everything for her himself. He declined the offers of help from both Wade and Natalie. Four years ago, however, when Ed wound up in the hospital with a heart scare, he agreed to let Wade and Natalie begin helping out. He has begun to rely on them more lately because he can no longer drive. Ed is very suspicious of hiring outside help and has never considered placing Hannah in an assisted living community or a nursing home, despite his own compromised health.

Natalie recently was diagnosed with cancer so she is not able to help as much as she once did—she now has caregivers of her own. With all the caregiving responsibilities now shifting to Ed and Wade alone, Wade is finding himself exhausted. He has even canceled some of his own health appointments because he is too busy driving Hannah to her medical appointments. He can't remember the last time he played golf. He wants to take a trip to visit his new great-grandchild but doesn't think Ed can handle Hannah's needs by himself. When Wade suggested to Ed that they could hire some help, Ed became furious. He accused Wade of not caring enough about his sister and of being selfish. He said he would never have "strangers" in his home and said he can't believe Wade would bail out on him now. Wade knows that Ed is totally burned out but does not know how to get him to see how unhealthy the situation is for everyone.

Clearly Ed and Wade are both dealing with global stress, but Hannah is also suffering the consequences of being made the center of their world. Hannah, who has always struggled with an anxiety disorder, worries constantly about Ed's health. She is terrified that Ed is going to die before she does. The resentment she sees building between Ed and Wade also upsets her. She hates that her husband and her brother who used to be close always seem annoyed with each other. Because Ed has been so protective of her, Hannah does not see many other people. And now that Ed is increasingly in a surly mood, their friends rarely stop by anymore. So not only is Ed isolated from others, but also Hannah is isolated as a result of being made the center of his world. Hannah has also stopped doing some things for herself that she used to, such as laundry and dishes, because Ed has "a system" of how he likes the chores to be done.

Ed is even short with her at times, which is upsetting for them both. When Ed snaps at Hannah, he feels guilty afterward.

In reality, Ed's making Hannah the center of the world has not been good for him, Wade, Natalie, or even for Hannah. Hannah sees how tired everyone is, and she feels bad about that. Natalie is now struggling with her own health problems. Wade and Ed both deserve to have leisure time to refresh themselves. They also should be making their own health a top priority. Ed's health is already at risk; doing too much is only putting him at greater risk. Caregivers like Ed think they can go on forever just as they are. Unfortunately, they sometimes die well before the loved one they are caring for.

Although most caregivers are well intentioned and loving, making an older loved one your only priority can destroy families. When the older person is the only priority, the family dynamics shift out of balance. Families sometimes don't realize they are making the older person the center of the world until significant damage is done to other relationships. In this scenario, Ed and Wade's relationship is suffering, but more commonly when going overboard in this way, the hardest hit are the relationships of married couples and the bonds between siblings.

Making the older person the center of the world is a major caregiving misstep because it leads to caregivers neglecting themselves and the needs of other important people in their lives—who are sometimes part of the entire caregiving crew. This chapter helps the caregiver avoid or fix this situation by utilizing strategies to balance the needs of the older person with the needs of all other family members.

Prevent Overprioritizing Your Older Loved One

It is important that everyone in the caregiving crew hold each other accountable for self-care.

Hopefully by now you are convinced that making your older loved one your only priority is not good for anyone—not the older loved one or the caregiving crew. So how do you prevent this from happening?

It is important that everyone in the caregiving crew hold each other accountable for self-care. Ideally—early on—when caregiving begins, all caregiving crew members should discuss how they are going to hold each other accountable for taking care of themselves and the people and pursuits that are important to them. As you can imagine, most of the time this doesn't happen. Why? First of all, everyone is bogged down with caregiving duties, and the crew is not taking the time to plan anything out in an organized fashion. Also, some members of the caregiving crew may actually believe that the older loved one *should* be the only priority.

But as soon as possible during the caregiving voyage, it is best practice for the caregiving crew to have a discussion. Optimally, this conversation should be in person, but as we know in caregiving it can be very challenging to get everyone together at the same time. Can you do a conference call or Skype? While this can be done via email, I caution against that, because tone can be misunderstood. And even though it would seem logical for the primary caregiver to initiate this meeting, that individual is often the one who is bogged down and won't think to do it. Often it is good for a secondary caregiver to suggest and coordinate this meeting.

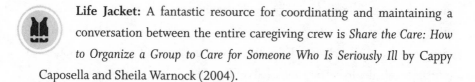

Life Jacket: A fantastic resource for coordinating and maintaining a conversation between the entire caregiving crew is *Share the Care: How to Organize a Group to Care for Someone Who Is Seriously Ill* by Cappy Caposella and Sheila Warnock (2004).

The purpose of this meeting is for all the primary and secondary caregivers to identify as soon as possible what their nonnegotiables are. Some caregivers still work, and a nonnegotiable for a working caregiver might be "I can't take a day off for a care emergency when I have to give a presentation at work." For another caregiver, her nonnegotiable might be that she needs to exercise at least twice per week. For other caregivers, especially for those dealing with chronic illnesses themselves, it might be that their own doctor's appointments are not to be canceled and rescheduled more than once.

What's nonnegotiable for you may not even be on my radar screen. Olivia and Jill are caring for their brother Zack. Olivia has a low-pressure job, so she can't wrap her head around why her sister Jill can't leave work before seven o'clock during the week. Jill doesn't completely understand why Olivia won't give up running a 10K race most weekends. But if both sisters simply accept that outside of a life-threatening emergency those are one another's limits, they will avoid overprioritizing Zack. Olivia's 10K runs are just as important as Jill's need to maintain long hours at work.

Have You Gone Overboard?

Beth Witrogen McLeod's book *Caregiving: The Spiritual Journey of Love, Loss and Renewal* says, "By definition caregiving doesn't affect your life; it *becomes* your life. Outside activities disappear; your friends disappear. In eight years, I have been to the movies three times" (McLeod 1999, 80–81). Can you relate to this? Obviously the caregiver quoted here enjoys movies. But maybe for you it's something else that you aren't doing that you'd like to be. Visiting the grandchildren more, going to family parties, going on vacation—the list goes on and on. Maybe it's simply that you can't remember the last time you read a book or went fishing. But if you can relate to the sentiment in the quote, it is likely that you are making the older loved one the center of the world.

A great way to gauge whether you are making your older loved one the center of the world is to assess your feelings on a regular basis. I created the following worksheet to use when I provide individual coaching to caregivers. It's a great barometer for assessing potential burnout and determining if a caregiver needs to course-correct the way she is doing things. The sheet that follows has one hundred words on it. Without overthinking it, take a couple of minutes to circle any word that expresses how you feel today or how you have been feeling in the past week.

Caregiver Feelings Worksheet

Directions: Make photocopies of this page, or go to my website, www .jenerationshealth.com, to print out additional copies for all the primary and secondary caregivers in your caregiving crew. Set a timer for sixty seconds (you can find one on most cell phones), and within that time frame, circle all the words that describe how each of you is feeling *today or felt during the past week*. This exercise works best if you don't think too hard about the word; go with your gut feeling as to whether a word describes how you feel *in this moment*.

angry	lonely	abandoned	betrayed
cheerful	comfortable	motivated	glad
supported	genuine	resilient	pleased
alone	irritated	peaceful	relieved
tired	resentful	worn out	useful
disgusted	annoyed	useless	frustrated
unappreciated	deserted	short-tempered	edgy
successful	respected	calm	sleep-deprived
low	manipulated	comforted	reassured
happy	confident	helpful	harassed
stressed	displeased	frazzled	prepared
fulfilled	mistreated	accepting	determined
effective	adrift	confused	loved
rewarded	appreciated	worried	valued
composed	mad	furious	grateful
blessed	refreshed	satisfied	guilty
lost	thankful	upset	disappointed
joyful	disoriented	honored	disgruntled
heartbroken	in control	dejected	nervous
distressed	glum	proud	worthy
emotional	deserving	sad	wise
tearful	competent	safe	moral
enraged	appreciative	positive	inept
burned out	special	important	controlled
delighted	hopeful	hopeless	panicked

Now count how many positive words you circled and how many negative words you circled. (Of the one hundred words and phrases listed, fifty are positive and fifty are negative.) Do you have more positive words or more negative words? Were you aware of all the feelings you had prior to completing this exercise? If you did the exercise without judging yourself, you should have an honest collection of words that describe how you are feeling *now*.

How do you interpret the results of this worksheet? While it's a subjective tool, its primary purpose is to alert you to when you are feeling out of balance. Obviously, if you circle fifty negative words and zero positive words, you need to make a change. But it's more about the words you circled.

If you are consistently circling many more negative words than positive ones, you want to consider how you are overprioritizing your older loved one and what you can do to shift. If you find yourself circling words like hopeful and appreciative, try to focus on why you feel that way. What activities are evoking those feelings, and how could you do more such activities? If you are circling words like heartbroken or lost, what is creating those feelings for you? How could you manage those difficult feelings better? Will making yourself and your needs more of a priority help you decrease those negative feelings?

I created this tool to use when I speak to groups of caregivers, and it's been my experience that most people who are currently caregiving circle a lot more negative words than positive ones. But people who circle more positive words than negative ones are usually doing something different from everyone else. For example, I recently presented to a group of working caregivers: managers and salespeople who in addition to working full-time take care of an older loved one. When I asked the group to complete this exercise, one attendee who was taking care of her mother raised her hand to share that she had circled three negative words and thirty-two positive ones! The rest of the exhausted faces in the room glanced over at her, and she immediately exclaimed, "I hired a home care aide for my mother three months ago!" This working caregiver had taken steps so her mother was not her only priority.

In using this worksheet with your caregiving crew, ask each other periodically what your "numbers" are. And don't be resentful if a member has few negative words; try to learn what he or she is doing or not doing so that you could report those numbers yourself.

Life Ring: This worksheet should be completed regularly to "take your temperature" about how you feel. Are you brimming over with negative feelings or are you more in balance? Consider filling out this worksheet monthly, weekly, or even daily. Encourage the rest of the caregiving crew to do the same.

Make a Course Correction:
Treat the Whole Caregiving Crew as Important

Every relationship, in order to be functional
and healthy, must have boundaries.

Every caregiver, particularly primary and secondary caregivers, must learn to develop boundaries. Boundaries need to be set not only with your older loved one but also with other members of the caregiving crew. This is easier for some people than for others. Most people who don't struggle with setting and maintaining boundaries have developed this skill. Whether you find it difficult or easy, to have a less stressful caregiving experience, it's really essential to create and enforce boundaries.

Every relationship, in order to be functional and healthy, must have boundaries. Don't think so? Don't you have boundaries with your children? Most parents have some nonnegotiables with their kids like bedtimes. Don't think there are boundaries between you and your spouse? A healthy boundary for spouses is that there will be no hitting.

Dianne Turpin, MBA, M.Ed., has more than two decades of experience working with older adults, mostly at Area Agencies on Aging. Dianne has worked with many wife caregivers who don't think they are entitled to prioritize anything else besides their spouse because of the traditional marriage vows "for better for worse, for richer for poorer, in sickness and in health" perspective. Many older wife caregivers in particular don't feel permitted to set any boundaries. It is quite reasonable for a wife taking care of her husband to want an afternoon off once a week to shop, exercise, get her nails done, whatever. But many wives, particularly those of the GI generation, or greatest generation (born 1901–1924), and the silent generation (born 1925–1942), don't think setting limits in caring for their spouses is an option.

Set Your Boundaries

My husband, Sean, helped take care of his dad when his father was terminally ill. He told his mom and sisters that he would do anything for his father but "wipe ass." This is a pretty clear boundary. Sean was willing to cook, administer medicine, run errands, or do almost anything else but help his father in the bathroom. Everyone in the family accepted Sean's boundary. Unfortunately in some caregiving crews, especially when the older loved one is the only priority, boundaries are less respected.

When you are trying to have a more balanced life and stop making your older loved one the center of the world, it is essential to hold firm to what you know will help restore balance to your life. Even if you anticipate pushback with a boundary you would like to set, it is important to follow through and set that boundary. The more boundaries you set, the less likely you will be to overprioritize the older loved one and their caregiving. It might help to anticipate how others will respond to the changes you are going to make. Consider who might have a problem with your boundaries. Remember—it may be your older loved one who has a problem with a boundary you set.

For example, you may say to others in the caregiving crew that you will do anything you can to help during the week, but you are not going to be available on the weekends. Some other members of the caregiving crew who are making the older loved one the center of the world might fight you on that, saying, "Why is it fair for you to have weekends off?" These conversations often take place in an effort to make things fair or even. But just because you said you couldn't provide care on the weekends does not mean the other person has to. Is there possibly yet another person, paid or unpaid, who can help with caregiving on weekends?

*You and your caregiving crew are going
to be happier and healthier if your older
loved one is not your only priority.*

One of the best strategies on course-correcting is to seek out other caregivers who are not making their older loved one the center of the world. Caregiver support groups can be a great place to find these people. There are all types of support groups. The Alzheimer's Association has support groups (to help people who are caring for a loved one with dementia) in nearly every community in the country. Many hospitals and other nonprofits also offer support groups as well. If you aren't sure where to find one that's appropriate for you, a great place to begin your search for a support group is your local Area Agency on Aging (AAA), which will be discussed in more detail in chapter 11.

Lots of people balk at the idea of joining a support group. It's understandable—a lot of us don't want to share our major stressors with a bunch of strangers. But Dianne Turpin encourages everyone—even people who aren't "joiners"—to at least try going to a support group. She believes the "single best thing you can do for yourself is go to a support group . . . you need to try it." After all, what's the worst thing that could happen? Dianne compares trying out a support group to trying on a dress at a store. Having raised daughters who are now grown, she reflects back on taking them shopping when they were younger. She remembers encouraging her girls to just try on a dress to see how it fit; it doesn't cost anything to just try it on. The same thing is true of support groups.

You and your caregiving crew are going to be happier and healthier if your older loved one is not your only priority. If you are still struggling with this concept, try to focus on the far-reaching consequences of making your older loved one the center of your world. Overprioritizing your older loved one negatively impacts more people than you probably realize.

Recall that at the beginning of the chapter you made a list of everyone you believe is currently being impacted by the fact that your older loved one needs care. Now that you've read this chapter, look at your original list to see if you need to expand it. Consider what changes you may need to make if caregiving and overprioritizing your older loved one is negatively impacting too many people. Likewise, review the list of activities you have put on the back burner. What will you reintegrate on your priority list once you've stopped making your older loved one the center of the world? In the next chapter, we tackle one of the most common caregiving challenges that comes up—moving in—which can make an older loved one the center of your world instantly if you're not careful.

Five

THINK REALLY HARD BEFORE MOVING IN

Gone Overboard: You're Living with Your Older Loved One, but It's Not Working

"Do you think Aunt Jane should move in with one of us? What if one of us moves into her house with her?" Too often, caregivers think that the best (or only) way to provide good care is to move in with the older loved one or have the older loved one move in with them. While this is not true, the caregiver and/or the older loved one commonly have this mind-set. Obviously, there are some caregivers who were already living with the older loved one before care was needed (e.g., a husband caring for a wife). But unless you were living with your older loved one long before care was needed, this chapter will likely be helpful to you.

This chapter helps you with the following concepts and tasks:

- Understand the reasons caregivers consider either moving an older loved one into their home or moving themselves into the home of an older loved one.

- Identify the pros and cons of living with an older loved one.

- Decide whether moving in is the right option for your situation.

- Course-correct if you've already moved in and it's not working out well.

Why Are You Thinking of Moving In?

The instinct to move your older loved one into your home (or move yourself into their home) is a natural one for many caregivers. (Please note that from now on in this chapter the term *move in* or *moving in* will refer to either a caregiver moving in with an older loved one *or* the older loved one moving into the caregiver's home.) Many caregivers think by moving in they will have more control of the older loved one's situation and will be able to deal with issues more efficiently. They believe their loved one will be better protected and properly cared for if they are physically nearby. Imagine an older loved one has Alzheimer's disease and has left the stove on one too many times, triggering fire department visits. Maybe your older loved one has been conned into buying an unnecessary item by a malicious telemarketer who has called the home. If your older loved one is depressed, lonely, or simply wants company, you may think living together is the easiest way to fix that. In some cases, caregivers worry about an older loved one's self-neglect or even a suicide attempt. Faced with such realities, caregivers often think that the only way to truly protect and take care of the older loved one is to reside under the same roof.

As we discuss in chapter 1, many people hear the term primary caregiver and immediately envision someone who has moved into the older loved one's home or someone who has moved an older loved one into her home. Of course, primary caregivers are not required to live with their older loved ones, but many consider it at one point or another. Often, secondary caregivers have the (I'm sure always genuinely altruistic) idea that *somebody* should move in with Mom— how about the primary caregiver! These types of conversations can be awkward at the least and exasperating at worst. This is a sensitive topic because there can be all kinds of turf issues that may arise. But, most caregivers have the instinct, at one point or another, to move the older adult into their home, whether on a permanent or a temporary basis.

This thought does not occur to the caregiver only. Some older loved ones expect that you, the caregiver, will move in to take care of them. Sometimes this expectation is cultural or simply historical. If your family comes from an African-American, Asian-American, Latino, or a number of other cultures, moving in is commonplace. Historically speaking, it may be that moving an older loved one in is just what has always been done in a family. Particularly when your family custom for five generations has been to move the older loved one in, it may be very shocking to break with this tradition. It will likely be really scary to even *think* about challenging this long-held cultural belief about what good elder care means. Nevertheless, it is important for all caregivers, regardless of their culture, to consider whether moving in is *right* for their situation.

Of course, there are times when the moving-in decision is based on financial reasons: Your older loved one has little or no money, and living together is the most cost-effective option to provide care. Your older loved one may own a home but is reluctant to sell it, especially if it is a home he or she has lived in for decades. Many caregivers don't want to sell their older loved one's house for sentimental reasons. Others don't want to sell their older loved one's house because they want to keep it in the family for future use. Finally, some caregivers may even want to preserve their older loved one's house for inheritance purposes.

WHEN YOUR OLDER LOVED ONE HAS *ALWAYS* BEEN "DIFFICULT"

Occasionally older adults with a lifetime pattern of being controlling, self-centered, or overly dependent on you have an expectation about moving in with a caregiver and assume an overly demanding attitude about it. If you are caring for an older loved one who is demonstrating this behavior, there may be a possibility that he or she has a widely underdiagnosed and undertreated lifelong mental health condition known as a personality disorder. Barbara Kane and Grace Lebow's book, *Coping with Your Difficult Older Parent*, provides advice to caregivers on how to set boundaries and improve communication with older adults who have been "difficult" their whole lives. Even though the title of this book refers to older parents, it is still relevant to any older loved one—not just a parent—that you may be caring for who has a personality disorder or personality disorder traits. Discussions with such individuals about changing the living arrangement can be especially difficult. It is quite possible she is going to be unreasonably angry, insulted, passive-aggressive, or even mean to you when you broach this topic. In this case it may be wise to work with a professional in this area. Consider consulting an aging life care expert, formerly known as a geriatric care manager (www.aginglifecare.org), an elder care mediator (go to www.mediate.com and under the drop-down menu that says "Select Type of Matter," select the word "Elder"), or even a psychotherapist on how to discuss with your older loved one possible alternative plans. Ann Morrison (RN, PhD), who is a former Johns Hopkins School of Medicine faculty member and director of their Alzheimer's Treatment and Memory Center Caregiver Family Program, is now a speaker with Jenerations Health Education. She warns that if your older loved one has always had a personality disorder or personality disorder traits, you should not expect anything new when you are her caregiver. Best practice, especially regarding a move-in situation, is to be prepared for how to handle a potentially unreasonable reaction.

~~~~~~

Pros and Cons of Living with Your Older Loved One

Let's assume you are currently living in a nice house that meets your needs, but someone offered to build you your dream home. Even though this is a very exciting, positive change, there will still be stress associated with that move. The associated stressors would include packing and unpacking your possessions, arranging for people to help you with the move, transferring utilities, changing your mailing address, and so on.

Other stressors might include determining whether all your belongings should be taken to the new home, determining if new items need to be purchased for the new home, saying good-bye to neighbors you consider friends, changing your kids' schools, or the gym you belong to. Even with a move you are looking forward to, there will be stress.

Contrast a move the family wants to make with moves that take place because of caregiving needs. Most of these moves are made in more of a negative mind-set: for instance, someone is sick, disabled, or dying. Major sacrifices are being made, and it's typically a move that is not looked forward to by either the caregiver or the older loved one. While many caregivers understand how stressful moving the older loved one can be for the older person, they dramatically underestimate how challenging it is when a move in takes place for caregiving reasons. Moving is stressful for everyone who's impacted by the move, both the caregiver, older loved one, and anyone else in the caregiving crew (or others who are important to the caregiving crew). Consider the benefits and challenges of moving in with an older loved one before making such an important decision.

Consider the benefits and challenges of moving in with an older loved one before making such an important decision.

And, as with everything in caregiving, it's important to think about your intentions before committing to something. Some caregivers make impulsive decisions based strictly on emotion. Other caregivers don't take the time to explore any other options; their knee-jerk reaction is that moving in is the only choice. Still other caregivers move in because they made some form of The Promise to their older loved one (as discussed in chapter 2). Regardless of the reason, moving is a big step; therefore, it's equally important to weigh both the potential benefits and the potential problems.

What Are the Potential Benefits?

There are certainly times when cohabitation between the caregiver and older adult makes sense. There are practical aspects of caregiving that must be considered, and location is certainly one of them. Perhaps your house is closer to healthcare services or the best-rated emergency department in the event she needs urgent care. It could be that your house is only one story, and it will be easier for your mom to get around. Each caregiving situation is different, but the different attributes of where caregiving takes place must be considered.

There can, of course, be some emotional benefits for both the caregiver and older adult in a cohabitation situation. Obviously, as a caregiver, you may worry less knowing that you will see your older loved one on a daily basis and can be available to handle emergency issues as they arise. If you are thinking that it would offer your young children more of an opportunity to spend quality time with their grandmother, this might be a good reason to move your mother into your home. The older adult may enjoy the more frequent interaction with family. Even older adults who may have been more emotionally distant with their own children may develop close ties with their grandkids.

WHEN MOVING IN WORKS OUT WELL: SMOOTH SAILING!

In many circumstances, moving in works out beautifully. Let's look at an example. Rose has had some struggles with an anxiety disorder, and she has suffered more and more panic attacks while living alone since her husband passed away. Rose's daughter, Maryann, and her partner, Erin, have always gotten along great with Rose. Maryann and Erin invited Rose to move in with them and their daughter, six-year-old Monica. While things are not perfect, Rose helps out around the house by doing laundry, and Monica absolutely loves taking walks with her grandmother after school each day. Having company and being less isolated has positively impacted Rose's mental health as she is suffering fewer panic attacks. She still takes medicine and sees a psychotherapist each week, but the new living arrangement is working out really well. It is a win-win for all four of them.

After years living apart, some caregivers may enjoy the concept of "going home" and spending time living with a parent. This can sometimes develop into a mutually beneficial relationship. For example, seventy-year-old Angela is a widow with an empty nest. Her eighty-nine-year-old mother, Helen, needed help. (She's suffered lots of recent falls, and she is legally blind.) Angela determined that by moving in with Helen it would be easier to provide care rather than visiting several times each week, and the two women—who have always had a respectful relationship—will provide each other with companionship.

While Angela has her hands full with care duties—driving Helen to doctor's appointments, doing most of the cooking, doing a lot of chores around the house, and sometimes even helping Helen with personal care—there is a gain for her in this arrangement as well. Angela feels good about her ability to help her mother. Another plus is that Angela was able to rent out her condo so she now saves more money for her own retirement/future care needs. While not a perfect arrangement—Angela and her mother do annoy each other at times—it is working out very well overall.

~~~~~~

Other potential benefits might be that Mom is not quite ready for nursing home care, and she has limited funds, so she would not be able to pay for assisted living for very long. Perhaps on a time-limited basis, it makes sense to move her in so her funds can be stretched. You could think about renting out her house to bring in some extra income while your mom stays with you. If there comes a time when she needs more extensive care, such as a nursing home, there may be more money for that kind of costly expense.

What Are the Potential Problems?

Wasn't everything perfect when you were growing up? Weren't your mom and dad flawless parents? Weren't you the ideal child? Yes, this is meant to be sarcastic; most of us had challenges and growing pains living under our parents' roof. Now let's add in that you've lived apart from your parents for decades, developed your own life (maybe with a spouse, partner, or kids of your own), and your parents have grown accustomed to a house all to themselves. What could possibly go wrong if you change all that? The list of challenges is lengthy, but I'll try to touch on a few of the more common ones.

There are some basic logistical issues to deal with when a caregiver decides to live with an older adult. It may be something as simple as space. You may not have an extra room where your mom could stay. What if you live in a cold weather climate, and your ailing parent's home is in San Diego? How would the longer winters affect her health? Changing locations can create major disruptions in a person's life—finding a new doctor and making new friends can take weeks, or months, to work out.

Taking care of someone in your home has a huge impact on your own life, maybe not as huge as you thought or would like to admit. But because of the obvious proximity, you will be more involved in the life of your older adult. If Mom falls in the middle of the night, you, or someone in your house, will be the one to wake up and deal with the situation. You may have to leave your office in the middle of the day because your mother left the house without her key and couldn't get back in.

Anyone who lives in the house will be affected by the caregiving situation. Suppose your hard-of-hearing dad moved in and stays up late to watch television. He turns up the volume so he can hear his program, but the loud noise prevents your nine- and seven-year-old children from getting to sleep. They wake up tired and cranky and have a hard time concentrating at school.

For some of you, this may not be hard to imagine, but suppose that your spouse has never gotten along very well with your mother, and you are considering moving her into your home. Or suppose your spouse wants your in-law to move in? How would you feel about it? Maybe the potential challenges you foresee are more benign. One might be that you and your spouse won't have as much "couple time" as you would like. While this is not as serious as tension between your spouse and your mother, you do want to think through how you would manage this change to your relationship. Will you have more date nights outside the home, for example?

Another challenge to moving in with an older loved one involves finances. Most people think that cohabitating will save money. It certainly can. However, what if your mother does not have much money, and you now have another mouth to feed? Electric and water bills for home usage may increase. If you had to move into your parent's home to provide care, your ability to work could suffer. Perhaps your commute is longer, and you are filling up the gas tank more often; or in a situation where you decided to move across the country to your mom's home, you may have had to quit your job. Finances need not be the determining factor when deciding to live with an older adult, but it's a subject that can affect your decision.

Why You Want to Think Really Hard Before Moving In

To illustrate the points previously mentioned, let's look at some examples. Elizabeth is eighty-five years old and recently suffered a stroke. Her daughter, fifty-eight-year-old Jessica, decided to temporarily move in with Elizabeth while she recovered. Jessica moved sixty miles away from her husband to take care of her mother. While Jessica feels like it was important for her to do this, her husband is not very happy about the situation. But Jessica felt an obligation to stay with her mother while she recovered even though other arrangements probably could have been made. Despite intending to move in with Elizabeth temporarily, Jessica has lived with her for nineteen months so far. While Elizabeth recovered nicely from the stroke, she began struggling with other issues like a bout with pneumonia, cataract surgery, and bursitis. It seemed like every time Jessica was ready to move home to her husband, Elizabeth had another concern that needed to be addressed. While Jessica's husband visits at least weekly, this separation has caused tremendous strain in their marriage.

Let's consider another example. Juan and Gloria are in their mid-forties and have two children in middle school. Juan's father, Julio, has been experiencing symptoms of dementia for quite some time, but now that his longtime lady friend with whom he had lived has died, the symptoms have gotten much worse. He was just diagnosed with Alzheimer's disease and has done some things in his home that have concerned Juan and Gloria. He was making a pot of soup one night and went to bed while the stove was on. This set off the smoke detectors and really scared him so Juan had to go over in the middle of the night. Also, after walking to the mailbox one day, Julio tried to get into a neighbor's home, thinking it was his house. The police were called and the misunderstanding was cleared up, but Juan thought his father should move in with them. So he moved Julio into his home.

Julio's dementia symptoms seemed to worsen even more once he moved in. He seemed more disoriented than ever before. Juan and Gloria's kids were a little afraid of their grandfather, especially when he would walk around inside the house in the middle of the night while everyone was sleeping. Because both Juan and Gloria work, nobody was home all day to supervise or spend time with Julio; he wound up getting into the same kind of trouble he did in his own home. But it gave Juan peace of mind knowing that Julio was with them. Eventually they brought in a friend of the family to sit with him during the day, to make sure he wasn't getting lost in the neighborhood or creating fire hazards.

You may see from these examples that moving in with an older loved one or having that older loved one move in with you does not always solve all the problems, and may introduce new ones.

What problems were solved in each case? What problems remained? What new problems arose once the caregiver and older loved one moved in together?

In the case of Jessica moving in with Elizabeth, the problem of Elizabeth needing help adjusting after the stroke was solved. But other problems occurred. It is possible that Jessica created increased dependency for Elizabeth. Instead of simply supporting Elizabeth and staying for a few weeks after the stroke, Jessica became a permanent fixture—so much so that Elizabeth began to feel unable to function without her. It is possible that Jessica liked feeling needed by her mother. The marital strain that Jessica and her husband feel is very common and is another problem that often arises during this type of arrangement. What other options could have worked better?

In the case of Juan, Gloria, and Julio, Juan made the emotional decision to move his father in, probably out of fear. Julio really did need more supervision because he was getting into some dangerous situations because of his Alzheimer's disease. So, while the problem of Juan being nervous and needing more peace of mind seemed to be somewhat solved, was Julio really better off? He was still getting into the same kind of trouble because he was alone during the day while Gloria and Juan were working and the kids were at school. When everyone else in the house was asleep, Julio was wandering around unsupervised, creating potential fire hazards, and theoretically able to walk right out of the house. Ultimately, because of the family's schedule during the week, Julio was probably spending fewer than ten hours a day supervised by them. Moving in really did not necessarily make Julio any safer, but it did make Juan feel less stressed initially.

What about the kids? This arrangement has been disruptive to them, and their relationship with their grandfather has suffered. Is Julio really any better off? Is Juan's family in a better situation? What other options could have worked better than moving Julio in?

How to Decide Whether to Move In

Choosing to move in with older loved ones or having them move into your home is a big decision and one of the great sources of stress for a caregiver. So, how do you decide whether relocation should be part of your caregiving voyage? If you are moving in with your loved one simply because you will feel guilty if you don't, that is probably not the best reason. Let's look at things to consider when making this decision.

Not surprisingly, many people leap to the conclusion that moving in is a great decision if they think the older loved one needs constant supervision. When someone has advanced dementia, twenty-four-hour care really is needed (as in the previously mentioned case with Julio). But stop to consider whether you will actually be spending significantly more time with your older loved one if you do move in. Let's look at a sample of a typical day:

- Commute to/from office: one hour

- Work: eight hours

- Daily errands/housekeeping: one hour (at least)

- Caregiver's sleep: seven hours

These numbers are actually pretty conservative estimates. Have there been times when you needed to stay late for work? Were there traffic problems that caused you to be late getting home? Were there long lines at the grocery store? Even with this sample schedule, a caregiver would have less than seven hours per day to spend time with the older adult. It's not like the caregiver can protect the older loved one while he or she is sleeping, at work, or running errands if the older loved one truly needs care twenty-four hours per day. But the caregiver thinks somehow this arrangement makes the most sense, and the older adult will be healthier or safer as a result of it. If your older loved one suffers from a chronic condition that really requires constant medical or specialized supervision, moving into a nursing home, assisted living, or hiring paid in-home help while keeping your older loved one at her home (without you moving in) may actually be better options.

It's important to assess the condition of the older adult and what type of care or services will be needed—and to consider how moving in might improve the situation. When you observe the older adult, what do you see? Is he having physical difficulty moving around? Is he constantly idle and spending most of his time watching television? In my experience, a great many older adults who have significant physical or cognitive limitations are doing one of two things all day: watching TV or napping. Observing and understanding their behavior can help you with your decision, but you probably could also benefit from the opinion of some trusted advisors. If the rest of your caregiving crew can be objective, they may be able to provide some valuable insight. Seeking the advice of the professionals noted in chapters 10 and 11 could likely be of great assistance. Emotions can skew your view about this critical issue, so it is important to obtain as much unbiased information as you can.

~~~~~~

IS MOVING IN A GOOD IDEA?

Here is a worksheet with ten questions that can help you determine whether moving in is a good idea. Please mark each item according to the following scale:

> 1 = Not at all true of my caregiving situation.
> 2 = Somewhat true of my caregiving situation.
> 3 = Very true of my caregiving situation.

___ My older loved one and I have a stable relationship.

___ My older loved one and I can have candid discussions about difficult subjects.

___ My older loved one respects my spouse/partner/children.

___ Those close to me believe moving in with my loved one would work out.

___ My older loved one genuinely cares about my well-being.

___ My older loved one and I have lived together previously, and it worked out well (growing up together, as roommates, etc.).

___ My older loved one is usually reasonable about most topics.

___ My older loved one respects my personal decisions.

___ There would be benefits (financial, emotional, psychological) for *both* my older loved one and me/my family if we move in.

___ I have seriously considered other options besides moving in.

Scoring:

- 22–30   Start packing!

- 17–21   It could be a good option.

- 11–16   Probably not a great idea.

- 0–10   Don't even think about it!

For more copies of this worksheet, check out www.jenerations health.com.

~~~~~~

Once you have determined the needs of the older adult, does moving in make sense? As much as you want to help, you need to be honest and figure out if you have the time and—more importantly—the energy to handle caregiving in such an intimate setting.

Many family members and older adults balk at the idea of relocating the older loved one to an assisted living or nursing home, but they later will admit that it was a great decision. The older person was more physically active and cognitively stimulated in the new environment that is set up for older persons struggling with limitations. Of course, the services at some nursing homes are better than others, but all of these types of residences are designed to deal with the challenges faced by older adults. We will cover how to evaluate communities like these in chapter 9.

The services available for senior care keep expanding, and many options are available. Perhaps the older loved one really does not need to go to an assisted living community or a nursing home because he really doesn't have a condition that requires twenty-four-hour care. Adult day care is often a wonderful option that can provide social engagement and medical oversight for the older person. If the person is more independent but wants or needs social stimulation, perhaps going to a senior center a few days per week would be beneficial. Some of these options may actually be a much better fit for your caregiving situation than moving in. You can typically find a list of local senior centers and adult day care centers through your local Area Agency on Aging (AAA), which will be discussed in more detail in chapter 11.

Who Makes the Final Decision about Moving In?

> *You might assume this decision lies exclusively*
> *with the primary caregiver. Caregiving affects*
> *a multitude of people, though, and involving*
> *others early in the process can help reduce*
> *the stress of those in the caregiving crew.*

Despite all the information available, some caregivers still think that if an older adult truly can't manage in her own home, moving in with family—or even friends—is the best option. This could be the primary caregiver or, more likely, another member of the caregiving crew. But before you start making moving plans, let's discuss who should be involved in making the decision. You might assume this decision lies exclusively with the primary caregiver. Caregiving affects a multitude of people, though, and involving others early in the process can help reduce the stress of those in the caregiving crew.

Who makes this decision? Ideally it is a consensus. But so much in caregiving is messy, and often various members of the caregiving crew have differing opinions about moving in. The older loved one is also likely to have a strong opinion about this issue. We've discussed the idea of an older adult who expects to move in, but there are many older adults who have absolutely no interest in moving in and giving up their independence. They don't want you living with them, and they don't want to move in with you! This surprises some caregiving crews, but this mind-set is quite common.

Ultimately, unless the older loved one has an advanced dementia diagnosis (which will be discussed in depth in chapter 12), her opinion should be honored *as long as it does not negatively impact the caregiving crew's quality of life.* In other words, if an older loved one who does not have advanced dementia wants to stay at home and not move in with a caregiver, her choice should be honored. By the same token, if she doesn't want you moving in with her—don't do it.

However, there are going to be times when you may have to set limits around her choices. For example, sixty-two-year-old Desiree's seventy-year-old brother Don has been diagnosed with cancer. Desiree lives about one hundred miles away from Don and very close to some excellent cancer treatment centers. Desiree and her husband, who have always gotten along well with Don, offered to move him into their large home where he would have his own suite. Don declined their offer, wanting to maintain his independence. But Don still wants Desiree to come to his chemotherapy appointments with him as often as she can. Desiree is frustrated by this because it is just too far away for her to travel on a regular basis while she's working. She feels irritated because Don easily could have moved in with her family. While it's not wrong for Don to have declined Desiree's offer, and it's very understandable that he'd rather not undergo any more changes right now (moving and finding new doctors near her house), expecting Desiree to travel weekly is not reasonable either.

It is important for Desiree to explain that she wants to be as supportive and helpful as possible but she may only be able to accompany him to chemotherapy once or twice per month rather than weekly. In this case it would make sense for Desiree to try to assist Don in finding other support closer to his home. So, while Don has every right to decline the offer to move in, Desiree has the right to set some limits too.

Bottom line? The discussion about moving in should obviously include the older loved one (barring an advanced dementia diagnosis) and any members of the caregiving crew (and those important to them) who will be impacted by the move.

If you still think moving in is the right thing (and it surely might be for your family), then consider discussing it as a temporary solution that will be tested out. Most caregivers will enter into these arrangements with the best intentions, but anticipating the effects it can have on the relationship is tough to guess. If an older parent is moving in, remember that the old parent–child dynamic will often play out and be magnified—even though the older parent might be sick and vulnerable. If the older loved one who moves in is an aunt, uncle, sibling, or friend, you may really not have any idea what to expect when he moves in. But whatever your relationship—good or bad—whatever might get on your nerves about that person likely will be magnified. So, agreeing to set a time frame for the arrangement, or at least a date to revisit how the arrangement is going, will help reduce stress.

Make a Course Correction: Consider Moving Out

Like everything in caregiving, you can almost always undo something that's not working. Moving in does not have to be permanent, even if you believed it would be. Even if you didn't set a trial period for the arrangement, it is always best to regularly examine the care your older loved one needs and what you are capable of providing. Course-correcting might mean that you should no longer live with your older loved one, or it could mean that you simply need to adjust some of the ways you are doing things. Always be on the lookout for better solutions to your caregiving situation, because there are usually a number of other options.

What Navigational Markers Should You Look Out for?

As a caregiver, you need to consider your mental and physical health as critical. After all, you are reading this book because you want to reduce the stress in your life. Remember the exercise in chapter 4 where you circled words to describe your positive and negative emotions? You will not be as effective a caregiver if your own emotional and physical stability are suffering. Let's try another exercise: true or false. Put a check next to each line that is true for you. How many of these statements did you mark?

❏ You never have a break from your older loved one.

❏ You and your older loved one argue frequently.

❏ You don't feel like you have enough personal time or personal space.

❏ You don't feel like you can be honest with your older loved one about how you feel.

❏ You are neglecting your own nutrition, exercise, sleep, or medical needs.

❏ You are suffering increased health problems.

❏ You don't see any other people besides your older loved one with whom you are living.

❏ People who care about you say they are concerned about you.

❏ There is significant tension in your household or within your romantic relationship.

❏ You don't do anything (e.g., golf, reading, watching a movie) for your own pleasure.

❏ You feel like you have to do most things for your older loved one.

❏ You find yourself having an emotional outburst (e.g., crying, screaming, losing your temper more than usual, hitting your pillow, stomping your feet, slamming cabinets) at least weekly, whether privately or in front of others.

If you marked even one of these questions as true, don't panic. It simply means you might need to reassess your caregiving situation. Circumstances can always change, and perhaps the plan you established for your older loved one needs to be updated. There is nothing a course correction can't fix.

*Circumstances can always change, and perhaps the
plan you established for your older loved one needs to be
updated. There is nothing a course correction can't fix.*

What Are Your Options for Course-Correcting?

Sometimes caregivers want very badly to get out of a move-in situation but don't know how. They are terrified of hurting the older loved one's feelings or perhaps even worried that the older loved one will stop talking to them if they broach this subject. Having a conversation about changing a living arrangement is never easy. Not many people look forward to telling someone that they no longer should live together. So, how do you start that conversation?

What may surprise you is that, in many cases, the older loved one also knows it is not working. Most older adults hate the idea that they might be burdening the caregiver or causing too much stress with their presence. Many older loved ones didn't want the move in the first place, but they did it because they thought it made the most sense. But sometimes the older loved one is just as amenable to changing the situation as the caregiver is.

If the living situation is negatively affecting one party more than another, changing course can be more challenging. Remember that move-in arrangements have an effect on many people, not just you and the older adult. For instance, perhaps your kids are struggling in school because you are constantly tending to their grandmother's needs and you are not available to help them with homework after school. Spouses, children, and grandchildren need to be able to voice their concerns so that all family members' needs are met (as I cover in chapter 4). So, it is important to discuss the arrangement with others.

To help give you the courage to confront the problem, remember this: things are inevitably going to get worse if you don't take some action. And there are different ways to approach this depending on your individual situation with your older loved one. Here are some suggested openings:

When you have the impression that your older loved one would rather not be living with you: Ask for her opinion. Say, "What do you think has been the biggest challenge since we began living under the same roof?" This will often open the way to have a dialogue about the concerns each of you has, which can further lead to an honest discussion about what your other options may be.

When you expect your older loved one will logically understand why you want to change the living arrangement but emotionally have her feelings hurt: In this case a good opening may be: "I care about you very much and want the best care for you. Unfortunately all of us living together is not working out as well as I'd hoped because _____."
Gently introduce the subject and plan to come back to it—allowing her to think about it for a few days or even weeks. Discuss whether her feelings are hurt and why. Focus on the logistical reasons the move is not working out. A common example I've heard from caregivers is that the older loved one shares a bathroom with three teenagers, which is becoming a source of contention.

When your older loved has a lifetime habit of being frequently unreasonable or overly dependent on you (potentially indicative of a personality disorder/personality disorder traits): When your older loved one falls into this category, it is important to be well prepared for the discussion. Brace yourself for the silent treatment, an angry outburst, or a *big* guilt trip. It is common for the caregiver to back down when an older loved one like this has a catastrophic reaction. But that would be the worst thing you can do. Therefore, it is critical for you to make your final decision *before* even broaching this topic and to have some alternative options set up. (Line up support ahead of time, either from your caregiving crew or other friends/family who will "give

you permission" to have this conversation and to follow through
with course-correcting.) If things are too difficult living together,
it is perfectly reasonable for you to course-correct and hold your
ground; otherwise, things *will get worse.*

Alternatively, there are going to be times when living together is not working
perfectly, but it doesn't necessarily involve a new living arrangement for someone.
Ask yourself whether the entire arrangement needs to be scrapped or if a little
tweaking might be the solution. Has the move-in situation worked out okay for
the most part and just needs a slight adjustment? Is it possible to hire some in-
home help from a home care agency or to consider sending your older loved to
adult day care a few days per week? If funds are an issue, perhaps someone from
her church can stop by a couple times a week to sit with your mother while you
tend to the children after school. A few small changes can greatly improve a
caregiving situation without having to start from scratch with a brand-new plan.
These types of small changes are also easier to communicate and generally better
received than is news about yet another move situation.

Living with an older adult who requires care can be extremely stressful for
both the caregiver and the older loved one. Feelings of guilt or concerns about
finances often lead caregivers into a situation that creates even more stress and
results in worse care for the older adult. Be sure to keep an open mind about
such a large decision and consider your own emotional and financial stability. As
I discuss in the next chapter, decisions about how to incorporate caregiving into
your life when you are employed can also be quite a challenge—but it's nothing
you can't handle.

Six

THINK REALLY HARD BEFORE YOU QUIT YOUR JOB

Gone Overboard: You've Left Your Job and You Regret It

Most working caregivers, particularly primary caregivers, have considered quitting work to focus more fully on caregiving. Maybe you've been retired for the past twenty years or you've never had a paid job outside the home. If so, you might be tempted to skip this chapter. Not so fast—even if you don't have a paid job currently, you might have something in your routine that you are considering giving up to be a better caregiver. Maybe you have a regular volunteer shift or play tennis every morning. While these do not technically qualify as a job, some of the concepts we are about to discuss in this chapter may be relatable to your situation.

But if you are like so many caregivers and are currently working or were working up until recently, this chapter will likely help you with some issues that may be on your mind. This chapter helps working caregivers with the following concepts and tasks:

- Determine if it makes sense for you to keep working while caregiving.

- Weigh the pros and cons of leaving the workplace.

- Realize why giving up work doesn't necessarily make you a better caregiver.

- Course-correct if you have left the workplace and think you have gone overboard and wish to return.

Why People Stop Working When They Become Caregivers

In my many years of helping working caregivers, I have heard numerous versions of the following laments:

> "I'm just breaking even if I place my dad in assisted living and keep working. It's like I'll be working just to pay the assisted living bill! I should just quit work and have him move in with me."

> "With all that I have going on with the kids and my in-laws who have been in and out of the hospital a lot lately, not to mention the dog, I may as well just stop working and focus on all of that."

> "I don't really like my job anyway, and if I quit I can focus on being there for my mother. She is having some health problems, and it's likely to get worse because she is in her late eighties."

But, contrary to popular belief, even if it seems like a great option at first glance, quitting your job does not always turn out to be simple or smart.

If you are a caregiver who stopped working because of caregiving, do any of these statements sound like your reason for leaving the workplace? Sometimes ceasing work seems like the simplest and smartest option. Isn't it really a no-brainer? Work equals stress. Caregiving equals stress. Getting rid of one of those sources seems like the opportunity to cut your stress in half. But, contrary to popular belief, even if it seems like a great option at first glance, quitting your job does not always turn out to be simple or smart. Let me explain why.

Why You Should Think Really Hard about Quitting Your Job

First off, let's not over-romanticize work. There is the old adage that says, "No one looks back on their life saying they wish they'd spent more days in the office." Work can be downright miserable sometimes. Why else do so many of us struggle with getting up on Monday mornings to go back to the daily grind? Many employees endure lousy commutes, micromanaging bosses, sabotaging coworkers, and they don't even feel like they are making much of a difference at their place of employment. But even if you identify more with some of the negative aspects of paid employment, here are some questions to ask yourself before you make the decision to quit a job to focus on caregiving:

- Besides the paycheck, what am I giving up when I leave my job?

- Even though working while caregiving has been stressful, have there been times when work has been a welcome distraction from caregiving worries?

- Are there reasons besides caregiving that make me want to leave my job?

- How long am I willing to be out of the workforce?

- What might I miss about working or my job after three to six months?

In her book *The Feminine Mistake: Are We Giving Up Too Much?*, *Vanity Fair* contributing editor Leslie Bennetts challenges a woman's decision to stay at home with small children while her spouse earns a good living. While I personally believe every woman needs to decide what makes the most sense for herself and her family, Bennetts makes some excellent points about working mothers that apply to both female and male caregivers. The bulk of her book makes a case for women continuing their careers throughout motherhood for financial reasons and for personal fulfillment. But you can draw many parallels to the decision of a caregiver to leave the workplace. It is really important to consider what you may miss if you leave your job behind.

Finances
Obviously, dollars and cents come to mind first when a caregiver thinks about quitting a job. Unless you are truly wealthy, finances play a pretty big role in caregiving decisions. When considering whether it might be more cost effective

to quit work rather than hire help or place an older loved one in assisted living or a nursing home, it is really important to look at much more than just a snapshot of today's financial picture.

Let's look at an example of a very common situation for caregivers. Marion, a thirty-year-old retail store assistant manager, and her husband Craig are paying three thousand dollars per month toward a home care aide for her sixty-nine-year-old father, Wendall, who is struggling with complications from diabetes. Craig and Marion have recently begun discussing whether it is worth it for her to continue working. Marion's paycheck brings in about $3,300 per month after taxes. Because Marion handles a lot of extra details for her father that the home care aide does not, she is perpetually exhausted. She has started to dislike some things about her work lately too. Because she works in retail, it is a really big deal when she arrives late on the days she takes her father to the doctor. Her coworkers are frustrated because they have more responsibilities when she is late. Because Wendall's doctor visits are not always scheduled ahead of time because of emergencies, Marion's manager has a hard time knowing when she is available for the retail work schedule, which varies on a biweekly basis. Speaking of her manager, Marion also has a new boss she doesn't particularly like. It seems like the perfect storm. Why put up with all this extra stress to walk away with only an extra three hundred dollars per month when Craig can support them with his salary alone?

Craig and Marion are having a hard time figuring out why Marion *shouldn't* resign. But they haven't yet considered the potential longer-term impact. Many people never consider the long term because the decision to quit often is made with short-term information and when the caregiver(s) is under extreme stress. By itself, losing an extra three hundred dollars per month may not seem like a life-changing event for many people. But, if Marion were to save that three hundred dollars and earn a modest one percent interest on it annually, she would accumulate nearly $126,000 over the next thirty years before she retires. Not so insignificant now, right?

Again, unless you are endlessly wealthy, quitting your job or retiring prematurely can have a ripple effect in the finances of subsequent generations in your family, too. Ultimately it may be your future caregivers who are stuck in a similar predicament if you don't have enough funds to pay for future care *you* may need. Let's look at another example to illustrate just such a situation.

James took an early retirement to care for his father, Francis, even though James really needed the additional income from working a few more years to put into his 401(k). After Francis passed away, James never went back to work. Now that he needs care, his daughter, Niki, is providing hands-on care because there is not enough money to hire a home care aide. If James had not taken an early retirement, there would have been more money to help support his own care needs, and this burden may not have fallen on his daughter. And because James did not particularly enjoy having to provide care for his father, he had been hoping that he would not put Niki in the same situation.

Many families experience this sort of thing, and it can be a vicious cycle. We frequently see generations of families failing to prioritize their own financial well-being and retirement in favor of supporting the older generation. But it only takes one person to discontinue this generational trend in a family. To prevent these financial repercussions for James and Niki, what might James have done differently? After all, early retirement was not his only option. Maybe James should have stuck it out at work for the next several years. He could have coordinated a plan with some paid help and some unpaid help (as I discuss further in chapter 10). Perhaps he could have taken a temporary leave of absence from his job through FMLA to coordinate a plan. (See the subsection titled "Consider Taking FMLA Time as a Test-Run" later in this chapter, and the FMLA box in chapter 2, for more details.)

Let's look at another instance of financial repercussions when the primary caregiver decides to quit working to become more involved in caregiving. This illustrates the potential issues that can develop between caregivers and other people in their lives.

Vince and Carrie are a married couple who have always both held full-time jobs. They are both in their fifties and have always kept their money separate. Now that Carrie has decided to take time off to care for her mother, Leah, there is some financial tension between Carrie and Vince. Carrie was accustomed to spending money freely, such as getting facials and buying clothes for their college-age kids whenever she wanted to.

Not surprisingly, Vince is frustrated when he sees Carrie's spending level now that she's not working. While there really is no financial emergency, Vince resents that he is now picking up all the bills and that Carrie has made no effort to curtail spending. This couple's new way of handling money is yet another change that must be added to the stress of caregiving.

Let's look back on the time Carrie told Vince she wanted to quit her job. It was made during an emotional moment when Carrie said she didn't feel like she was doing a very good job helping her mother. She had this big *aha!* moment about how her career was not nearly as important as her family. Vince told Carrie he would support her decision fully and that they didn't need to worry about money; they had plenty saved, and Vince earned a great salary. But they spoke in generalities. Vince was very sincere in his commitment to financially support his wife. He probably didn't even think about how this major change to their financial arrangement might cause tension. After all, one of the reasons the couple had decided to keep their money separate was because they had different spending habits.

Caregivers should routinely examine the
financial impact that comes with caregiving.

Ideally a more detailed discussion would have taken place. But how do you start that type of conversation? It is important to be honest and realistic not only with your partner but also with yourself. First, Vince and Carrie would need to acknowledge the difference in their financial situation. It is helpful to literally write down the amount of money you would be losing. Developing a budget and examining your spending habits can help you identify areas where you could spend less, like cutting out the premium cable package or finding a better deal on your cell phone. By taking a detailed look at their finances, perhaps Carrie would have seen that her spending habits could not be sustained if she quit her job.

But it's not too late now for Vince and Carrie to have that discussion to set up a better agreement. Caregivers should routinely examine the financial impact that comes with caregiving. There may be ways for Vince and Carrie to work out an arrangement that they can both live with. For example, they could agree to a set discretionary amount each month for "fun stuff" that Carrie can spend on herself and their children.

If you get out of the workforce to be a caregiver today, how would that affect your long-term plans? How hard will it be for you to get back into the workforce if you want to get out only temporarily? Will you be able to command the same salary when you return in six months? A year? What if Marion or Carrie quit today and wanted to get back to work years from now, after their older loved ones have passed away? Would they command the same salary? If you are over the age of forty-five, there is always the chance that you could face age discrimination when you try to rejoin the workforce at the salary and seniority level you desire. What if you work in the technology field? Would you be up to date with the latest technology after being out of the industry for a year—much less five years?

Personal Fulfillment

Paid employment means a variety of things to different people. For some, work is simply all about the compensation. They work only to bring money in or for the health insurance, pension, or other benefits provided by their employer. But for many workers, paid employment provides so much more than just the dollars. Work provides socialization; many workers have friends, or at least friendly acquaintances, they see on a daily basis. Work gives you a routine, a place to go every day, a place where you are expected. For many it also provides a feeling of accomplishment, especially for people who consider their work a career or vocation. Let's also not underestimate that quitting, retiring, or cutting down hours (even if for the right reasons) can introduce *yet another* change in your life.

Going back to Bennetts' thoughts on mothers, she highlights the fact that many women who love being mothers and opt to stay home do not feel completely fulfilled overseeing the development and growth of their child. Many also want careers so they can utilize the skills and talents they have developed through education and years of experience. The parallel to caregiving is obvious. If a mother is not always fulfilled with mothering duties that she happily and willingly signed on for, and often still longs to use other skills, many caregivers will feel similarly. Simply being a caregiver may not be enough. And let's not forget that caregivers are taking care of an older loved one who is not growing and developing; that person is typically failing and declining. Many mothers say that you never stop being a mother. In contrast, however, when you are a caregiver for an older loved one, there will come a time when your caregiving duties will end.

> *This may surprise you, but the physical routine of going to a job actually can help reduce the stress of caregiving.*

A caregiver—like a working mother—should not underestimate other needs that may be met by a job, such as socialization and routine, which add to an individual's personal fulfillment. Many people don't consider that a lot of their social life and interactions with people come as a result of a job. How many of your friends did you meet at work? Are there people that you enjoy seeing or talking to everyday? Whether you work from home, an executive office suite, in a retail store, or from a cubicle, you engage in some social interaction at your job. That socialization you get from going to work may also provide you with a needed break from your care duties.

This may surprise you, but the routine of reporting to a job actually can help reduce the stress of caregiving. Even though everyone experiences work-related stressors, it may be that working is the only outlet you have that gives you a real break from caregiving. Some workers don't realize how much the routine of a job keeps them centered, especially if they've held a job for a very long time. Many studies have indicated that when people retire without a plan, they flounder. Nancy Hooyman and H. Asuman S. Kiyak's book *Social Gerontology: A Multidisciplinary Perspective*, ninth edition (2010) summarizes the research by indicating one factor that retirement satisfaction is contingent upon is "activities that offer autonomy, sense of control, and chances to learn and feel useful." Even if you don't necessarily love your job, it grounds you. You know what to expect each day. Disrupting your routine can be a very difficult thing to become accustomed to, especially when that routine is being disrupted so that you can provide caregiving.

Becoming a caregiver is a major change in your life. When you add leaving the workplace to provide caregiving, you have two huge changes going on. You need to consider the potential domino effect that leaving the workplace is going to cause. You may think that leaving your job to become a full-time caregiver affects only you. As we just explored, however, the effects are widespread. If a member of the caregiving crew is contemplating leaving her job, it's crucial to discuss the possible ramifications with the rest of the caregiving crew *and with those important* to the caregiving crew.

What Are Your Options Other than Quitting?

So, you've sat down and made a list of the pros and cons of leaving your job to become a full-time caregiver. You have looked at the financial impact, both long and short term. You've carefully considered how much your social life will change and how you will deal with the role of full-time caregiver. You've discussed how your decision will impact others, including people outside the caregiving crew. It is still not an easy decision, is it? There are some ways you can make working while caregiving less stressful, though, which I describe in the sections that follow.

Communicate with Your Employer

While you don't need to share every painstaking detail with your boss, it is important that she knows you are a caregiver and understands a little bit about what that involves for you. Often, working caregivers are reluctant to share this detail, much the way some working mothers are reluctant to discuss childcare issues because they don't want their boss to doubt their commitment to the job. In reality, however, some employers are willing to make special arrangements to retain you based on your individual needs—especially if you are a top performer at your job. But, at the very least, your boss should recommend that you contact human resources and look into FMLA.

Check with Human Resources Personnel

You often hear that the only stupid question is the one not asked. Are you familiar with all the benefits your company offers? In addition to FMLA, some companies offer leave for employees to deal with caregiving issues or have backup care available when needed. Many organizations have Employee Assistance Programs (EAP) you can be referred to through human resources as well. EAP was designed to help employees struggling with substance abuse, mental health issues, or other personal problems. Caregiving is typically an area that EAP specialists are knowledgeable about. Speak with your manager or someone in the human resources department to see if there are programs available to help you.

Some employers allow their staff to use paid sick and vacation leave to deal with caregiving situations. Some companies even allow their staff to purchase additional vacation days, and other companies allow coworkers to donate their unused vacation time to another employee. These may be only temporary solutions, but they can provide you with the chance to assume the role of a full-time caregiver without fully committing to it permanently.

Consider Taking FMLA Time as a Test-Run

Take a minute to think about two big decisions that people commonly make in their lives: purchasing a car and buying a home. Before buying a car, you would take it for a test-drive, wouldn't you? You'd want to get a feel for how the car moves and whether you are comfortable driving it. If you were going to buy a house, you'd insist on a home inspection before signing the legally binding paperwork at closing. The home inspection helps you identify potential issues with the home that you may not be able to see just by being shown through the rooms.

It's the same thing when you're considering becoming a full-time caregiver. Choosing to be a full-time caregiver is a big decision, yet there are proven ways to help ease you into that transition and to help you understand what you are about to undertake.

Under the Family Medical Leave Act (FMLA), private for-profit and nonprofit organizations with fifty or more employees, as well as all government agencies, are required to offer twelve weeks of unpaid leave to care for a family member. Before you even consider quitting your job or taking early retirement, it is crucial to ask your employer about this option and discuss what's involved in at least trying it out. Exercising FMLA gives you the freedom to test how you would manage as a full-time caregiver while maintaining a safety net so that your job will still be there if you want it.

You might take three weeks of FMLA and say, "No way! I am not cut out for taking care of my mother full-time." But others may think, "Wow, life sure is easier when I don't have to juggle so much." While most caregivers' reactions to taking FMLA aren't quite so polarized, you will at least get a taste of what life might be like if you opted to be a caregiver full-time.

Get Paid by Your Older Loved One

If you do decide to quit your job, consider looking into getting paid by your older loved one to care for him or her. An experienced elder law attorney can help you draw up an agreement by which you get paid by your older loved one for the caregiving you'll provide. In most states this is a legal arrangement where you can be paid very modestly (typically at the rate of a home health aide) for taking care of your older loved one.

Some states have legal ways in which paying a family member to provide care can count toward a potential Medicaid spend-down (talk to an experienced elder law attorney in your area for specific details). The funds paid to the caregiver(s) may not be a lot of money, but they could help defray the financial disadvantages of quitting your job.

Like so many other areas in caregiving, of course, this can arouse friction within a family and/or the caregiving crew. Sixty-three-year-old Carys, for example, is a teacher who is considering retirement. Carys has also been taking care of her father, Fred, diagnosed with emphysema a few months ago. Carys and Fred discussed the situation with an experienced elder law attorney and had an agreement drawn up so Carys could be paid by Fred to take care of him. This is an asset-protection strategy that some families will consider so that money spent paying Carys will not be counted if Fred ever needed to apply for long-term Medicaid (more on this in chapter 10). When Carys shares that she will retire to take care of their father under this arrangement, her brother, Nathan, explodes. "If you need the money so badly, why are you going to retire in the first place?" he asks. His argument is that Carys has no right to be paid for doing something "for family." This plan just doesn't sit right with Nathan. Carys is shocked that her brother had such a strong negative reaction; she assumed that he'd be thrilled they didn't have to hire a stranger to help out.

But in other situations, the rest of the caregiving crew "gets it." They realize that rather than hire a home care aide or place the loved one in an assisted living community (both of which cost money), it may be nicer to simply pay one of the existing caregiving crew members instead.

Change Your Work Circumstances

Many working caregivers find that changing positions within their company, finding a new job entirely, or figuring out a way to work for a more accommodating manager can make a huge difference in their quality of life. Sometimes remaining in the workforce while working part-time is the best option of all.

Minimize Everything Else

If you continue to work while caregiving, let go of everything else you can that doesn't absolutely have to be done or doesn't bring you utter joy. For instance, stop volunteering for every committee at your child's school. Decline social functions that you don't have a burning desire to attend. Set clear boundaries with colleagues regarding your ability to take on extra projects and work additional hours.

Create a Plan B

Emergencies come up *both* at the office and in caregiving. Figure out who your backup is for picking up the kids, taking Mom to her doctor's appointments, or attending that unplanned but mandatory business meeting.

Make a Course Correction: Keep Working as Long as You Need (or Want) To

Many stay-at-home caregivers believe their older loved ones would be devastated if they were not at their beck and call. Yet, for many older adults this is not so. They do not want their caregiving crew to be inconvenienced by their needs. The most important thing to do in terms of course-correcting is to start out by talking to your older loved one.

If your older loved one is upset by the idea of you not being around all day every day, it may make sense to set a deadline for how long you will continue to be available full-time. But it is important to have a discussion about *why* you are returning to work full-time. Your reasons for returning to the workforce could be financial (you need the money), emotional (you miss work), or medical (your older loved one requires medical care that you cannot provide). Conveying a reason that you need to step back from full-time caregiving helps an older loved one feel less abandoned because there is a basis for your decision. Depending on why you want to go back to work, there are different strategies for course-correcting.

If you need the compensation you were making previously, start a full search for a job that will again meet this need. Then make a commitment to coordinate the appropriate in-home help or make plans for your older loved one to go to assisted living or a nursing home. Most adults, including older adults who need care, understand the concept of financial stress and can understand why you may need to return to work.

> *When you speak with your older loved one, you*
> *can explain that your caregiving is not going*
> *away. You are simply making some adjustments*
> *or supplementing it with outside help.*

It may be that quitting the job is just fine; it's just that full-time caregiving does not fulfill you. If you are struggling with the lack of socialization and/or routine, but don't truly need the money or feel the need to jump back into your career, figure out how to get some items on your calendar right away. Start taking an exercise class three mornings per week at 8:00 a.m. Volunteer at the local elementary school every Wednesday afternoon. Have a standing lunch date with your friends each week. Arrange adult day care or care in the home for when you will be busy with your new activities. When you speak with your older loved one, you can explain that your caregiving is not going away. You are simply making some adjustments or supplementing it with outside help. As much as the older adult cares for you and needs your help, she may look forward to the prospect of having some time away from you.

Generally, an older adult's health will decline with time, not improve. While you may have been able to provide adequate care for a number of years as a full-time caregiver, your older loved one's physical condition may have deteriorated to a point where she needs professional care. You may have been comfortable giving medication or handling routine tasks around the house, but what if your older loved one needs physical therapy after a fall? If you want to provide the best care for your older loved one, sometimes you need to utilize professionals.

In addition to having this conversation with the older adult, it is helpful to speak with other members of the caregiving crew. Although some crew members may object and question your decision, having identified your reason for changing the caregiving arrangement can reduce the stress of having this conversation.

Leaving the workplace prematurely and feeling like it is the "only way" may very well be a symptom of a bigger problem. It may signify that the caregiver has surrendered to caregiver martyr syndrome. The next chapter helps you avoid this condition and offers tips to course-correct if you have fallen overboard.

Seven

DON'T BE A MARTYR
(BECAUSE MARTYRS DIE)

Gone Overboard: Someone in Your Caregiving Crew Has Caregiver Martyr Syndrome (Is It You?)

As you learned in the opening chapter, caregiving works best when there is a solid crew consisting of one or two primary caregivers, several secondary caregivers, and many more tertiary caregivers. Caregiving is never a job for just one person. When one member of the caregiving crew (typically a primary caregiver) tries to do it alone or do more than he or she can reasonably handle, that person may be suffering from what I refer to as "caregiver martyr syndrome."

Caregivers of older adults can seem like the most selfless people in the world. They sacrifice money, energy, and time to assist an elderly loved one. But is it possible to be too selfless as a caregiver? Absolutely, and when it becomes caregiver martyr syndrome, it can have grave consequences that can include physical and mental health declines for the caregiver, conflicts and estrangements among the caregiving crew, and even—though unintentional—possible damaging abuse and neglect of the older loved one.

Merriam-Webster's online dictionary defines a martyr as "a person who sacrifices something of great value and especially life itself for the sake of principle." Caregiver martyr syndrome, then, in my definition, is sacrificing one's whole life in favor of caring for an older loved one. Not only do caregiver martyrs put the older loved one above everyone and everything else, including themselves (going overboard in chapter 4 addresses making your older loved one your only priority). They also believe they are the only ones who do caregiving "right."

This chapter helps you with the following concepts and tasks:

- Understand what caregiver martyr syndrome is.

- Recognize and manage a martyr in your caregiving crew.

- Recognize martyr syndrome in yourself so you can utilize strategies to change.

Why Do Caregivers Fall Victim to Caregiver Martyr Syndrome?

Once a family member commits to caring for an older loved one, it is common for the caregiving to consume that person's life initially—at least for a period of time. In chapter 4, we discussed why it's so important for the older loved one not to become the *only* priority of any one caregiver. But some caregivers do go down this road and eventually come to believe they are the *only* ones who can care properly for the older loved one. Tunnel vision takes over, and caregiving becomes their identity.

> *Caregivers, and those who love caregivers,*
> *need to understand that too much selflessness*
> *inevitably leads to caregiver martyr syndrome.*

Unfortunately, sometimes one caregiver does the job alone, without significant help from others, and there are major consequences to these solo providers. Some studies (Berglund, Lytsy, and Westerling 2015; Perkins et al. 2013; and Thomas, G. et al. 2015 to name a few) suggest that caregivers who don't enjoy help from others may experience more illnesses, injuries, and possibly increased mortality than their counterparts in the same age group who are not providing care to dependent loved ones. Caregivers, and those who love caregivers, need to understand that too much selflessness inevitably leads to caregiver martyr syndrome. The following caregiving scenario illustrates caregiver martyr syndrome to a tee.

Ashley is the primary caregiver for her father, Joe, who has Lewy Body dementia. (Lewy Body dementia is a fatal progressive condition; the symptoms include memory loss, hallucinations, sleep disturbances, and balance/gait problems.) Although Joe is still in the earlier stages of the disease and is able to live alone in his home, Ashley has been over at his house every day for the past year. She has a part-time job, is recently divorced, has grown children, and has made taking care of Joe her main priority.

Stephanie, Ashley's sister and Joe's other daughter, is the secondary caregiver. While Ashley complains about being exhausted and needing more help, she criticizes Stephanie's way of caregiving. When Stephanie helps out, Ashley still comes over to their father's house, looking over her sister's shoulder, monitoring even small tasks like what kind of food she prepares for Joe. Stephanie had hoped that when she came over Ashley would take some much-needed respite time to go for a walk or have coffee with a friend. Instead, Ashley hovers over her. Stephanie is tired of being criticized and has started to back off from helping out with Joe. Ashley has become angry that Stephanie is helping out less and cannot see things from Stephanie's perspective. Ashley does not understand why Stephanie doesn't want the best for their father like she does.

If you guessed that Ashley is the one who is in the throes of martyr syndrome you would be correct. Now, it would be reasonable (and absolutely necessary) for Ashley to intervene if Stephanie had been giving their father the wrong medication. But for smaller things, like how she's cooking his eggs or what time they eat dinner, it would make more sense for Ashley to back off. Ashley might truly be better at some of the caregiving tasks. But if she thinks her way is the only way to provide acceptable care for Joe, and she allows martyr syndrome and her need to control all his care to run wild, she will alienate Stephanie. Many secondary caregivers in Stephanie's position are going to throw up their hands and back off. Sadly most caregivers experiencing martyr syndrome genuinely do not see that they are pushing their secondary and even tertiary caregivers away.

TOTAL SELFLESSNESS IS NEVER GOOD

Ideally a primary caregiver welcomes the help of many secondary and tertiary caregivers. Unfortunately sometimes the primary caregiver gets into a dysfunctional caregiver martyr syndrome mind-set that doesn't benefit her or the older loved one. The martyr syndrome mind-set involves distorted thinking such as *Nobody can take care of her like I can*. Now it's true that nobody will take care of your older loved one *exactly* as you would. But others don't have to do it exactly as you would for it to be decent care.

Sometimes members of the family or even friends are trying to offer their help as secondary caregivers, but the primary caregiver dismisses them. The primary caregiver doesn't want help and thinks she can do it all better than anyone else. When a primary caregiver refuses help, it is a huge mistake and creates additional stress.

It is certainly reasonable for the primary caregiver to have some boundaries as to what kind of help she wants to accept. Marie is taking care of her husband, Dan, who recently had hip replacement surgery. Marie's sister, Kathy, offers to stay with Dan while Marie goes to a wedding. Dan and Kathy don't have the best rapport so Marie declines this offer, knowing that Dan would be miserable with Kathy at the house all night. But perhaps Kathy can do something else to help. Could she shop for the wedding card and gift so that task is taken off Marie's plate?

Further, maybe because of Marie and Dan's comfort level, Marie decides she is the only one who will provide personal care such as bathing Dan. But what additional things can she be open to allowing others to help with? Can their son, Bob, take Dan to doctor's appointments?

In other situations, the primary caregiver appears to be doing just fine, and nobody else in the family offers help. The other family members don't think their help is needed; the primary caregiver has it all under control. Meanwhile the primary caregiver, quickly losing steam, is headed for a crisis. The primary caregiver goes overboard by not asking for help.

In this situation, the primary caregiver is often inside her own head furiously thinking, *I can't believe nobody is offering to help!* When the primary caregiver is privately seething, she should honestly reflect on whether she has turned down help in the past. This can be similar to a party's host who is frustrated that she's doing all the shopping, cooking, and decorating but realizes she declined the offer of several guests who wanted to bring side dishes and desserts.

~~~~~~

A common problem in caregiving is the primary caregiver becoming too controlling and allowing his or her ego to dictate care plans. Sometimes members of the family or even friends are trying to offer their help as a secondary caregiver, but the primary caregiver dismisses them. The primary caregiver doesn't want help and thinks she can do it all better than anyone else. Or, as with Ashley, the primary caregiver accepts help but then micromanages and critiques how that help is given.

How to Spot Caregiver Martyr Syndrome in Your Crew

What can be done to pull a caregiver like Ashley from the depths of martyr syndrome? It can be a real struggle. Often the caregivers are in denial about their overcommitment to caregiving. A useful exercise can be to carefully consider each symptom category: physical, emotional, psychological, spiritual, social, relationship, and financial. What kind of issues is she (or are you) having within each category?

Physical Symptoms

Often the first symptom of caregiver martyr syndrome is a physical problem. The caregiver may struggle with headaches, stomach problems, muscle tension, and excessive fatigue. The caregiver is likely not sleeping or eating well. Exercise has gone out the window. Ironically, while this is happening the caregiver is typically focusing intently on the medical problems of the older loved one.

Instead of seeking help from their own doctors, caregivers are frequently canceling and rescheduling their own regular checkups and other appointments. While they would not dream of treating their loved one's health so casually, caregivers are often downright negligent about their own well-being.

Emotional Symptoms

Caregivers often experience feelings of anger, resentment, guilt, frustration, sadness, and loneliness. Caregivers who are feeling bombarded by negative feelings on a daily basis—especially when they don't acknowledge or discuss them—are suffering from martyr syndrome. What's worse, the caregiver often will feel bad about the presence of these negative feelings, which leads to a distressing emotional cycle. What's worse is that when you feel bad or guilty about your own irritation at your older loved one or the caregiving situation, it tends to worsen those feelings.

 Life Ring: Back in chapter 4 you completed the "Caregiver Feelings Worksheet." I encourage you—again—to download that worksheet from www.jenerationshealth.com or to make copies of the version in this book. Identifying negative feelings and accepting that they are part of the caregiving process may help you prevent developing caregiver martyr syndrome. And, should you find yourself in the throes of the martyr syndrome, this worksheet might help point that out to you (or others in the caregiving crew) by the sheer number of negative words you've circled. Periodically complete this exercise to touch base with how you truly feel.

Psychological Symptoms

Caregivers with a history of mental health concerns such as clinical depression and anxiety disorders find themselves susceptible to increased symptoms while they are providing care for a loved one. Even people who have sought treatment for such conditions previously and found their mental health condition was stable may find themselves struggling. Anyone who has struggled with a mental health condition can tell you that their symptoms can be exacerbated during periods of excessive stress or major disruptions to routine. But because of their responsibilities, caregivers can be reluctant to seek treatment, even when they recognize that old symptoms are flaring up.

The stress of caregiving can also trigger brand-new mental health diagnoses. Because caregivers are focusing on their loved one's medical issues, contacting a doctor about their own new mental health symptoms is often last on their list. Denial—particularly for people who have never suffered with a mental health concern previously—also contributes to the refusal to seek treatment.

WHO IS AT PARTICULAR RISK FOR DEVELOPING CAREGIVER MARTYR SYNDROME?

Do you ever wonder if you are someone who is likely to show signs of the caregiver martyr syndrome? Put a check mark next to any of the following characteristics that you think apply to you. Do you—

- ❑ Identify or do others identify you as a "control freak"?

- ❑ Have no major outside interests/people in your life (spouse, children, or grandchildren, job, hobbies, projects)?

- ❑ Find tremendous purpose/gratification in caregiving (e.g., spiritually, personally)?

- ❑ Have very rigid ideas of what good caregiving is and what bad caregiving is?

- ❑ Have a history of not asking for help when your older loved one could benefit from it?

- ❑ Have a history of always being stubborn?

- ❑ Have a history of wanting to fix things, be a hero, or save the day?

- ❑ Have a history of other adults being overly dependent on you (adult children or grandchildren, staff you supervise)?

- ❑ Have an extremely close relationship with your older loved one?

❏ Have a history of being passive-aggressive or negative?

❏ Micromanage others at work?

If you checked the box next to one or more of these qualities because you identified with the statement, and you think you may be a caregiver martyr, try to think of what small step you can take today to change. Maybe, for today, it's just admitting that you have martyred yourself. Maybe tomorrow you can begin talking to loved ones about your self-discovery. By the time you realize that you are in the throes of caregiver martyr syndrome, it's likely those who care about you recognized it long ago. Let your support system know you are ready to take steps to readjust your approach to caregiving.

~~~~~~

Spiritual Symptoms

Most Americans describe themselves as spiritual, religious, or both. When these individuals are caregivers, they will regularly experience interruptions to their plans to attend religious services or to honor spiritual routines (yoga, meditation, prayer, etc.). Some changes to a caregiver's traditional practices may be subtler than others. For example, a Catholic caregiver whose attendance at Sunday Mass is erratic because of her mother's needs may notice the loss sooner than does a caregiver who has gradually stopped meditating regularly. This is likely because the churchgoer has others who have noticed that she has missed services; whereas, someone who meditates is often accountable only to herself.

People rely on spiritual practices like yoga, meditation, prayer, and religious services to help them deal with stress and uncertainty and to increase inner strength. While caregiving, many people need their spiritual practices more than ever, but during this time they are likely to be minimized or even abandoned totally.

Social Symptoms

If a caregiver cannot remember the last time she did something fun with others, it's a sure sign that the social symptoms of the martyr syndrome are present. Is the caregiver turning down lunch or dinner invitations with friends? Perhaps she is taking care of her husband and doesn't want to go out without him, worried about being a third wheel among other couples.

Caregivers who have abandoned activities they previously found enjoyable—swimming, biking, movies, book club, or playing cards—are in the process of isolating themselves. This is detrimental because socialization and scheduled breaks from the dependent loved one are so beneficial during this stressful time.

> *Caregivers who have abandoned activities*
> *they previously found enjoyable are in*
> *the process of isolating themselves.*

Socializing is important because it strengthens both close and casual relationships and reduces isolation. Numerous studies (Kroenke et al. 2012; Seeman et al. 2011; Teo et al. 2015) have lauded the importance of building relationships and not isolating yourself for good overall health and mental health. Maintaining relationships is particularly important when you are under the stress of caregiving.

Relationship Symptoms

When a caregiver is in the throes of martyr syndrome, most of his or her relationships are suffering. A caregiver might stop having meaningful conversations or physical intimacy with his or her spouse or partner. Perhaps you and your sister used to get your nails or hair done together regularly, but now most of your interactions with your sister are strained ones that have to do with your mother's declining health.

Furthermore, the caregiver martyr syndrome impacts your relationship with your older loved one. Maybe you used to turn to the elderly uncle you are caring for to ask for advice. Although he is physically sick, he's still mentally as sharp as a tack and may still give you great advice. But you don't see him that way anymore; you view him primarily as someone who is enfeebled and needs you to care for him.

While many caregivers admit to relational problems with their close loved ones, they underestimate the impact these relational problems can have on their casual relationships with others. For example, for the past two decades you enjoyed catching up and laughing with your neighbors on the weekend while all of you were out doing yard work. Because you are now neglecting your yard work because of caregiving, you don't really chat with your neighbors much anymore. You also get the feeling they're not thrilled you've let your yard go. Or maybe at work you eat lunch at your desk rather than going out with your work buddies so you can run out the door precisely at five o'clock. You are missing out on the camaraderie at work that most of us take for granted after a while.

Another sign of martyr syndrome are estrangements that arise because of disagreements on how to provide the best care. A primary caregiver not talking to his sister who is serving as secondary caregiver is an example of this. I believe that all families, even the happiest and healthiest ones, are dysfunctional in *some* way. Even if you have four adult children who genuinely want the very best for their aging mother, there is likely to be discord between the siblings at some point. But when the discord arises to the point of estrangement, it may be a sign that one or more of the caregivers has succumbed to martyr syndrome.

Financial Symptoms

Even if the elderly loved one is completely financially independent, caregivers may find themselves struggling with financial concerns. A caregiver employed outside the home is more likely to reduce hours or even consider resigning or retiring early to ensure that care for the older loved one remains uninterrupted, which we discussed at length in the previous chapter.

When the older loved one has limited funds, the caregiver frequently will pay for necessities and even little luxuries that will improve the quality of life for the senior. This obviously reduces resources available for the caregiver and her immediate family, which can lead to financial difficulties and, potentially, resentment.

Caregiver Martyr Syndrome Symptom Checklist

Directions: Take a quiet moment and look at this list. Think about the past six months of caregiving. Without judging yourself, circle all the symptoms you have experienced. Feel free to make copies of this checklist for your caregiving crewmates too. You can also download this worksheet at www.jenerationshealth.com. For example, have you noticed

- stomachaches (P)
- estrangements or significant tensions that have occurred in your family since caregiving began (R)
- weight change (P)
- feeling more anxious, restless, or nervous than usual (M)
- increased use of alcohol or recreational (street) drugs (M)
- increased use of prescription drugs to counter anxiety (benzodiazapenes) or sleep aides (M)
- headaches (P)
- sleep problems (P)
- exhaustion and fatigue (P)
- aches and pains (P)
- flare-ups of chronic conditions (arthritis, back pain) (P)
- arguing a lot with others in your personal/professional life (R)
- reduced sexual activity (P)
- spending most of your time alone or *only* with older loved one/other members of caregiving crew (R)
- unable to relax (M)
- feel disconnected from spouse/partner/significant other (R)
- onset or exacerbation of depression (M)
- resent friends/family who aren't caregiving (R)
- regularly turn down social invitations you'd love to accept (F)
- feeling out of balance (S)
- often upset with other members of the caregiving crew (R)
- haven't gone on vacation during this time frame (F)
- flare-ups of a mental health condition other than anxiety disorder or depression (M)
- eating poorly (P)
- not exercising (P)

- haven't participated in a hobby you enjoy lately (F)
- missing your doctor appointments (P)
- spending money on your older loved one that your spouse/partner is not comfortable with ($)
- missing appointments with mental health provider/psychotherapist (M)
- not taking your medication as directed (P)
- left workplace for caregiving *despite* financial repercussions to self/partner/children ($)
- borrowing from your retirement to take care of your older loved one ($)
- missing religious services (S)
- spending more money than you can comfortably afford on items/services for your older loved one ($)
- not making time for prayer/meditation/yoga (S)
- anger with God (S)
- not spending time in nature (S)

Did you circle none, some, or the maximum in each of the following categories? Take a moment to add up how many you circled for: financial, fun, mental health, physical health, relationships, and spiritual needs.

$ = Financial (0–4)
F = Fun (0–3)
M = Mental health (0–7)
P = Physical health (0–12)
R = Relationships (0–6)
S = Spiritual needs (0–5)

....

Then add up how many total items you circled on this list. If you have circled more than five items, you are likely experiencing significant caregiver stress. If you have circled more than eight items, you may be on the verge of caregiver martyr syndrome. If you circled more than twelve items, it is likely you are in the throes of caregiver martyr syndrome.

To set a different course in these choppy waters or shoals, add up how many items you have in each of the categories. The more you have in any given category, the more important it is for you to focus on making a course correction in that area. If you circled the maximum of twelve having to do with your physical health, start to make changes immediately by scheduling a doctor's appointment and *keeping* it!

Make a Course Correction: Just Say No to Being a Martyr

So far during this chapter we've talked extensively about how to recognize martyr syndrome in yourself. Obviously the best strategy is to avoid falling overboard in the first place. But if it's too late for that, you will find some tips here on course-correcting.

Avoid Caregiver Martyr Syndrome in the First Place

As a primary caregiver, you can avoid caregiver martyr syndrome by following the advice in this book. Rely on a solid crew of secondary and tertiary caregivers as discussed in chapter 1. And, as reinforced in chapter 4, resist making your older loved one the center of the world indefinitely.

If you recognize caregiver martyr syndrome in yourself, congratulations! The reason I say congratulations is because you can now come out from under the weight of this burden.

Here are four steps for releasing yourself from caregiver martyr syndrome:

1. Tell your caregiving crew (assuming you've assembled one) that you recognize you have caregiver martyr syndrome. If you recognize it in yourself, it's likely they have seen it well before you did! Consider apologizing if you have rebuffed their offers of help. *If you don't already have a caregiving crew, start building one today.*

2. Give yourself permission to be an imperfect caregiver.

3. Assign one of your caregiving crewmates the task of researching which of the services discussed in this chapter (Area Agency on Aging, Alzheimer's Association, aging life care experts, etc.) might be most helpful to you right now. Begin utilizing some of these resources.

4. Commit to doing one thing immediately to take better care of your physical, emotional, psychological, spiritual, social, relational, or financial self. Commit to one additional thing each week until you are starting to feel like yourself again.

Nip Caregiver Martyr Syndrome in the Bud

Throughout my many years as a professional in the field of elder care, I can't tell you how many times I have been pulled aside to hear complaints in hushed tones from caregivers *about another caregiver* in their caregiving crew. Molly, the primary caregiver, laments how her brother, Bobby, a secondary caregiver, "does nothing." The next week I will hear from Bobby that Molly "won't let anybody else do anything." The point is that if your expectations of the others in the caregiving crew are not being met, resentment is likely brewing. In cases like this, it can be very valuable to work with an aging life care expert (formerly known as a geriatric care manager), a mediator, or a family therapist who understands caregiving issues. Sometimes when an objective person helps you sort out everyone's expectations and needs, it can feel like you are experiencing a miracle. Caregiving is an emotionally and physically draining undertaking throughout which small misunderstandings and resentments can be magnified if they are not caught early and addressed.

> *When an objective person helps you sort out*
> *everyone's expectations and needs, it can*
> *feel like you are experiencing a miracle.*

 Life Jacket: To find an objective professional who can help you nip caregiver martyr syndrome in the bud, check out the following organizations' websites:

- **Aging Life Care Association (www.aginglifecare.org):** Lets you search for aging life care experts (formerly geriatric care managers) who are typically private nurses, social workers, or gerontologists.

- **Mediate.com (www.mediate.com):** Under the drop-down menu that says "Select Type of Matter," select the word "Elder."

Make a Course Correction: Crewmates, Just Tell It Like It Is

When you recognize caregiver martyr syndrome in a caregiving crewmate, it can be very frustrating. You may have a hard time understanding why this person is doing this to herself. But it's in the best interest of your older loved one and the whole caregiving crew to be patient and to persist in trying to help this person course-correct.

Find Out Why Your Crewmate Has Developed Martyr Syndrome

More often than not, the primary caregiver experiences martyr syndrome and a secondary or tertiary caregiver observes this happening. Dr. Ann Morrison, former longtime director of the Johns Hopkins Alzheimer's Treatment and Memory Center Caregiver Family Program, associate speaker for Jenerations Health Education, and coauthor of *Caring for a Loved One with Alzheimer's Disease: A Comprehensive Guide for the Home Caregiver,* suggests, "Try to figure out psychologically why the primary is in martyr syndrome." What might be going on with that person that they are focused so exclusively on caregiving? Is caregiving meeting a specific need for the *caregiver?* Perhaps the caregiver needs a project because she is now retired. Or in the situation of a caregiving wife, is she so paralyzed with anxiety that she is genuinely afraid if she leaves her husband with someone else for just a moment he will die?

Try This Exercise

Dr. Morrison observes that some primary caregivers truly believe they have nobody else, even when this is not true. When she encounters a caregiver who stubbornly holds on to this perception, Dr. Morrison asks her or him to imagine the following scenario:

> You, the primary caregiver, are in an accident and then taken to the hospital. You are told that you must participate in rehab for a full six weeks. At this point there is no physical way you can carry out all your usual caregiving duties. Someone else will have to take care of your older loved one.

Dr. Morrison says she typically asks, "Who could help out in your place during this crisis?" She then gives the caregiver about ten minutes to write a list of people who could be a primary caregiver. Yet, during this exercise, many caregivers balk and still say, "There's no one!"

But Dr. Morrison persists. She reminds the caregiver that this scenario is a real emergency; there is no way the individual can continue caregiving after this accident. Sometimes after a caregiver writes down a few names she'll probe further, asking, "Is there anyone else you can add? Anyone from your church or neighborhood you can add to this list?" Inevitably each caregiver will acquiesce and come up with *some names.* Dr. Morrison doesn't just focus on the issue of the primary caregiver needing these other people as part of the caregiving crew to avoid burnout, however. She reframes the exercise from a different angle. "Forget everything I just said about you being in the accident, but look at this sheet of paper here. See the names of all of these people you're not allowing into your mom's life? You're shutting them out! Have you ever seen it that way?" Often what comes out in this conversation is that a caregiver felt she was doing "these other people" a favor by sparing them having to help with caregiving.

When you attempt this exercise with a primary caregiver (or with a secondary or a tertiary caregiver), think ahead about how you can personalize it a bit to make the emergency scenario more realistic. For example, perhaps the primary caregiver has a chronic health condition that has previously required hospitalization. Maybe your sister, who is taking care of your mother, has diabetes and has been in the hospital for a week at a time with complications.

Discuss the emergency scenario in vivid detail. You might say, "Remember the last time you were in the hospital? What if you had been caring for Mom then? Who would have stepped in?" Or you could discuss some health condition that eventually could cause an interruption to caregiving. For instance, perhaps the caregiver has bad knees and for the past two years his doctor has suggested a double knee replacement. "You know, with all the running around you're doing for Dad, it's likely there's even more wear and tear on your knees. What if your doctor insists this is the year for the knee replacement? Who would you call to help out with Dad while you're recovering?"

It may even be an acute health problem like a very bad flu bug that knocked Dad on his butt for two weeks last year just before his wife needed so much hands-on care. You might say, "Dad, what happens when or if you were to get a bad case of the flu again? Remember how weak you felt? How you could barely get out of bed all those days in a row? I know that you really don't want to ask others for help, but if you were laid up with the flu again and you were desperate, who would you consider calling?"

Offer the Kind of Help the Crewmate Would Most Likely Accept

Maybe the primary caregiver in martyr syndrome has refused your offers to take your older loved one to the doctor or to stay with him while she goes out to dinner. That might seem to be too grand a gesture. But sometimes you can nudge someone out of martyr syndrome by starting with some very small gestures. Could you, for instance, drop off treats from the primary caregiver's favorite bakery? What about going over with your lawnmower to take care of her yard? Sometimes when the person in martyr syndrome gets used to accepting small favors, the secondary and primary caregivers can build up to offering greater degrees and types of help.

Point Out What You Are Observing

Rather than continuing to offer help or to lecture the crew member with caregiver martyr syndrome, consider pointing out what you are observing. Here are a few suggestions of how to phrase your observations:

"I've noticed you don't seem to sit down and eat a proper meal."

"You keep saying you haven't been sleeping."

"I bumped into your neighbors that you usually walk with each morning and they said you haven't been out with them in months."

Sometimes simply mentioning such observations will stimulate the caregiver martyr to think more about self-care and changing her ways. Odds are if you are mentioning these things, someone else might be too. Sometimes when several people are sharing such observations, the caregiver martyr will think more about making a change. While you want to give honest feedback, of course, you want to be equally mindful of your tone and word choices. Most people are going to become very defensive if you mention they look tired or they appear to have gained weight.

Point out the way their behavior is making you feel (along with a suggestion). As Dr. Morrison reminds us, sometimes caregiver martyrs don't realize they are excluding others from the older loved one's life by not allowing them to participate. Consider the following conversation starters:

"I feel bad because I am not doing more. What one thing can I do to make a difference with Mom's care in the next week?"

"I feel left out because I live so far away. I would love to be more included in helping with Uncle Glenn's care. I know I can't be here as much as I'd like to, but maybe I could make phone calls for you. I know you are always on the phone with the insurance company, the pharmacy, and the medical equipment company for the oxygen. Would it help if I handled some of those calls for you?"

"It breaks my heart watching you do so much for Nana while the rest of us do so little. If I paid for a home care aide for six hours a week, would you consider using a service? I know it's not much, but it would give you a little break."

You may have noticed that this section does not recommend telling the caregiver martyr *everything you are feeling*. If you are angry, frustrated, annoyed, or want to tell the caregiver martyr that you think she is being manipulative, that's okay. But it's unlikely to be productive to express *those* strong negative feelings when someone is in the throes of caregiver martyr syndrome; such a person is unlikely to be able to respond rationally to vents like that. It will likely be more productive for you to discuss these feelings with another member of the caregiving crew, a therapist, or a friend who has nothing to do with the caregiving situation. Remember that caregiver martyrs are often in an unreasonable headspace and won't be able to logically respond to what they'll perceive as attacks.

Be Persistent

It is very possible that your primary caregiver crewmate is not going to "hear" your concerns the first time you discuss them with her. While you don't want to nag your crewmate every day, keep the dialogue open. Unfortunately, many secondary and tertiary caregivers give up after broaching the subject once or twice because they become frustrated, which is understandable. But know that a message that the crewmate martyr is unable to act on today may be something she is ready to hear in six months or even in six years. But some caregiver martyrs *never* recognize the damage they are doing to themselves, their older loved one, and the rest of the caregiving crew. If your message is received six years after you've been trying to get it through, remember it's better late than never.

Some Caregivers Don't Want to Let Go of Their Martyr Mind-Set

Does the caregiver martyr you are concerned about have a history of feeling sorry for herself, alienating and blaming others, and/or passive-aggressive behavior? If so, she may unconsciously feel most comfortable playing the role of the caregiver martyr. While you want to try to persist and offer help, it is very possible this caregiver martyr does not want the circumstances to change, in which case, we can accept what we can't change or bring in the big guns.

Accept What You Can't Change

Unfortunately, many caregiver martyr syndrome sufferers do not make a change until they become very sick or are ready to collapse from exhaustion. Some of these caregivers are literally forced to change their approach to caregiving only after they themselves suffer a major health setback such as a stroke or a fall. Some secondary and tertiary caregivers drive themselves nuts worrying about a primary caregiver with a martyr mind-set. While you want to be persistent with your crewmate, you really need to let it go unless you believe the older loved one is truly being abused or neglected in some way. Some signs of abuse or neglect can be bruises, bedsores, or the older loved one appearing nervous or afraid of the primary caregiver.

If you have any genuine concerns about possible abuse or neglect, call your local Adult Protective Services—you can call them anonymously—right away. To find your local Adult Protective Services, check out the National Adult Protective Services Association website at www.napsa-now.org. Many crewmates are reluctant to make such a call because they view it as a really drastic measure. But remember this: If you suspect true abuse or neglect is going on, even if it is unintended by the caregiver martyr, it needs to be stopped. Even if what you are observing does not fall into the category of abuse or neglect, sometimes a visit or call from Adult Protective Services is enough to jolt the primary caregiver with a martyr mind-set into making a change.

~~~~~~

SOMETIMES THE CAREGIVER MARTYR SYNDROME IS WELL HIDDEN

Sometimes the primary caregiver appears to be doing just fine, and nobody in the family offers help. The other family members don't think their help is needed; the primary caregiver has it all under control. Meanwhile the primary caregiver, quickly losing steam but hiding it well, is headed for a crisis. If a primary caregiver seems to be humming along just fine with no help from anyone else, be a bit suspicious and keep an eye on that person. Some martyrs hide it well until they have a meltdown of some sort: losing their temper with someone on the caregiving crew or experiencing a serious health crisis, for example.

~~~~~~

Bring in the Big Guns

Another option for friends and family members of the caregiver is to enlist the help of professionals who may be able to convince the caregiver to lighten the load. Friends and family can always contact the caregiver's physician, financial planner, spiritual advisor, or psychotherapist to share their concerns. While these professionals won't be able to share with the friends and family any response from the caregiver suffering from martyr syndrome, due to confidentiality, often they are willing to accept information about the caregiver. Often a caregiver will take a warning from a professional more seriously than they will from friends or family.

If friends and family members of a caregiver are unable to offer direct help, there are many resources in the community that can provide hands-on help to a caregiver. Each of the following national organizations can link a caregiver to local services all over the country:

- **Aging Life Care Association (www.aginglifecare.org):** Links caregivers to private aging life care experts, formerly known as geriatric care managers (typically nurses and social workers), who assist with managing care of an older loved one.

- **Alzheimer's Association (www.alz.org):** Links caregivers to support groups and services for people who are dealing with irreversible dementia diagnoses.

- **Argentum (formerly Assisted Living Federation of America; www.alfa.org):** Offers a database of assisted living residential options.

- **Continuing Care Retirement Communities (www.ccrcs.com):** Offers a database listing continuing care retirement communities (CCRCs).

- **Medicare.gov (www.medicare.gov):** Offers a database of nursing homes.

- **National Adult Day Services Association (www.nadsa.org):** Links caregivers to adult day care centers in the community. Adult day care centers are sites that offer meals, activities, and sometimes medical care. Adult day care centers exist so an older person with physical or cognitive health problems can interact with others and receive good care while their caregivers work or just take a break.

- **National Association for Home Care & Hospice (www.nahc.org):** Offers a database of home care agencies that can provide private pay aides to help with non-medical care like bathing, housekeeping, meal preparation, companionship, and transportation.

- **National Association of Area Agencies on Aging (www.n4a.org):** Links caregivers to local city and county Area Agencies on Aging (AAA), which is the first place a caregiver for an older loved one should check for help. We will get into much more detail about how the AAA can help you in chapter 11.

Now that we have covered what caregiver martyr syndrome is and how to deal with it, let's move on to the next chapter to learn about when our expectations for our crewmates need to be adjusted.

Eight

FELLOW CAREGIVERS: THEY ARE WHO THEY ARE

Gone Overboard: Expecting Too Much (or Too Little) from Your Crewmates

A major cause of stress that caregivers experience is expecting too much (or perhaps not enough) from others in the family or the whole caregiving crew. Caregivers often go overboard because they set unrealistic expectations for themselves, their family members, and others in the caregiving crew.

Please note that I have intentionally used the terms "family" and "caregiving crew" separately because they often have different meanings. As we previously discussed, just because certain people are family does not mean they are active members of the caregiving crew, and vice versa. When you are a caregiver (especially a primary one), it is common to have unfair or unrealistic expectations of many people—relatives and other caregivers included.

When you are a caregiver, it is common to have unfair or unrealistic expectations of many people— relatives and other caregivers included.

Recall that in chapter 1 we defined the three main categories of caregivers: primary, secondary, and tertiary. The caregiving crew is comprised of a primary caregiver and—optimally—many secondary and tertiary caregivers. By this point I hope you have not only identified which type of caregiver you are but also the roles of others in the caregiving crew. Once you recognize your role and what category your fellow caregivers fall into, it helps you determine how you can reduce stress by expecting just the right amount from others in your caregiving crew.

Typically the primary caregiver and at least one secondary caregiver are close relatives such as spouses, adult children, grandchildren, in-laws, nieces, or nephews. There are, of course, some cases where family members don't fall into any of these roles and the caregiving crew is made up mostly of friends, neighbors, and perhaps extended family members. Regardless of their relationship to the older loved one, the caregivers most at risk for going overboard in expecting too much or too little from others are the primary and secondary caregivers. And, in most cases, these roles are filled by family members but not always.

This chapter assists you in managing expectations of your crewmates. Use the information presented here to help you as caregivers:

- Understand why your (usually primary caregiver's) expectations of others in the caregiving crew are often impractical and even harmful.

- Identify situations where you are expecting too much or too little of others.

- Develop more practical expectations, implement productive solutions, and communicate with your other crewmates.

Too Much or Not Enough: What to Reasonably Expect from Others

Have you ever participated in a work project where you felt a teammate was not doing his or her fair share? Ever had a boss who made decisions that you thought were way off base? Ever have trouble agreeing on which movie to see when you went to the theater with a friend? Not everyone sees things the same way. Caregiving is no different. Whatever role you play in the whole caregiving crew, at some point it is likely that you will view things differently than your crewmates do. Whether you think others are doing too much or not enough, the stress of caregiving can naturally lead you to second-guess everything. Although this second-guessing typically applies to primary and secondary caregivers, occasionally it extends to a tertiary caregiver as well. This section helps you if you ever have, or might experience, these common thoughts and feelings.

Some people feel the pull to become the primary caregiver by default because "nobody else will do it." Typically primary caregivers are the culprits who expect too little from others in the family or caregiving crew. They often dismiss the idea that certain family members or friends could assist with caregiving for a variety of practical reasons, such as geography, age, or financial considerations. Perhaps the primary caregiver has concerns about the relationships among family members or whether other caregivers are uncomfortable with certain tasks, such as bathing an older loved one. Because of these concerns, many primary caregivers place the entire burden of caregiving on themselves. This is called martyr syndrome, which is discussed in great detail in chapter 7. Unrealistic expectations go hand in hand with some primary caregivers' penchant for maintaining a martyr mind-set and not asking for help when they really want or need it. This can lead to situations where a primary caregiver has very low, if any, expectations for others in the caregiving crew.

Almost never are the caregiving duties split equally between all members of a family or caregiving crew.

In contrast, some primary caregivers think other members of the caregiving crew could do more. Unfortunately, primary caregivers sometimes embrace a dysfunctional mind-set of being angry with other family members, who are functioning well in secondary or tertiary roles, by expecting them to rise up and become an equal primary caregiver. Almost never are the caregiving duties split equally among all members of a family or caregiving crew. When the primary caregiver has this expectation, it is rarely met with satisfaction. If you can identify with this feeling, you are especially ripe for burnout. Sometimes a primary caregiver expects others in the caregiving crew to have the same level of commitment to the older loved one. The primary caregiver may also have a certain philosophy on how the care should be performed, which she expects the rest of the caregiving crew to embrace. Let's take a look at how this played out for Holly and her family.

Three years ago, Holly's mother moved into the home where Holly and her husband reside. Holly has reduced her hours at work so she can spend more time taking care of Mom. Holly's three siblings are secondary caregivers. They each visit Mom once or twice per week, and they will help out with errands and other chores when Holly requests. Three years into this situation, Holly is now finally burning out. She is furious that her brother and sisters are not doing more. She starts asking them to give up their weekends to stay with Mom so she and her husband can have a break. They refuse. Their stance is that they love their mother but are giving all they can. They have jobs, small children, and are not interested in being more hands-on. They are glad to continue providing their current level of support but aren't willing to do more.

Because Holly is so burned out, and Mom has the resources to afford assisted living, the siblings suggest that they all have a serious conversation about this. Holly is enraged. She responds that she would never put *her mother* in an institution. They suggest hiring home care aides. Holly responds that she does not want strangers in her home.

While Holly's request for more help is reasonable, so is the response of the siblings. They know their limits and are not willing or able to do more. If Holly wants to keep Mom at home, that is her choice. But it is also her siblings' right to suggest other options that will relieve the burden from them all.

Holly's fantasy of perfect care for her mother involves four primary caregivers: where she and all her siblings share the job equally. However, her siblings have refused but are willing to help her look at other options. Holly is wedded to the idea of Mom staying at home and will not consider other ideas. As a result, Holly is developing issues. She has been crying a lot, feeling alone. She and her husband are arguing more than usual, even though he supports the idea of keeping his mother-in-law at home. Holly is losing weight, her arthritis is acting up, and she is getting colds frequently. This is common with caregivers; health and mental health suffer more when a caregiver is overwhelmed.

While many of you may relate to how Holly feels, it's important to recognize that other members of the caregiving crew are not being unreasonable. Holly does not have the right to expect her crewmates to have the same level of commitment (constant daily hands-on care) and philosophy (Mom must be kept at home!). Holly has every right to her level of commitment and philosophy, but she must also respect her crewmates' boundaries.

Secondary caregivers can also harbor unrealistic expectations of their fellow crewmates. In this situation, Holly's siblings did recognize and appreciate her struggles and have offered valid alternatives. But sometimes, secondary caregivers underestimate the amount of work the primary caregiver is currently doing. Sometimes they try to take over the primary caregiver role without cause, and they second-guess or criticize the primary caregiver. To illustrate why this can happen, let's look at another example of how this scenario plays out in real life.

Dawn is the primary caregiver for her eighty-seven-year-old father, Jon, who lives about twenty miles away. Jon is terminally ill with cancer. Dawn has been arranging the home care and hospice and has dealt with numerous hospitalizations over the course of Jon's illness for the past five years. Jon's other daughter, Dawn's older sister Casey, lives five hundred miles away. For the past five years, Casey visited every two to three months, about four to six times per year; she has been a very good secondary caregiver on which Dawn has relied. Until recently, Casey and Dawn have generally been in agreement about the course of Jon's treatment. But now that everyone has been told Jon is truly nearing the end, Casey has been a bit more critical of the way Dawn is caring for their father. When she is not in town, Casey calls Dawn every day for an update. She has suggested that Dawn look into a different hospice provider because Casey didn't like the bedside manner of one of the nursing assistants she encountered during her last visit to Jon's home. She is concerned that Dawn is giving Jon too much morphine; she complains that he is overmedicated when she visits. When Casey is in charge of administering the medication when she is in town, she decreases the morphine dosage so her father isn't so "doped up."

Casey is expecting too much from Dawn because she is counting on her sister to care for their father the way she herself would. Dawn is not doing anything wrong or malicious; actually, she is doing the best she can for her father. Why do you think Casey is acting this way? Take a moment and write down at least three ideas.

What did you come up with? Did the majority of your ideas have more to do with Casey or Dawn? Very often, the reasons secondary caregivers expect more from primary caregivers have more to do with their own feelings than to do with the level of care the primary caregiver is providing. Let's look at some common reasons secondary caregivers expect too much from the primary caregiver. In this scenario, Casey—

- Is having a hard time accepting that her father is dying.

- Feels guilty that she is not there all the time.

- Doesn't understand the pain her father is experiencing, because she has not had as much direct contact with him.

- Doesn't see how Dawn can view their father as needing more, rather than less, medication. (What Casey doesn't realize is that Jon might be putting up a good front when she is in town. Often the patient rebounds a bit when a new person visits or is helping out.)

- Is trying to get back a sense of control by suggesting finding a new hospice provider.

- Is trying to make up for the fact that Dawn has done more caregiving than she has thus far.

Are you seeing the theme? The reasons Casey is expecting too much from Dawn have much more to do with what's going on internally with Casey than they do with Dawn's care of their father. Secondary caregivers, especially in situations with a terminal diagnosis, often feel a sense of guilt or denial about the situation. These feelings are then directed at the primary caregiver, an easier target than their terminally ill older loved one.

Life Ring: Be aware that at times you may judge those you are closest to more harshly than you would other people. That's because, humanly speaking, your past history and relationship with another caregiver impacts your expectations of him or her. For example, Casey may not have judged an aunt or uncle caregiver as harshly as she did her sister. And, obviously, the emotional component of their father dying led to Casey's critique of Dawn's caregiving, but it's likely that an older sister dynamic may have come into play as well.

While it's probably hard to find time for counseling in a situation like this, it would likely benefit both Dawn and Casey to try to talk to someone about their challenges with each other. Ideally, a professional skilled psychotherapist could help. But if not, talking to an objective friend or spiritual advisor might help each see the situation from the other sister's perspective.

Make a Course Correction: Rein In Unrealistic Expectations

Communication among members of the caregiving crew is essential for success. Whether you are a primary caregiver who is burning out or a secondary caregiver who wants to help more, you need to discuss your expectations and limitations. Caregiving for an older loved one is a fluid experience; therefore, just because you were able to handle certain tasks by yourself a few months (or even weeks) ago doesn't mean you can't revisit the caregiving plan now.

Caregiving for an older loved one is a fluid experience. Just because you were able to handle certain tasks by yourself a few months... ago doesn't mean you can't revisit the caregiving plan now.

Life Ring: Each member of the caregiving crew only has complete control over his or her own choices and actions. *You can't control your crewmates.*

If you find yourself expecting too much or too little from other members of the caregiving crew, one of the first steps in course-correcting is to remind yourself to accept that you have control only over *your own actions*. You can't control what others in the caregiving crew are doing or are not doing. But, you have to take stock of yourself to see how your possibly out-of-whack expectations are impacting other caregivers.

It's good for a caregiver to talk things out with a trusted friend or family member who is objective and not involved with the older loved one's care. A spiritual advisor may also be a good person to call upon during this time. Of course, it would be ideal for all caregivers to see a psychotherapist to deal with issues that may arise, but it can be challenging to find time for counseling sessions in the throes of caregiving. Before you start speaking with others about their roles in the caregiving process, try to make sure you have an understanding of your own feelings and behavior. Because it's so important to pick your battles in these cases, having a third party weigh in on whether you are being reasonable is invaluable.

Surprisingly, sometimes it's the older loved one who attempts to limit the number of members on the caregiving crew. Madelyn Campbell, LCSW and senior social worker at a large Philadelphia-area continuing care retirement community (CCRC), states that a main reason people over the age of sixty-two move to a CCRC is so they don't need to "burden" their adult children. Campbell notes that it is "not unusual for residents who need additional caregiving crew members to refuse to allow a social worker to contact their children."

While this happens when paid staff, such as CCRC social workers, are trying to increase support for the older patient, primary caregivers may experience this with their older loved ones as well. Sometimes the older loved one has predetermined who is "too busy" to help out with care. The older loved one may also not want certain friends and family members involved because of feelings of embarrassment about the situation. When this occurs, it is critical for the primary caregiver to discuss how essential it is for the well-being of both to have more help.

It's important to explore any legitimate concerns when an older loved one is particularly resistant to adding a friend or family to a caregiving crew. For example, Luke really did not want his daughter-in-law helping out with his personal care, even though she was a nurse. The family respected that this was a major dignity issue for Luke and found other ways for his daughter-in-law to help out.

Course-Correcting for Primary Caregivers

Generally, among the members of the caregiving crew, finding ways to provide sufficient elder care is the task that falls most heavily on you—the primary caregiver. If you have previously declined help, perhaps some of your potential secondary and tertiary caregivers really do think you have it all under control. But in reality you are finding that so many issues contribute to your stress as a primary caregiver. These might not have seemed like a big deal to you before, but the cumulative effects of caregiving stress may eventually catch up with you.

*The cumulative effects of caregiving stress
may eventually catch up with you.*

Because of the tremendous stress primary caregivers are experiencing, when they do decide to ask for help they often do so in a haphazard way. They say things like "I really can't do this alone anymore" or "I need help with your father." According to Dianne Turpin, former Area Agency on Aging staff person, one of the best ways to ask for help is to be sure you are asking the *right person for the right thing.* And to accomplish this you need to be strategic. That means you must first identify some of the tasks that are adding to your stress level. Rather than just saying in general that you need help, it is important to really think about what kind of specific help you want and are willing to accept.

If your sister loves to cook, ask her to provide a meal for you each week. If your niece is in nursing school, she might be a good person to ask to provide hands-on care like feeding or bathing. Matching needs with available resources can greatly improve the quality of life for both the caregiver and the older adult.

....

Use the MET Exercise to Relieve Your Stress

Money, energy, and time are the most precious resources to caregivers. When a caregiver or an entire caregiving crew is struggling, it is almost always because they don't have enough money, energy, or time. Typically, when someone else offers one or more of these resources, caregiving burdens are relieved. Because of this, I created a simple exercise for caregivers to do so they could get more money, energy, or time from someone else. I call this the MET exercise because it helps you get your needs and your older loved one's needs "met." When I provide consultations to individual caregivers, they often begin experiencing some stress relief immediately upon completing this exercise.

To do this exercise, you need to set aside about twenty minutes to sit in a quiet place with some paper, a pen, and a timer (most cell phones now have them). Do this when you have a short block of uninterrupted time. This simple exercise helps you identify areas that create stress and some available options you have for handling it. You will be surprised at how using these twenty minutes can greatly reduce your stress as a caregiver.

Set the timer for five minutes. Write a list, emptying your mind of all the tasks you are stressing about. These chores might be directly related to caring for your older loved one, such as, I can't forget to pick up Dad's prescription refill today, or they might include some of your own needs, such as, I really should find out more about the Alzheimer's Association's Safe Return program, or even, I really need a haircut. Caregivers encounter increased stress not only because of the demands placed on them by caring for the needs of an older adult but also because their own personal needs are not receiving enough attention. Remember, your stress can be reduced by having people take over some caregiving duties for you or by doing things that directly help you. Be sure to think about both of these when you work on this exercise. This first list you create is your "Need Help With" list.

Set the timer again for two minutes. Without regard for age, finances, geography, or anything else, write down as fast as you can at least twenty people you can think of who *care about you*. Don't limit yourself to immediate family or neighbors.

Anyone is fair game: your hairdresser who always asks how you are doing, the old college roommate you still call occasionally, or maybe even your financial advisor or lawyer. Label this second list "My People."

Set the timer again for two minutes. Again, without regard for age, finances, geography, or anything else, write down as fast as you can at least twenty people you can think of who *care about the older loved one you are caring for*. Don't exclude people you put on the previous list. The purpose of this is to identify *all* the people who care about the older loved one you are caring for. Again, don't limit this to your immediate family. Your older loved one probably has friends, neighbors, or former coworkers. Try to cast a wide net when you do this exercise and don't censor yourself—write down anyone who pops into your head! This is list number three, which you want to call "Her People" or "His People."

Review the "My People" and "Her People" lists. Likely there will be some overlapping names: perhaps you wrote your son's name on both the list of people who care about you and about your terminally ill husband. Usually you'll have at least twenty-five to thirty people, total, between the two lists. Merge lists "My People" and "Her People" into a new list you'll call "Possible Helpers."

The next step is to review the names on your Possible Helpers list to see what each person will most likely be willing to help you with—money, energy, or time. Place the letter M for money, E for energy, or T for time next to the name of each person on your Possible Helpers list so you'll later be able to readily match her/ him to one of your needs. In some cases you might find that you can put MET (all three!) next to a given person.

Let me give you an example to illustrate how to approach this step. Maybe on the Possible Helpers list you have a nephew who is a stockbroker on Wall Street, and your first thought, naturally, is to ask him to contribute financially to his grandmother's assisted living costs. So, you put an M by his name. Not so fast, though. You need to keep an open mind as you work through this review. Although you want to reach out to your nephew for money, don't assume he has tons of it. He could have a lot of debt that nobody knows about. Or it's possible that he can afford to help financially but chooses not to for personal reasons. In addition to the M, you might also place a T next to his name because your loving family oriented nephew might be the perfect crew member to visit once a month to give you a hand.

Now take your Need Help With list and place it next to the Possible Helpers list. Try to match up the needs you have listed with the people you have listed as potential helpers. Sometimes you will get really lucky and have an obvious match. For example, maybe your hairdresser is on the Possible Helpers list and on the

Need Help With list where you indicated you needed a haircut. Could you ask your hairdresser to come to your house so you don't have to find care for your husband while you get your hair cut?

Sometimes the matches might be a little less apparent. Perhaps your granddaughter who resides in another state is on your Possible Helpers list. What is she good at? What does she enjoy? Maybe she is great with computer skills. Perhaps on your Need Help With list you indicated you needed someone to research how the Alzheimer's Association's Safe Return program (www.alz.org) works. It may make sense to ask your granddaughter to help you with that.

....

Often if you ask someone you care about to help you by doing something they are already good at, they will be happy to do it. Let's look at a great example of how this worked out for a family whose circumstances might sound familiar.

Avery is caring for her aunt June full-time. When Avery did this MET exercise, she put a T next to the name of her brother Bill, who lives in another part of the state and has recently retired. She looked at her list of needs as a caregiver and what Bill might be able to help her with. Avery has been meaning to make an appointment with an experienced elder law attorney, but she doesn't know how to start the vetting process. She keeps putting it off because she finds the whole business of finding the right attorney overwhelming.

Because Bill retired from a job where he managed hiring vendors, he seemed more than qualified to handle the vetting process for Avery. With this in mind, she decided to ask Bill to research elder law attorneys within a twenty-five-mile radius of where Avery and June live. Avery called Bill with this very specific request, and he was happy to help. Within a week, he had identified the elder law attorney who was the best match and had set up an appointment for his sister and his aunt.

Does this process work perfectly every time? Of course not. But caregivers are frequently thrilled with how this brief twenty-minute MET exercise can give them ideas on the kinds of things to ask for help with and who might be the best candidates for secondary or tertiary caregiver tasks.

Again, the best way to use the MET exercise is to keep an open mind. You may think your cousin might be able to stay with your mom once a week for an hour, but you find out she is busier than you initially thought because she recently picked up more hours at work. While you may be disappointed to hear the cousin can't help you with time, you may be stunned when she gladly offers to kick in a one-time financial contribution toward adult day care costs! Alternatively, there will be times when people on your Possible Helpers list will disappoint you terribly by not helping at all. But more often than not, you will be surprised by how many people want to help you and will if you ask them for something they feel capable of doing. To download a ready-made template for the MET exercise, please go to www.jenerationshealth.com.

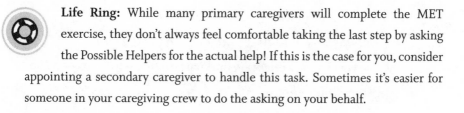

Life Ring: While many primary caregivers will complete the MET exercise, they don't always feel comfortable taking the last step by asking the Possible Helpers for the actual help! If this is the case for you, consider appointing a secondary caregiver to handle this task. Sometimes it's easier for someone in your caregiving crew to do the asking on your behalf.

Course-Correcting for Secondary Caregivers

Secondary caregivers need to course-correct sometimes, too. One of the most common primary caregiver complaints concerns secondary caregivers swooping in and criticizing her actions. Even the slightest hint that the primary caregiver is not doing a good job can create a war within the caregiving crew. Despite the horror stories we have all heard about abusive and exploitative caregivers, most caregivers of older loved ones have the very best intentions. However, helping out with or providing care for an older loved one is one of the most daunting challenges a person can experience. Unless secondary caregivers see something that is truly dangerous, unsafe, or hazardous to the older loved one and/or primary caregiver, they should keep their mouths shut.

That's right. Shut up. Most of the time the primary caregiver is doing the best she can. A secondary caregiver pushing an agenda on the primary caregiver— however well intentioned—is almost never well received.

Secondary caregivers need to course-correct when they're guilty of assuming rather than asking. Don't assume what the primary caregiver needs or wants help with. It's great to anticipate, but don't assume. Remember the example in chapter

7 where Kathy assumed her sister, Marie, would attend an upcoming wedding and generously offered to stay with her brother-in-law, Dan, who was recovering from surgery? Marie declined the offer and suggested another way Kathy could help—and Kathy should have thick skin when her offer is rejected. If Kathy is able to pick up the card and gift for Marie to take to the wedding, that's great. But if Kathy is unable to do so, that's okay, too. Ultimately it's just important for Kathy as a secondary caregiver to communicate often and clearly with Marie and to ask what other help is needed, rather than assuming she knows what the primary caregiver needs.

> *. . . Providing care for an older loved one is one of the most daunting challenges a person can experience. Unless secondary caregivers see something that is truly dangerous, unsafe, or hazardous, they should keep their mouths shut.*

Secondary and tertiary caregivers can also conduct their own version of the MET exercise. Take a few minutes and think about ways your money, energy, and time could be used for caregiving. Consider listing some routine or simple tasks that the primary caregiver may think are insignificant, and thus won't think to ask someone else to do. Such a list could give secondary caregivers an *aha!* moment.

While it can be a helpful and an eye-opening experience for each member of the caregiving crew to complete the MET exercise, it is almost inevitable that most caregiving crews will need something at some point from the "system." When I say the "system," I am referring to the professional senior care field. You will likely need to work with some or all of the following: home care agencies, assisted living communities, nursing homes, public and nonprofit agencies that help older adults, hospice, etc. When you approach them, it's important to have reasonable expectations for them as well. While we've touched on some of these resources in many of the preceding chapters, the next chapter helps you understand the best resources for you in greater detail.

Nine

THE SENIOR CARE SYSTEM: IT IS WHAT IT IS

Gone Overboard: Expecting the Senior Care System to Be Perfect

The senior care system is flawed. Accept this. The sooner you do, the less stressed you'll be.

Expecting the senior care system to be perfect can be a major cause of stress for caregivers. The senior care system includes home care, home health care, adult day care, assisted living, nursing homes, outpatient rehabs, hospice, elder law attorneys, aging life care professionals (up until recently known as geriatric care managers), the local Alzheimer's Association, the local Area Agencies on Aging, and Adult Protective Services. Plus, a variety of other new services seem to be popping up every day that serve older adults and their families that may be considered part of the senior care system. Some of these newer offerings may include money managers, professional organizers, and smaller local nonprofit organizations that are indigenous to a geographic area.

The senior care system is flawed.

The senior care system is comprised of human beings serving human beings. Whenever that is the case, the obvious result is an imperfect system. Furthermore, the senior care system is comprised of imperfect people frequently providing services to and taking care of often physically or cognitively *vulnerable* older adults and their very stressed-out family members. However, the vast majority of these imperfect people do care about you and your older loved one and are doing their best—with exceptions that unfortunately tend to get lots of media attention. These hyped-up, media-sensationalized stories, by the way, are not the norm in the senior care system. More often than not, professionals working in the senior care system care very much about helping older adults and their families, but sometimes they will make mistakes. This chapter helps you with the following concepts and strategies:

- Understand what organizations and people are part of the senior care system.

- Establish reasonable expectations for the senior care system.

- Be content with the senior care services you utilize.

- Figure out how to course-correct if you still have unrealistic expectations about all or part of the senior care system.

Why Do We Expect Perfection from the Senior Care System?

No industry is perfect. We don't like this fact, but we often have a bit more patience with industries other than eldercare. It's frustrating when our cell phone dies unexpectedly. It's irritating when we have to return a container of milk that is spoiled. It's annoying when a clerk at the gas station is not terribly friendly. But customers' anger can have a longer fuse when dealing with frustrations like these.

Why, then, are so many caregivers so impatient when it comes to the imperfect world of the senior care system? First, caregivers are often irritated that they or their loved ones are paying for the service they were expecting to be free or covered by insurance. Even if they accept that they have to pay, it is often much more expensive than they were anticipating. Whether they or their older loved ones are paying cash out-of-pocket, utilizing their long-term care insurance, Medicare, Medicaid, or other benefits, they understand that the bottom line is an exchange of money for service.

Often caregivers perceive this cost to be extreme. Marie O'Shea, a community sales director with Brightview Senior Living with more than twenty years of experience, shared her thoughts with me on why caregivers frequently have sticker shock about assisted living. "I think they forget that it's a twenty-four-hour-a-day business. You're paying staff twenty-four hours a day. The insurance—the liability insurance on assisted living—is astronomical. You're heating and cooling a building twenty-four hours a day. The cost of the generator system that we use, which we have to run every week, for example, is something I don't think families realize, nor do I think they *should* have to think about."

This sticker shock also extends to home care. If a caregiver is paying what she thinks is a very high amount to a home care agency, the expectation is often that the aide will function as a personal butler instead of as just a professional healthcare provider. A lot of this stems from the caregiver expecting Medicaid or Medicare to cover more than they do (this concept will be discussed further in chapter 10). Frequently the caregiver resents that, as one put it, "My dad worked all those years and put taxes into the system. Shouldn't he be entitled to more now that he is old and sick?"

To put this unreasonable expectation in perspective, let's look at a few ordinary everyday examples of frustrating moments. We've all experienced a variation on finding the container of milk that's spoiled, the broken cell phone, and the rude gas station attendant that grates on our nerves, yet most people will agree these aren't life-and-death situations. That's why such things annoy us, but we usually don't "lose it." But when they are talking about even small slipups by a senior care professional, many caregivers have a tendency to turn them into catastrophes. They amplify small mistakes and misunderstandings in the senior care system and sometimes even base their expectations on assumptions conjured out of thin air. For instance, have you ever expected the aging life care expert you hired to call you in the morning to discuss your next appointment, but she didn't phone until the afternoon, apologizing that she was tending to an emergency? Even though she had not designated a specific time when she would call, you begin making assumptions: "If she is not making us, new clients, a priority, what will happen once we've been working with her for a while?"

Often this is all exacerbated by the fact that the caregiver is under significant stress. Unfortunately, when a caregiver begins the process of trying to obtain services from the senior care system, he is in crisis. Frequently the caregiver finds the process of actually researching and obtaining services too daunting. Noelle Wilson, former executive director and marketing director for Arden Courts, a specialized memory care assisted living community, shared a story about the son of a prospective male resident with advanced dementia. Upon meeting with Wilson and touring the community, the son said, "I don't think my father's ready for this; I think we need to find a better way to help my mother cope." It was lost on the son that moving his father to an assisted living situation *was* the way for his mother, the primary caregiver, to better cope!

Another challenge is caregivers getting sidetracked by the aesthetics and amenities of a community, and focusing less on what the true purpose of a senior living community is. Sometimes very upscale senior living communities look so beautiful, and the service seems so elegant, we forget the bottom line: It's a healthcare organization. While many senior living communities do offer lovely amenities and fantastic food, they are not supposed to function quite like a five-star hotel. Their priority really needs to be the health and safety of the residents living there.

Expecting Perfection Is a Major Stressor

Expecting the senior care system to be perfect is a major stressor because it is unreasonable. While you have every right to expect the senior care system to offer clean, safe, health-focused professional and polite service, it will never be perfect. When we focus on smaller imperfections, we add to our frustration as caregivers. This chapter helps the caregiver adjust expectations and understand when it is reasonable to ask for more or advocate for better service or outcomes.

Senior care services are unique. We can't compare them to the service we'd get from a plumber, dry cleaner, or a cashier. We can't compare them to the service we'd get from our accountant or financial planner. And we surely should not compare them to the service we'd get at a hotel or restaurant.

The senior care system is growing every day. We have nursing homes, assisted living communities, continuing care retirement communities (CCRCs), home care agencies, adult day care centers, and the list goes on. Most of these organizations are trying to do the best they can to offer quality services to older adults and their families, but they make mistakes every single day. Expect them to offer high quality and hold them to that standard. Just don't expect them to be perfect.

Let's look at a couple of examples of caregivers who expected the senior care system to be perfect—and how it affected them.

Andrew picks his mother up from her nursing home every Sunday morning so they can go to church together. On one particular Sunday, he arrives to find that his mother is not ready for church because another resident spilled lukewarm coffee on her a few minutes before he arrived. The staff decided to give Andrew's mother another shower because of the accident. Andrew is irate because now they will be late for church.

Is this inconvenient? Is this disrupting the Sunday morning routine? Of course. But these types of things *will happen* in senior living. Actually, these types of imperfections should not merely be tolerated, they should be expected. Families who learn to flow with these imperfections tend to be happier overall. It would benefit Andrew to reframe his interpretation of what happened. The staff cared enough to not only change his mother's clothing but also to make sure she was showered so she wasn't sticky all day from the coffee spill.

Sandy is taking care of her husband, Jim, and has a home care company come in twice each week to give her a break. Sandy has been using this home care company's services for six months with no problems. Today she has a great day planned for herself: meeting friends for lunch, getting some holiday shopping done, and then going to see her granddaughter's basketball game. About five minutes before the home care aide is scheduled to arrive, Sandy receives a call from the home care company indicating that the aide was in a fender bender. They assure Sandy that they will have another aide over to her house as soon as possible. Sandy is very angry and hangs up on the agency caller without saying good-bye.

Although it makes sense that Sandy is really disappointed, it would help her to remember that having merely one case of tardiness in six months' time is not unreasonable. Plus, the agency acted responsibly; they phoned to inform Sandy there was a problem and promised to have a replacement aide at her home as soon as possible. This type of imperfection is reasonable.

There will always be mistakes when human beings are serving human beings.

Sandy would also probably be well served to remember the advantage of using a home care agency, because it is their responsibility to find a replacement for the aide. If she had hired an independent aide who got into a car accident, that aide may not have had the ability to arrange a replacement, and Sandy's day out of the house would likely have been canceled completely rather than just delayed.

Caregivers will be less stressed and happier if they strive to forgive such imperfections in the senior care system.

How to Choose the Best Service Provider

While it's important to acknowledge that the senior care system will never be flawless, you can minimize the impact these imperfections have on you and your older loved one by reducing the potential for some mistakes as you search for a service provider. When looking for a service provider (nursing home/assisted living/home care agency), how do you narrow down your search so you are likely to be *closer* to perfect?

Identify Your Must-Haves—or Nonnegotiables

While perfection will never occur in the senior services field, we get closer to it when we identify our must-haves—or nonnegotiables. When you are choosing assisted living, a nursing home, or home care or other services, make a list of everything you want that service to be or to provide. Make this list as long as you like. Then, narrow it down to three nonnegotiables.

You may be familiar with this concept in other areas of your life. My uncle Pete still jokes about the list I wrote when I was young and single of my "nonnegotiables" about the man I would someday marry. Many of you probably created a must-have list with a real estate agent when purchasing a home. On a slightly smaller scale, others of you can probably relate to making such a list when planning a vacation.

Maybe your top three must-haves were a beach town accessible by a direct flight, a hotel on that beach, and staying within a specific budget.

As with life partners, buying a home, and vacations, nonnegotiables for senior care services are different for everyone. For example, if your older loved one has multiple serious chronic health problems and you are considering assisted living, looking at nursing coverage may be important.

Cheryl Burris, RN, owner of Senior Living Geriatric Care Management Services, advises families to confirm that there is twenty-four-hour on-site nursing coverage if that's a nonnegotiable. Many assisted living communities offer nursing coverage during the day, but only an on-call nurse is available in the evening.

Other nonnegotiables that families have frequently insisted on may include items like these:

- A certain geographic location

- A Kosher menu

- A fitness center or exercise classes

- Transportation to shopping, doctor's appointments, or cultural centers

- Affiliation with a certain religion

- Staff who speak a specific foreign language

Another common nonnegotiable comes up for men who are seeking assisted living or nursing homes—they want there to be other male residents! Because women live longer, there are generally significantly more females in nursing homes and assisted living communities. But a nonnegotiable for some men is that they want to be able to hang out with and make new men friends when they are considering a new residence. Of course, there are other men who don't care about this at all. The point is, what's a nonnegotiable item for one older person or caregiving crew may not be relevant at all for another.

Who makes this list? I hope it's obvious that this list can't exist without the input of the older loved one. The older loved one should make his wishes known and discuss them with members of his caregiving crew. If this older loved one has advanced dementia, of course, it is important to consider what that person would want if he was able to articulate it. But typically the primary caregiver and the older adult should be making this list with some input from the secondary caregivers.

Don't Read Too Much into Tax Status

Frequently caregivers make assumptions about an organization based on its for-profit, nonprofit, or government status. No senior service organization is perfect, regardless of its status.

> *Both good and bad care . . . occurs at all types of organizations, regardless of their tax status.*

Negative and positive stereotypes are associated with all three of these types of organizations. On one hand, some people believe that for-profit organizations are only concerned about the almighty dollar. On the other hand, some caregivers assume that a for-profit nursing home will do a better job because they assume that staff are paid better. This in turn may lead to the assumption that the for-profit nursing home has attracted the very best people who will make no mistakes.

Certain caregivers have the preconceived notion that a nonprofit or a government organization won't be of high enough quality. Alternatively, other caregivers might assume that a nonprofit with a religious affiliation will offer better care because the people who work there follow specific religious teachings. Some might assume that a government nursing home or hospital will offer better care because they are more highly regulated by the government.

Both good and bad care as well as mediocre care occurs at all types of organizations, regardless of their tax status. Try to judge each individual organization on its own merits. Don't rule out (or rule in) an organization simply because of its tax affiliation. Regardless of tax status, mistakes happen.

Don't Maintain Fixed Assumptions about Brands

If you have ever been to a franchise or chain store, restaurant, or hotel, you know that every location does not always offer precisely the same quality service, food, or surroundings as another. I am a Platinum Marriott member and have stayed at Marriotts around the world. But I have to say I favor some Marriott properties more than others. One of my favorite hotels is the Marriott Renaissance Vinoy in St. Petersburg, Florida. But just because I love that hotel does not mean I should expect every Marriott hotel to be precisely the same as that property. Keep this in mind when you hear that the "Smith" chain of nursing homes is fantastic but the "Jones" chain is terrible. You really must evaluate each service or organization on its own merits. There are many large franchises and chains of nursing homes, assisted living communities, home care organizations, etc. Keep in mind that a good experience at one does not guarantee a good experience at another (and vice versa).

Use Your Senses—Literally

Our five basic senses can tell us a lot about senior care services when we tune in to them. Sometimes caregivers are so stressed that they aren't tuning in to very obvious signals:

> **Nose around.** That is, literally take some deep breaths through your nose. Dr. Rabins says, "Places that smell bad . . . that makes me worry." Taylor Penvose, who holds a bachelor's degree in gerontology and has more than fifteen years working at Arden Courts, a specialized memory care assisted living community, concurs, "Smell is the biggest thing." Like Dr. Rabins, Penvose believes an unpleasant smell says a lot about a senior living community. The community should smell clean. Spills and accidents with incontinence do happen, but are they cleaned up quickly? If residents are sitting around in soiled Depends, you will likely smell it. It is not okay for a senior living residence to consistently smell like urine or feces. The aroma of baked goods or delicious food cooking, plants and flowers, or *simply nothing at*

all is what you want to smell. A building that consistently smells of overpowering air fresheners is another scent to be wary of; it is likely masking something unpleasant.

Use your eyes. Watch the staff very carefully. Dr. Rabins suggests watching how staff treat other residents. He asks, "Do they treat them like a person?" Are the staff well groomed? Do they look harried and exhausted, or are they handling the frenetic pace of a senior living community with patience, flexibility, and a smile? If not quite smiling, are they at least not frowning and grimacing? How do the residents look? Are they clean and well groomed? Are they engaged in activities or simply sitting in a chair alone in the hallway? Louise Montgomery, ADC/MC CDP, director of recreation and engagement, assisted living, for Bayleigh Chase, recommends viewing how the staff interact with the residents. Montgomery believes this is more important than how the senior living community looks aesthetically.

Observe touch. How do the staff handle the residents? Does an aide lend an arm to help a resident walk to the dining area, using a gentle yet firm touch? That's ideal. Grabbing or pulling a resident in a rough manner should never occur.

Listen. What are you hearing? If you hear music that the residents are singing or dancing along to, that's a good sign. If the residents seem to be simply tolerating the music, that is not good; this signals that the music is for the benefit of the staff and not the residents. In most senior living communities, you want to hear less Rihanna and Eminem and more Frank Sinatra and Nat King Cole. (As the baby boomers move into senior living communities, we are probably going to want to hear more Motown and Rolling Stones playing in the halls.) Gentle, pleasant tones of voice are good signs. If you witness staff yelling at each other across the room, consider it a red flag.

Taste. Sample the food and ask yourself whether you would enjoy eating it every day. Is the food attractively plated? Are food items your loved one likes included or not included on the menu?

Ask Good Questions

Before you choose a senior living residence, Marie O'Shea recommends that you ask staff what they like about working there. She emphasizes how important it is to speak to the staff involved in the direct care of the residents: that is, the nursing assistants, the medicine aides, etc. "There's nothing you can't ask. People may not answer, or may not give you the true answer, [but] . . . just ask." Just don't ask questions over the phone. Marie thinks by watching the staff person's body language you can get an idea if that person is being truthful. Look the staff member in the eye and observe.

Christine Levy, who has fifteen years of experience in senior living sales, suggests asking, "Would you put your mother here?" Again, you may not get an answer from the staff person, but the lack of an answer will tell you something. Even if the staff person answers positively, you will get signals from her body language and tone of voice that will guide you to assess the reliability of the answer.

Sherry Gilde, sales counselor with Five Star Senior Living, says that families ask her this question often. While she wholeheartedly believes in the care at the assisted living community in which she works, she tells them that she would not place her loved ones there. She then goes on to explain that while she knows her own loved ones would receive excellent care, she would not want to blend personal matters, such as the eldercare of a family member, with professional matters at the place in which she works. Sherry's explanation makes sense and is genuine. The moral here is that you want to listen fully to the explanation or answer the staff person offers. Sherry's thoughtful explanation is more valuable than someone who gives a pat answer like, "Absolutely! I would place my mom here." Sometimes it's not the answer that we read into but the explanation and body language that go into the staff member's answer to our question.

Dr. Rabins thinks it's important to ask about training for the staff. Are they, for example, getting good training in dementia care? This is clearly important if your loved one has dementia. It's a good idea to ask very specific questions related to your loved one's situation. If your loved one has a serious allergy to nuts, how knowledgeable are the staff about dealing with accidental exposure? If your loved one has serious mental health issues like depression, bipolar disorder, schizophrenia, or an anxiety disorder, it would be important to ask how much continuing education the staff receive about those issues. At a minimum, it's a good idea to make sure that staff are following the state regulations for training and continuing education.

When talking to staff, ask your question(s) and then be quiet. Listen to their full answers. Don't try to fill in the gaps in conversation. You will get much more if you simply give them time to talk.

Look at Longevity

For employees at a senior living residence to have two or three years at the same job may actually be pretty impressive, especially for direct care staff. Five or ten years at the same organization is remarkable. "Turnover is pretty rampant in a lot of nursing homes, except your star centers," says Stephanie Goldstein, LBSW, director of social services for Genesis HealthCare. While longevity of staff certainly doesn't guarantee anything, it is a unique characteristic of an organization if a team stays in place a long time. Goldstein acknowledges that there are rare occasions where a staff person has been working somewhere a long time but isn't a very good worker. But most of the time, staff longevity can be a very positive sign. Geriatric care manager Cathy Lonas, RN, BSN, MSBA, and owner of Advocate 360 (an aging life care/geriatric care management company) in the Washington, DC, area, says she finds it interesting to ask staff, "*Who is your motivation?*" Often the most dedicated direct care workers (nursing assistants, activities assistants, etc.) will reveal who in their family they think of when providing care to an older loved one. Many will share stories about taking care of older parents, grandparents, or other loved ones or their efforts to treat older patients as they'd like their older loved ones to be treated. This can offer some personal insight as to whether a direct care staff member views her work as just a job or as more of a vocation.

Review State Surveys with a Grain of Salt

There is no question that state inspections are important. Nursing homes, assisted living communities, adult day care centers, and many other organizations are monitored by the states in which they are registered, and a public report often called a survey is issued. It is important to examine these inspection results carefully but not to put all your assessment eggs in that one basket. Inspections may rate everything from fire safety and food safety to patient clinical records to family satisfaction. Overall, leadership and staff at all senior care organizations take these formal checks extremely seriously.

If you ask healthcare employees in the senior care industry, most could tell you a horror story about a community that is currently highly rated. They could often also tell you a wonderful story about a community that is rated poorly or has multiple "deficiencies."

Levy recommends looking into why a senior living residence got a poor rating and not ruling out a place immediately only because of a low rating. Goldstein also advises caregivers to take the report into account but not to rely on it exclusively. She jokes that sometimes a community where a lot is going wrong can get lucky. Perhaps the state representative reviewed the one well-maintained resident chart. And it is possible for the opposite to happen as well. For example, the report might indicate that a patient was given the incorrect medication. But the report may have failed to indicate that there were no adverse effects on the patient. While we don't ever want medication errors on a state survey, it is important to realize that it unfortunately *does sometimes happen* in healthcare settings.

Make a Course Correction: Should I Stay or Should I Go?

The more you research services and providers before you need them the less likely it is that you will need to make a change. But sometimes no matter how carefully you vet a senior care provider, the service or the provider is not a good match, and there was no way of predicting that. If you think a service is simply a poor match for your older loved one or for you and your family, it may make sense to simply change services. But before you do that, consider what *you* might be able to do to make it work with the current service provider.

Denise Manifold, regional vice president of sales with Brightview Senior Living, suggests giving your older loved one breathing room to adjust to the new setting or service provider. Sometimes hovering caregivers make the transition to utilizing the new service or adjusting to the new residence very difficult. It also could be that you haven't properly shared your concerns with the staff. Most good service providers and senior living residences welcome feedback and want you to be happy. Sometimes caregivers want to avoid confrontation, so they simply decide to change providers without even letting the current organization know what's wrong. Manifold recommends not letting your concerns build up and to address them sooner rather than later to see if your dissatisfactions may be resolved.

If you still believe it's necessary to change service providers, chart this new course cautiously. Remember there is definitely a downside to moving your older loved one to a new residence. Often there will be significant adjustment challenges in dealing with yet another new environment. And switching home care providers can be traumatic, especially if your older loved one has just begun to trust one of the in-home workers. This can particularly be an enormous hassle if your older loved one has a dementia like Alzheimer's disease and is a resident at a specialized memory care assisted living. When an older loved one has advanced dementia, you want to think very carefully about disrupting his world (more on this in chapter 12).

But sometimes it is necessary to make a change, and that can be an opportunity for you to learn from the mismatch. Consider ways to "shop smarter" for a match now that you know better what you are looking for.

. . . Be careful not to look more at
aesthetics than at care.

Perhaps your original list of nonnegotiables didn't focus on the most important things for the older loved one. This often happens when primary and secondary caregivers focus on features and benefits a service provider offers that *they* would like rather than on what the older loved one truly needs. Lisa Chapin Robinette, certified senior advisor (CSA) and former sales counselor with Five Star Senior Living, encourages caregivers to stop considering services from their own point of view. They should be careful not to look more at aesthetics than at care.

Robinette acknowledges it can be hard to view senior services intellectually rather than emotionally, but it is important to make this effort. Take into consideration both how "at home" or comfortable you feel with a service provider or organization and the facts about care when making your selections.

When Reese was deciding where to place her elderly father, Lowell, she selected the most expensive and elaborate assisted living community in the suburbs. Lowell protested, but Reese insisted; after all, she wanted the best for her dad. But it turned out that her father was really uncomfortable with how "fancy" the other residents were. Lowell had been raised on a farm and really preferred a smaller group-home setting in a rural area. Reese admits now that she was so impressed with how gorgeous the first option was that she talked her father into it. Rather than thinking intellectually about what was best for him, she made an emotional decision based on the belief that if she spent more money on a "nicer" place she'd be doing a better job as a caregiver.

Perhaps your mother just doesn't have "chemistry" with the aging life care professional you hired to oversee her care. The aging life care professional, for example, earned her nursing degree at Duke University, a fantastic school. She has over twenty-five years of experience. On paper, when you looked at it intellectually, this person looked great, but your mom just isn't comfortable with her personality.

Alternatively, it may not be that the service or provider is a bad match; it is just that they are *bad*. While I believe that the vast majority of senior care services and professionals are doing a great job, there are bad services, facilities, and service providers out there. They are the exception, not the rule. If you have truly witnessed unsafe, unsanitary practices that you objectively assess as having put older patients in a dangerous situation, it is acutely important to report this to the proper authorities. When in doubt about where you would report misconduct, abuse, or other concerns, you can usually find the correct entity if you ask your local Area Agency on Aging (AAA) for guidance (more details on this in chapter 11).

> *Don't expect perfection in this exceedingly*
> *flawed system. Reshape your expectations*
> *to accept good enough.*

Depending on the situation, it may make sense to cease using the service or remove your older loved one from the care of an organization before making a formal complaint to a regulatory body. But there are other cases (when your older loved one's or another patient's life is truly in danger) where it makes sense to complain immediately.

While truly life-threatening and exploitative incidents can and do happen in the senior care system, you are more likely to experience problems that are *disappointing rather than dangerous.* The most important course correction to make as a caregiver engaging senior care services and providers is to know the difference and act accordingly. Don't expect perfection in this exceedingly flawed system. Reshape your expectations to accept good enough.

We discussed several examples in this chapter about spending money for care. While Medicare and Medicaid do sometimes pay for services that your older loved one needs, many caregivers are under the impression that those programs pay for more than they do. The next chapter outlines what Medicare and Medicaid do pay for and how to plan financially for what is not covered by those programs.

Ten

CARE COSTS MONEY!

Gone Overboard: Expecting Medicare and Medicaid to Pay for Everything

I can't begin to estimate the number of caregivers I have worked with who incorrectly assumed that Medicare or Medicaid would pay for something their older loved one needed. Medicare typically does not cover nearly as much as many caregivers believe it will. For instance, many caregivers assume that Medicare would cover an assisted living or an extended nursing home stay, yet that is *never the case*. It's a heart-wrenching moment when that realization sinks in, particularly when older loved ones have not planned well financially for their retirement years.

Although caregivers and their older loved ones who have limited financial resources will probably be very interested in this chapter, everyone can benefit from this information. After all, money can be a very emotional topic for people who have plenty of it and for those who do not.

This chapter helps you with the following concepts and tasks:

- Learn the *basics* about Medicare and Medicaid (also known as Medical Assistance).

- Identify places to look for additional money and benefits.

- Figure out how to make the most of the financial resources your older loved one does have.

Medicare 101

For the most up-to-date and specific information on Medicare, check out www.medicare.gov, which is actually quite straightforward and user-friendly. In the meantime, here are the *basics* about Medicare in plain English.

The reason people sixty-five and older gain access to this benefit is because they've paid into it through their work history or their spouse's work history. In this way, Medicare is similar to Social Security because it is considered an entitlement. Most of us are automatically entitled to it because we paid into the Medicare system through automatic mandatory workplace deductions. Many of us noticed this when we had our first jobs in high school and wondered how Medicare and Social Security wound up with so much of that precious hourly, minimum wage we were working hard for!

The Medicare entitlement program is a federally funded health insurance benefit that nearly all adults over sixty-five qualify for. (It is also worth mentioning that some persons younger than sixty-five also qualify for this program if they have certain disabilities.) The way it works for the sixty-five-plus population is that there are four parts, known as Parts A, B, C, and D.

Original Medicare

Medicare Parts A and B are also known as Original Medicare. Part A often covers an overnight stay at the hospital, for example. Part A also may cover *short-term* nursing home stays (e.g., if you need rehab after hip replacement surgery). Part B typically covers services like a visit to the doctor's office. Original Medicare is administered by the federal government. (Those enrolled in Original Medicare have also frequently enrolled in Part D, which offers prescription drug coverage.)

Medicare Advantage Plan

But some older adults don't have Part A, B, or D at all; they've opted for Part C. Part C is better known as a Medicare Advantage Plan. When someone has enrolled in a Medicare Advantage Plan, it means that the person has opted to have Medicare administered through a private company such as a health maintenance organization (HMO) or a preferred provider organization (PPO). In essence, Part C typically offers the same services as Part A, Part B, and Part D combined.

THIS TIME YOU *DO* WANT TO JUMP (ONBOARD) SHIP

To understand Medicare and insurance options in greater depth and how they apply to your older loved one specifically, it can be very helpful to seek the free assistance of a State Health Insurance Assistance Program (SHIP) counselor at your local Area Agency on Aging (AAA). To find your local AAA, go to www.n4a.org and plug in your zip code. SHIP is just one of the free programs offered at your local AAA. To better understand SHIP, check out www.shiptacenter.org.

Medigap

Many older adults also purchase supplemental insurance policies that will cover some costs not included in Original Medicare or a Medicare Advantage Plan. These additional policies, known as Medigap policies, typically cover items like co-pays and deductibles. For more extensive details on what Medigap policies cover and how to find the best policy for you or your older loved one, again check out the user-friendly www.medicare.gov website.

Medicaid 101

For the most comprehensive information about Medicaid, visit www.medicaid .gov. In the meantime, here are the *basics* about Medicaid in plain English.

Medicaid (also known as Medical Assistance) is a benefit program funded by both the federal government and individual state governments. Unlike Medicare, Medicaid is *not* coverage that older adults receive automatically. Medicaid is a needs-based (i.e., you must demonstrate that you need it) benefit that an individual must apply for. Although the federal government contributes to Medicaid, this program is administered by and applied for in the state in which the older adult resides. The most common reason older adults apply for this benefit is that they need to use it for an indefinite, long-term nursing home stay. But some states permit Medicaid to be used for other services such as adult day care, and some even allow it to be used for certain types of assisted living or home care services. In the states where Medicaid can be used for assisted living and home care services, there are frequently long waiting lists.

While you can apply for Medicaid online or even by phone (www. longtermcare.gov), Stephanie Goldstein, director of social services at a Genesis HealthCare center, highly recommends that you meet with an elder law attorney to help you with this process, particularly when the older adult who requires care is married. An elder law attorney may be able to help approach the Medicaid application so that you legally protect some of your assets (money, property) for yourself or your spouse if you are married. Because Medicaid has a "five-year look back" period, assets spent during the sixty months prior to a Medicaid application may need to be explained.

Evan Farr, CELA (certified elder law attorney) and author of the best-selling book *The Nursing Home Survival Guide*, recommends that any older adult with assets in excess of fifty thousand dollars consider consulting an experienced elder law attorney to do some estate planning so they can accurately submit a Medicaid application. Farr is fond of sharing a quote by the United States Supreme Court that calls the Medicaid laws "an aggravated assault on the English language, resistant to attempts to understand it." And because Medicaid law is so complex, when many older adults and their caregivers attempt to complete the application, they make major mistakes that can result in the application being rejected or in a delay of their eligibility. When an elder law attorney with expertise in this area is involved, the fees spent securing those elder law services can actually save you money (and aggravation) in the long run. Farr reports that some clients who *don't* have assets over fifty thousand dollars will retain the services of an elder law attorney to simply complete and submit their Medicaid application properly. Farr also shares that sometimes caregivers handling the application on their own forget about assets their older loved ones have. When the caregiver reports an honest mistake like this, there can be a retroactive disqualification of Medicaid benefits. An elder law attorney with experience in this area may help caregivers avoid this.

Ultimately, you want to remember that Medicaid coverage is not automatic and typically does not cover as much as many caregivers expect. Be prepared— even if your older loved one does qualify, the application process itself is extensive and, potentially, expensive.

Paying for What Medicare and Medicaid Won't Cover when Your Older Loved One Has Little Money or Few Assets

Now that we have clarified some basics about what Medicare and Medicaid cover, let's discuss how to fill in those gaps. Because many people don't give any thought to what Medicare or Medicaid does or doesn't cover until they are put in the position of taking care of an older loved one, the financial implications are typically unplanned for. These financial complexities often come as a surprise, even to the most savvy and highly educated people. As Kevin Knapp, owner of a Right at Home franchise (national in-home senior care company based in Omaha, Nebraska) says, "Generally, anything that's going to be ongoing 'custodial care' is going to be paid for privately." Further, he observes that typically anything that is *not* time-limited will be out-of-pocket. As we discussed earlier, often Medicaid will pay for a long-term nursing home stay after a complex application is filed and approved. But what if you want some other type of long-term service? Those types of ongoing services require funds that you or your older loved one will need to pay for directly and privately.

Let's look at an example of how a typically responsible and savvy couple are blindsided by the cost of elder care. This scenario compares how well prepared this couple was for caring for their newborn but how significantly less prepared they were in caring for an older loved one.

Mark is a forty-year-old political consultant and his wife, Tracy, is a thirty-seven-year-old attorney who recently gave birth to their first child. Of course, they read all the popular first-time parenting books like *What To Expect When You're Expecting* prior to their baby's birth. The nursery was freshly painted, furnished, and stocked with diapers, wipes, formula, and adorable pink clothing when they brought their beautiful daughter, Madeline, home from the hospital. They had heavily researched and selected the day care center where Madeline would be cared for when Tracy's maternity leave ended. Although the day care center was very expensive, it was the one most highly recommended by friends. The couple even began planning for Madeline's future by setting up a college fund to which their friends and family members could contribute.

Fast-forward eighteen months. Mark's seventy-four-year-old widowed father,

George, suffers a major stroke. He had been living independently in a small apartment, but now he requires more hands-on care. Up until the stroke, George had been financially self-sufficient, living off of his small pension, Social Security income, and some modest savings.

Mark and Tracy decided to move George into their home. The couple also looked into adult day care because they both work and George needs help and supervision most of the time. They were stunned to learn that Medicare does not cover adult day care. While some of the adult day care centers they looked at do accept Medicaid, George does not qualify at this time (although he might be able to qualify with the help of an experienced elder law attorney).

It is startling how frequently this type of scenario plays out in the United States. While Americans are making assumptions that general health insurance, Medicare, or Medicaid will cover whatever their elderly parent is going to need, nothing could be further from the truth. According to the Pew Research Center (Parker & Patten 2013), "Nearly half (47%) of adults in their 40s and 50s have a parent age 65 or older and are either raising a young child or financially supporting a grown child (age 18 or older)." So sandwich generation caregivers like Tracy and Mark also have to be concerned with the day-to-day economics of raising growing children (and even potentially financially supporting grown children). The obvious point here is that naturally Tracy and Mark did not expect Madeline's day care to be free. They wanted the best and were willing to pay for it. They prepared for the arrival and responsibility of caring for their infant. Financially they were ready for her when she was born and were even preparing for her bright future by setting up the college fund. In contrast, they were completely unprepared for the arrival and responsibility of George.

While some of George's monthly income covers the costs of adult day care, Tracy and Mark still had to make adjustments to their budget to cover the difference. Furthermore, because the adult day care center is only open daytime hours during the week, they have had to hire home health aides to help out on the weekends and some evenings. They were also shocked to find out that Medicare and George's Medigap did not cover the hourly wages of home health aides.

You may sympathize with this couple. I sympathize with this couple. Some readers may even feel a little indignant that Tracy and Mark were put in this situation. Why should they have been preparing for the prospect of having to care for one or more of their parents? Isn't it George's job to have planned better for retirement and to have his affairs in order in case he needs help during his senior years? Of course. Many people regard taking personal responsibility for and taking care of oneself as a high value. But keep this in mind: When George was growing up, saving and planning for long-term care services as you aged was not as heavily emphasized in our society. When George was a kid, people weren't likely to consider that they'd live nearly as long as they do now!

Most caregivers are just as unprepared as Tracy and Mark were for what happened to George, both financially and otherwise. Even the wisest, most savvy and financially responsible adult children are almost never totally prepared for the financial reality of elder care. If you have been caught off guard by the responsibility of elder care, it is not too late to better prepare yourself for all the additional financial challenges you will continue to face.

Like Mark and Tracy, if you are a primary caregiver, you have to figure out how to deal with the financial implications. And if you currently relate to the story of Mark and Tracy, you may be headed—just as they are—overboard. What are three things you can think of to do today to prevent that from happening? Write them down before you read further.

Did you write down any of the following?

- Set up a consultation with an experienced elder law attorney.

- Determine how *much* money you can realistically afford to contribute to your older loved one's care each month.

- Determine how *long* you can afford to contribute to your older loved one's care each month.

- Begin a comprehensive search of community resources, starting with the Area Agency on Aging, to determine whether there is anything else your older loved one qualifies for.

- Seek out other friends and family who may be able to contribute finan-cially to your older loved one's care.

- Do an exhaustive search of your older loved one's financial records. Some-times there are bank accounts or other assets that have been overlooked.

- Consider other resources that may be less expensive than the current ser-vices you are using for your older loved one's care (e.g., in George's case adult day care and home care) to determine whether the funds are being spent efficiently. Of course, you would be gauging the money spent versus the quality of the care your older loved one is currently receiving.

Make a Course Correction: Face the Financial Reality

Once you understand and accept the limits of Medicare and Medicaid, it's important to figure out how you and/or your older loved one is going to afford services. Some strategies include creating a realistic budget, mining community resources, and deciding to spend money on services now that might help you save money in the future.

Have a Budget and Stick to It

If the caregiving crew chooses to contribute money toward their older loved one's care, it is important to have a budget. Determining how much money you can realistically afford to contribute to your older loved one's care each month and how long you can afford to contribute is critical. Budgeting and planning ahead is essential, even if you consider yourself financially well-off. Money goes fast when paying for older adult services. When you go over the amount you can comfortably afford, there are countless spin-off problems that occur. Just a few include arguing with your spouse or partner about the amount spent; not having enough for your own care when you are older and thus putting your younger loved ones in the same difficult situation; feeling resentful toward your older loved one because of the money you are spending. You get the idea. You are much less likely to go overboard if you take a step back and think realistically about what you can afford.

Look into Your Local Community Resources

Begin a comprehensive search of community resources, starting with the Area Agency on Aging (AAA), says Dianne Turpin, who has worked at two AAAs during the course of her career in senior care. (We will discuss the role of the AAA in more detail in chapter 11.) Turpin then recommends that you contact your local health department and your local department of social services. Turpin shared a story about a family member she once worked with who was frustrated that community services for older adults are not well advertised. She encouraged this caregiver to begin his search by making the analogy that we don't notice car dealerships having sales unless we are shopping for a car. You don't know it's there until you need it. But when you open your eyes and start looking for services geared toward older adults, you start to see them everywhere. There's actually a term for this: the Baader-Meinhof phenomenon. So start your search for resources and see how many possible local services you can find. Make a contact at organizations like your local AAA, health department, and department of social services.

Very occasionally there will be a free resource that will absolutely blow your mind, such as grants or legacy programs that will offer free services to caregivers. For example, for several years I was able to refer families to their local AAA for a three-year grant called the ROSE Program. This grant was available through a partnership between nonprofits and the government. It offered $1,500 *per year* to someone who was caring for a loved one who had an irreversible dementia diagnosis. This money could be used to pay for adult day care, home care, or even to engage someone to come in and help the caregiver with cleaning or mowing the lawn. It was a simple one-page application, and there were no financial questions or constraints. So, regardless of how much or how little income or assets the older loved one or caregiver had, any caregiver could receive this grant. The only requirement was that the person had to be caring for someone with an irreversible dementia diagnosis. And this was available three years in a row, so the individual could receive up to $4,500.

Now, in the grand scheme of taking care of an older loved one, $4,500 over a three-year period is not exactly a windfall. But it sure helped a lot of people make their lives easier. The point is, you never know what your local nonprofit or government agencies may have available financially while you are a caregiver. In this case, caregivers who were in touch with their local AAA and/or Alzheimer's Association were the first to learn about it even though it was open to anyone and everyone.

While there is no guarantee something like this awaits you, you never know until you do the research. I can't stress enough how it's always a best practice to begin with your local AAA and other local government agencies like the health department and the department of social services; but don't forget about other nonprofits. In the case of the ROSE Program, the Alzheimer's Association was involved. But if your older loved one has cancer, make contact with the American Cancer Society. If your older loved one has heart disease, get in touch with the American Heart Association. You get the idea. Most major diseases and conditions have at least one nonprofit that offers education, programs, and other services. While you can use Google to search for this information or go to your hard copy of the Yellow Pages, your local AAA is typically going to be able to refer you to the most appropriate nonprofits for your situation.

Colleen Walker, CTRS (certified therapeutic recreation specialist) and executive director at a Brookdale Senior Living assisted living community, concurs with Dianne Turpin in recommending that you check for any and all types of government assistance that may be available. Walker has seen a number of families access veterans benefits to pay for some assisted living costs or other services. Some veterans qualify for what is known as Aid & Attendance, and often this benefit can be used toward assisted living. Many experienced elder law attorneys can also help caregiving crews navigate this program. For more detailed information, check out www.va.gov.

Ask People Who Love Your Older Loved One for Assistance

If financial resources for the older loved one are very limited, and you've exhausted all possible government and nonprofit resources, go back to chapter 8. Do the MET exercise. This exercise is really important for your caregiving crew to take seriously because it helps you determine who in your network of friends and family may be able to contribute. Some in your network may be able to offer funds, while others may be able to contribute by handling certain tasks so you don't have to pay privately for them.

Dig Deeper into Your Older Loved One's Paperwork

Sometimes there are bank accounts or other assets that have been overlooked. I even worked with a client once who had not yet settled his deceased sister's estate, and the sister had passed away several years prior! Look everywhere to see if there is any money or assets that may have been overlooked. This will also help if and when you ever do need to apply for Medicaid, as Evan Farr, CELA, cautioned about earlier, because you'll need to make sure you disclose all assets on an application.

Consider Approaching Care from a Different Angle

To determine whether you are spending your funds efficiently, examine other resources that may be less expensive than the current services you are using for your older loved one's care. Recall the example of George in the beginning of this chapter. It might be more cost effective for him to move to a small assisted living or group home rather than staying home with his son's family, which means paying for home care and adult day care. While you may not actually want to follow through with a less expensive option for any number of reasons, it is important to know what else is out there and what it costs in case a decision is ever made to adjust the care plan.

Use Private Pay Consultants Strategically

We've discussed the potential advantages of working with an experienced elder law attorney. Even if you are not sure it will be worth the money for these services, at least set up a consultation (many experienced elder law attorneys offer an initial consultation for free to assess your situation and explain their services). Colleen Walker recommends that you talk to your accountant about any and all tax credits the caregiver may be eligible for. She specifically mentions that there are tax breaks for taking care of someone with an irreversible dementia as a primary diagnosis. There are also write-offs for long-term care residences (nursing home) stays. She cautions that not every accountant will know about this, but more information about it is available in IRS Publication 505. Further, it may be very helpful to check out https://www.irs.gov/Help-&-Resources/Tools -&-FAQs/FAQs-for-Individuals/Frequently-Asked-Tax-Questions-&-Answers /IRS-Procedures/For-Caregivers. It may be prudent to talk to an accountant who has experience working with older adults and their caregivers. As Evan Farr puts it, "Why not pay a little bit now to save in the long run?" This concept of paying for one or two consultations with private pay experts applies to lots of services, including aging life care experts (which I will discuss more in the next section).

Help the Older Loved One Scale Back in Other Areas

This one was not mentioned in the scenario with George because he lived with Tracy and Mark, so it probably wouldn't apply. But sometimes when funds are needed for care, it is really advantageous to help the older loved one go through the monthly budget with a fine-tooth comb. I have worked with older adults who have extremely expensive cable packages for their television but claim they don't have money for prescription co-pays. Now, if someone is bedbound, giving up that luxury of a great cable package may be out of the question. But sometimes there are small expenses here and there that can be cut to meet care costs.

Paying for What Medicare and Medicaid Don't Cover when Your Older Loved One Has Significant Money or Assets

Caregivers of older loved ones who don't have much money may sneer at this section. *What problems could people who have money possibly be dealing with,* you may be thinking. Is being a caregiver easier if you and/or your older loved one has a good deal of money? If you have funds, it often makes caregiving a heck of a lot easier because you can afford the many more options for help that are available.

But don't assume that just because the older person or the caregivers involved have money, the caregiving situation will be smooth sailing. I have interacted with countless members of caregiving crews whose older loved one had money, yet the caregivers opted not to spend it! Money is an emotional issue, and there are lots of reasons an older loved one and/or her caregiving crew does not spend it even though they have it.

But skimping when your older loved one does have money can be another example of going overboard. Let's look at what happened to a family that did just that.

Maggie is a fifty-seven-year-old woman who lives 250 miles away from her eighty-nine-year-old father, Ron, who lives alone and is having a number of health problems. Because she lives so far away and can't be with her father very often, Maggie called Ron's local Area Agency on Aging (AAA) for advice about how to help him. When Renee, the AAA worker, asked about the family's financial resources, Maggie was tentative with her answer. She mentioned that her father "does have some money," but she wouldn't be specific. When asked about the value of his home, Maggie did disclose that it was valued in the neighborhood of one million dollars and there was no outstanding debt on the home.

Maggie described that she really needed someone to have their "eyes and ears" on Ron almost daily or, perhaps, even daily. In response, Renee suggested to Maggie that she consider hiring an aging life care expert (up until very recently known as a private geriatric care manager) to help her select a private duty home care aide. Because Maggie was far away and there were funds, Renee thought this would be an efficient way for Maggie to get an aide who was the best match for Ron. After all, Maggie's description of the services she was looking for exactly matched what a typical aging life care expert could provide. Renee went on to explain that the aging life care expert could monitor Ron's situation and report back to Maggie regularly. The aging life care expert could also go to doctor's appointments with Ron if Maggie desired.

Maggie was thrilled to hear this type of service existed and began looking for an aging life care expert in Ron's area on www.aginglifecare.org. Her delight faded, however, when she realized that this type of service was private pay. She called Renee back and said she didn't want to pay an aging life care expert; she wanted the AAA to help her for free. After all, Ron had paid into Social Security his whole life. Ron has Medicare! Why wouldn't the local AAA be able to cover this service? When Renee explained the types of services the AAA could offer,

Maggie deemed them insufficient. She wanted to know why it would take two weeks for someone from the AAA to assess her father. Maggie also could not understand when Renee explained that the AAA does offer some home care services in certain cases, but the type of long hours Maggie wanted to have someone at Ron's home would never be available free of charge for anyone in the AAA's jurisdiction.

Renee did exactly the right thing by assessing Maggie's needs, assessing Ron's assets, and suggesting that Maggie consider hiring an aging life care expert. The worker assessed correctly that the older adult could afford the service. While the AAA does have many programs, daily "eyes and ears" is typically not one that is available—especially free of charge!

Can you think of at least three reasons Maggie was so indignant when she was told about what the AAA could offer and what would be private pay? Take a moment to write some down before you read any further.

Did any of these make your list?

- Maggie wants to inherit Ron's assets. There may be a variety of reasons for this, including—

  - She may be counting on living in his house someday or even using it as a vacation home.

  - She may be planning to use his assets to fund her own retirement.

  - She may want to use his assets to pay for her son or daughter's college tuition.

  - She may be in debt currently and want to use a potential inheritance to deal with that problem.

- Maggie is simply very frugal and wants to try to get services for free or as low-cost as possible.

- While Ron's house is an enormous asset, Ron does not have a large monthly income. Maggie has no idea how to go about accessing cash from Ron's house.

- Ron's father (Maggie's grandfather) lived until he was 101. Maggie is terrified that Ron could outlive his assets and wants to very careful about spending his money.

- Ron is legally competent, and therefore Maggie has no right to spend his assets. But Maggie is confident that although her father wouldn't think twice about buying lavish presents for his children and grandchildren, he would never agree to pay fees for an aging life care expert or home care aide, which he would deem a waste of money.

So even when your older loved one does have plenty of assets or money, making caregiving decisions does not always *feel* simpler and easier. For Maggie to get what she wants to meet Ron's needs, she is going to have to make a course correction in her mind.

Make a Course Correction: Address the Miser in the Crew Head-On

Your first step in correcting your course is to identify which party—your older loved one or a member(s) of the caregiving crew—is reluctant to spend the money or assets, and why. Then address those issues head-on.

Many healthcare providers report it can be easier to work with an older adult who has no money than with one who has plenty but won't spend it (or the person's caregiving crew won't). While many of the free and low-cost services that we've discussed are wonderful, there can be waiting lists and limits to what those programs can offer. Not spending money when it is available is probably going to make your caregiving experience much more stressful. As Kevin Knapp mentioned earlier, when a service is long term it is most often going to be private pay. Gail Yerkie, RN, BSN, director of Kent County Medical Adult Day Care Center, recommends that caregiving crews make peace with the fact that if the older loved one has money, it is probably going to need to be spent on care needs. In Yerkie's experience, she has seen caregivers become resentful that care costs for older loved ones may be chipping away at their inheritance.

But sometimes even if it is the older loved one who is reluctant to spend her money, it may make sense for people in the caregiving crew to absorb some expenses if they can afford to and want to. Let me share a personal story to illustrate my point. For a long time, my grandmother was able to afford to pay her own rent, but because of her anxiety about her money running out, my father paid it each month with his own money. Also, because of some health concerns and fall risks, it became obvious that my grandmother would benefit from a medical alert system. After discussing it with her and determining that she would like to have the service, I secured it for her but refrained from telling her the price when she asked. Knowing her, I realized she would consider the fee unreasonable. So I paid it with my own money even though she could have afforded it. Some caregiving crews who choose this option may want to arrange for the older loved one to leave the equivalent amount of money they have spent outright to that caregiver in a will. While this was not done in my family, it would have been very reasonable for my father to suggest that my grandmother bequeath him the amount he has spent over the years for her rent.

Maybe *you* are the one who is reluctant to spend your older loved one's assets. Think about why this is, particularly if you don't already know. If you are afraid that your older loved one will outlive her money, then see an experienced elder law attorney so you can establish a plan. If you are counting on your older loved one's assets so you can inherit, you are not alone. A lot of people are hoping their parents or other older loved ones will leave them money to help pay for kids' college or even to supplement their own retirement. But it's important for you to make peace with the fact that your inheritance may not be what you were hoping for. Even if your older loved one really wants you to inherit the assets one day, it may not be in the cards if you want to have a less stressful caregiving experience where your older loved one gets the best care possible.

Private Pay Consultants and Services

I am a big proponent of using paid consultants, even when money is tight. I am an even bigger proponent of using paid services when money is *not tight*. When you hire the right consultant, you may actually save some money, energy, time, or all three. Think back to Maggie who was trying to arrange care for her father who lived close to a four-and-a-half-hour drive away. If she actually goes ahead and hires a good aging life care expert, it may be possible for her to actually save money and time. The same thing applies when a caregiving crew consults with an elder law attorney about asset protection or a Medicaid application.

This chapter focuses on reining in your expectations about Medicare and Medicaid and where to find help when those programs don't pay for services your loved one needs. The next chapter helps you better understand how to rein in your expectations for the doctor and how to augment the doctor's services.

Eleven

THE DOCTOR DOESN'T KNOW EVERYTHING

Gone Overboard: Expecting the Doctor to Be the Only Resource

While most of the information in this chapter is targeted at the primary caregiver, the entire caregiving crew can use it to prevent the primary caregiver from going overboard and needing to implement a course correction.

This chapter helps caregivers reduce stress by utilizing the following strategies:

- Identify reasonable and appropriate expectations for primary care doctors and other physician specialists.

- Find experts and resources you can utilize in addition to your older loved one's doctor or team of doctors.

The Doc Is Just One Person with One Perspective

A good doctor is invaluable, and appropriately utilizing the services of doctors can make the caregiving experience significantly less stressful. But older patients frequently pin all their hopes on their doctor or doctors. Caregivers also sometimes expect to hear *all that is necessary* to best care for their older loved one from the doctor. Caring, competent physicians will give patients and their caregivers as much information as they can about the patients' diagnoses, prescriptions, and treatment options. But it's unrealistic for patients and caregivers to expect physicians to be able to do more than that. Doctors are not supposed to do it all; they are just one of many resources for the older loved one and the caregiving crew.

Michael, an eighty-one-year-old, has suffered with chronic depression for more than fifty years. Since his wife died a year ago, he has experienced worsening symptoms. Michael has always refused to see a psychiatrist because he says he's "not crazy." But Dr. Burke, his primary care physician who is not a specialist in the area of depression or mental health conditions, prescribes antidepressants. (It's worth noting that while most older adults are reluctant to see a psychiatrist, many do obtain mental health medications at their primary doctor's office. A major study [Maust, Kales, & Blow] published in the July 2015 issue of the *Journal of the American Geriatrics Society* found that older adults have a higher psychiatric medication usage than do younger persons, but they see psychiatrists and psychotherapists significantly less frequently.)

Michael's son Josh is concerned because he notices that his father's symptoms are not getting any better. Josh knows that Michael refuses to see a specialist such as a psychiatrist and that he has also refused to attend therapy or counseling. Having recently read an article about how yoga can be helpful for people who are struggling with depression, Josh thought his father might consider trying yoga. Because Michael has always been an athlete and even still works out at a gym, Josh looked into this further and found that several yoga classes were offered in their community—even one at Michael's gym. Michael responded, "It was all girls" in the yoga class at his gym and, "If yoga could help me, Dr. Burke would have already told me about that."

At this point it would be great for Josh to say, "Let's ask Dr. Burke what she thinks about yoga for depression." It's very possible Dr. Burke might think yoga would be a great add-on to Michael's treatment plan. But because she—like so many general practitioners—didn't bring it up in the first place, her older adult patient Michael—like so many others his age, and even some of their caregivers—assumes it isn't worthwhile.

Doctors are usually not typically *qualified* to do more than diagnose and offer treatment options for a physical, cognitive, or mental health condition. Further, physicians almost never have enough time to impart all the relevant information, even if they happen to possess all the knowledge needed in each case. So even if Dr. Burke were aware that yoga can be a great supplement to depression medication and thought it was a good idea, she may not have thought to mention it during the typical brief doctor's appointment. This may surprise many older adults—particularly those born before 1940—who grew up during an era when the physician was unconditionally revered and respected. This way of thinking often persists during the course of these older adults' lives. Many healthcare providers joke that their oldest patients consider their doctors to be deities. While those born after 1940 respect doctors as well, they have a tendency to view doctors as being a bit more human.

The general belief (though there are exceptions, of course) is that the older the patients and caregivers, the less they will question the doctor. And the younger the patients or caregivers, the more they will view the doctor as more of a partner or even a vendor! But regardless of how you view the doctor—as a god, a teammate, or an employee—it is important to know that he or she can only offer a finite amount of help. While it may not feel natural for many older adults to shift to this more collaborative perspective, it's important to know that changing the way you view doctors does not mean you have any less respect for their abilities.

When to See the Primary Care Doctor

Let's start with what issues you should be going to the doctor about. After all, the patient's relationship with the primary care doctor (also known as an internist, a general practitioner, or family doctor) is often one that the older patient has had for many years. Therefore, most older patients are comfortable relying on their doctor to treat them or—if appropriate—to coordinate their care with specialists. Clearly any new or existing medical issues should be examined, diagnosed, and treated by the primary care doctor. Very often, older adults correctly seek the expertise of numerous specialists, but the primary care doctor should be aware of everything a specialist is recommending, prescribing, or coordinating on behalf of the older patient. (Depending on the type of insurance/Medicare plan that the older loved one has, a referral to the specialist by the primary care physician may be required in many cases.)

Life Ring: The primary care physician typically will refer you to the appropriate specialist your older loved one needs. But you are not always limited to the specialist the primary care physician suggests. You can often ask the physician to refer you to a specific specialist that you request. Keep in mind you have the option of doing your own research. Some ways to find specialist options include (1) asking friends and family for recommendations; (2) reviewing the list of specialists your insurance company works with and then looking at the individual specialist websites; or (3) considering online reviews as posted on sites like www.angieslist.com, www.yelp.com, or www.healthgrades.com.

When to See a Specialist

It's important to see a specialist when there is something going on that the family doctor can't adequately diagnose or treat, because it is not his or her principal area of expertise. Again, in many cases you will need a referral, but even if a referral is not required, it is a best practice to ask the primary care physician to provide one. Most often, referrals are provided for physical conditions, cognitive and mental health concerns, and geriatric-related conditions. Let's look at each of those categories in greater depth.

GERIATRIC SPECIALIST PHYSICIANS

Geriatricians are physicians who have specialized training and credentials in working with older adults. The American Geriatrics Society's Health in Aging database—http://www.healthinaging.org /find-a-geriatrics-healthcare-professional/—includes only doctors who have been board certified in geriatric medicine or hold a certificate in geriatric medicine.

Geriatric psychiatrists are physicians who have specialized training in working with older adults who need assistance with cognitive health/ memory issues such as Alzheimer's disease and other irreversible dementias; psychiatric diagnoses such as anxiety disorders, depression, bipolar disorder, schizophrenia, and personality disorders; and substance abuse problems (including prescription drugs).

The Geriatric Mental Health Foundation database—www.gmhfonline .org—includes only doctors who are members of the American Association for Geriatric Psychiatry. These are psychiatrists with interest and expertise in treating older adults.

The American Academy of Neurology—https://patients.aan.com /findaneurologist/—offers a database for patients to locate an AAN member neurologist in their area. *Note*: For older adults concerned about memory, it would be best to search under the subspecialties "geriatric neurology" or "vascular neurology and stroke" to find a neurologist who has both an interest and experience in working with older adults and memory issues common to them.

~~~~~~

Physical Conditions

As much as many older adults like and trust their primary care physicians, we almost never hear about an older adult relying solely on her family doctor when there is a serious chronic or acute *physical* condition. Typically, the primary care physician will refer the older loved one with a heart condition to a cardiologist. The older patient then sees a cardiologist for the heart issue in addition to the primary care physician who oversees the whole-person care.

This is also true with other chronic and acute conditions. Do we see older patients with cancer being treated only by their primary care physicians? Of course not. Actually, if a primary care physician does not recommend an oncologist in such cases, it would be considered negligent.

But, oddly enough, there seems to be a resistance to seeing a specialist when the older adult's problem is perceived to be less physical and more psychological or cognitive.

Life Ring: More details on how irreversible dementias like Alzheimer's disease are diagnosed will be covered in chapter 12. It's crucial to understand that not only are conditions like Alzheimer's disease a cognitive and memory problem, they are debilitating physical conditions as well.

Cognitive and Mental Health Concerns

Start with the primary care physician when there is any concern at all about chronic or unexplained mental or cognitive health symptoms. Even world-renowned Alzheimer's disease specialist Dr. Peter Rabins says, "I do think that in general people should start with their primary care doctor." But, just as you would do if there were a physical problem, it's typically a best practice to also see a specialist. Many older adults struggling with significant memory impairment may be wondering if it is Alzheimer's disease or another type of irreversible dementia. Just as in the case of an older adult with heart disease symptoms who sees a cardiologist, the patient should move on to a specialist if the primary care physician is unable to diagnose and treat the problem.

For example, Vanessa went to her primary care physician concerned about her memory, worried that she had Alzheimer's disease. Her primary care physician did a full assessment, including blood and urine tests. It turned out Vanessa had a major B12 deficiency. Once treated, Vanessa's memory returned to normal. This is a great example of a primary care physician being able to diagnose and treat the problem. If, after a full assessment, the primary care physician was unable to identify the root cause of and treat the memory loss, however, Vanessa should have moved on to a specialist. At this point a good specialist like a geriatric psychiatrist or a neurologist who specializes in memory would be able to dig further and possibly diagnose an irreversible dementia like Alzheimer's disease if that accurately fit the symptoms. While that would be a worst-case scenario, a specialist who has more experience in this area may also be able to find a reversible cause for Vanessa's condition that the primary care doctor had not considered.

Sometimes a primary care physician will screen out reversible causes of dementia and tell a patient or family that there is irreversible dementia. But that is as far as the diagnosis will go. Shouldn't the older patient and family know what type of irreversible dementia she is struggling with? Unfortunately this practice is quite common. The Alzheimer's Association recently publicized that less than half of people with Alzheimer's disease (or their caregivers) were told about the diagnosis by their physician. Unfortunately many persons with Alzheimer's disease simply know that they have memory problems but never are officially diagnosed with any condition.

If you were told that you have cancer, wouldn't you immediately inquire about what type? Of course you would, and for a variety of important reasons. What is the best treatment? Who is the best physician I should see for this type of cancer? Is there a family history link I should be letting my children and grandchildren know about? Are there clinical trials I may want to consider participating in with this diagnosis? How can we learn as much as possible about this particular type of cancer so the best choices can be made?

The same questions should be asked when irreversible dementia is diagnosed. While Alzheimer's disease is the most commonly diagnosed irreversible dementia, there are dozens of others. Seeing a specialist such as a geriatrician, geriatric psychiatrist, or neurologist specializing in geriatrics would be worthwhile just as it would in the heart disease–cardiologist scenario.

WHEN IS IT TIME TO SEE A GERIATRIC PSYCHIATRIST OR NEUROLOGIST?

Consider seeing a specialist like a geriatrician, geriatric psychiatrist, or neurologist specializing in memory when

- your older loved one is experiencing one or more of the following cognitive or mental health symptoms;

AND

- the primary care physician can't find a treatment that minimizes or eliminates them;

OR

- the primary care physician cannot determine the root cause of symptoms like these:

  - tearfulness

  - angry outbursts

  - excessive worrying

  - sleeping too much or not enough

  - poor judgment

  - unexplained changes in personality

  - dressing differently without explanation

  - forgetfulness

  - change in eating habits

  - unplanned excessive weight gain/loss

  - ruminating/obsessing

  - not enjoying things he/she used to

  - getting lost in familiar places

  - seeing things that are not there

  - becoming more pessimistic or negative than usual

  - withdrawing from others/isolating himself/herself

Doctors—both primary care and specialists—certainly are invaluable pieces of the caregiving puzzle, no matter what diagnoses the older adult faces. But if you are relying mostly on doctors for help, you are at a distinct disadvantage and at risk for more stress. Simply put, primary care physicians have a working knowledge about copious areas of medicine. Specialists know a lot about a smaller area of medicine. But it's important to recognize how much other types of professionals in addition to doctors can help you.

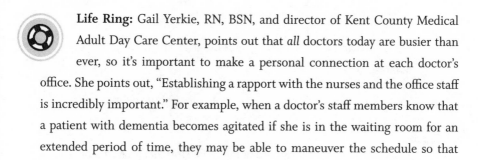

Life Ring: Gail Yerkie, RN, BSN, and director of Kent County Medical Adult Day Care Center, points out that *all* doctors today are busier than ever, so it's important to make a personal connection at each doctor's office. She points out, "Establishing a rapport with the nurses and the office staff is incredibly important." For example, when a doctor's staff members know that a patient with dementia becomes agitated if she is in the waiting room for an extended period of time, they may be able to maneuver the schedule so that patient's wait time is minimal.

When to Seek Other Resources Besides a GP or Specialist

Physicians are not intended to be the only professionals that older persons and their caregivers consult. There are many other organizations and ancillary professionals (with different types of education and experience) that support or augment the work of the doctor. Some ancillary organizations include the local Area Agency on Aging, the Alzheimer's Association (www.alz.org), and the American Diabetes Association (www.diabetes.org). Pharmacists, physical therapists, occupational therapists, speech therapists, elder law attorneys, geriatric care managers, psychologists, nurses, social workers, and case managers are just some of the complementary senior care professionals that well-informed doctors may refer the older adult and her caregiver to.

If your older loved one's doctor does not recommend other resources such as these, or is not particularly connected to community organizations, it is critical for the caregiver to become savvier about these services.

WHEN SHOULD YOU SEEK HELP FROM OTHER SOURCES?

While I believe that every older loved one and their caregivers can benefit from services and professionals besides the doctor, seeking out additional help is crucial, especially in situations like the following:

- You are disappointed with the way your older loved one's treatment for a condition or illness is progressing.

- You are having trouble getting your older loved one to follow the doctor's orders.

- Your caregiving crew has "all hands on deck" but you still need more help.

- You are not sure how you are going to pay for certain items or services you think your older loved one may need.

- You need a better understanding of what the typical voyage will be like with someone similar to your older loved one.

- You don't like your older loved one's doctor, but you can't "fire" the doctor because your older loved one likes him.

Keep in mind that just because the doctor doesn't know about a resource, it doesn't mean it's not worthwhile. New resources for older adults and caregivers are popping up all the time. And just because a doctor doesn't suggest a resource, it doesn't mean you shouldn't investigate or ask him about it. As with the earlier example of Michael, even though his primary care physician hadn't suggested a yoga class, that didn't mean she wouldn't be in favor of it as a supplement to his depression treatment. Doctors are experts in medicine, surgery, diagnosing, and medical treatments—not necessarily in community resources. They are not always well versed in all the different options that could make the road easier for the older patient and caregiver.

WHEN IS IT OKAY TO BID THE DOCTOR GOOD-BYE?

It is essential as a caregiver that you view your relationship with the doctor as a partnership. For example, a good manager typically refers to her staff as people who work *with* her rather than *for* her. While the manager is the boss of her staff, she looks at them as her team members or partners. Similarly, don't forget that you hire the doctor (even if your older loved one does not acknowledge that). You want to be reasonable and respect the doctor's time when you have an appointment. You want to avoid calling the doctor after hours with non-urgent questions. Reasonable expectations for a doctor are that she takes your or your older loved one's concerns seriously; that she respects your older loved one's privacy and confidentiality; and that she is up front when she doesn't know the answer to a question you have. It is also reasonable for the older patient and caregiving crew to receive respectful treatment from the doctor *and* from the doctor's office staff.

But you also need to remember that if your doctor is not open to answering basic questions, or simply refers you to a place where you can get more information, it might be time to fire the doctor. Some older loved ones and caregiving crews are reluctant to even consider firing a doctor, but if you find these basic needs unmet, it may be time to partner with a new physician.

Occasionally you will find the whole package in a physician's office. One outstanding example is Dr. Allan Anderson, a geriatric psychiatrist who specializes in dementia and the mental healthcare of older adults. He is continually in touch with the other resources that complement his services. He regularly refers to the Alzheimer's Association, speaks at their conferences, and refers to psychotherapists who help patients with cognitive and mental health diagnoses as well as their caregivers. Previously in private practice, Dr. Anderson currently practices in the Samuel and Alexia Bratton Memory Clinic at Bayleigh Chase, a continuing care retirement community, which is one of four Integrace communities.

~~~~~~

HITTING A SANDBAR: STUCK WITH A DOCTOR YOU REALLY DON'T LIKE

If you feel like you are stuck with a doctor you can't communicate or partner with effectively because your older loved one feels a sense of loyalty to or reverence for this doctor, you will probably need to do your own homework. As discussed earlier, "doctor worship" is a common practice among persons born before 1940. This unwavering deference to the doctor appears to be lessening as the baby boomers are moving into their older years. But if a caregiver is feeling stuck with a doctor who is not meeting all the older person's needs, it is even more critical for the caregiver to become informed about other resources.

You also may find yourself with a doctor that you and your older loved one really like; she is good at diagnosing and treating your loved one's conditions, but she is not particularly familiar with other supplemental services and resources. Here, too, you need to do your homework. Fortunately, this chapter has given you a big head start on where to find these resources!

~~~~~~

Doctors who are very knowledgeable about community resources and often refer their patients to them generally believe that such resources help their patients tremendously. They also realize such referrals free them up to focus on what they are best at: diagnosing and treating the physical, cognitive, or mental health issues they are uniquely qualified to deal with. If your older loved one is seeing a physician like Dr. Anderson, he and his staff are likely going to refer you to many outside resources that can make your caregiving journey easier. If you find yourself working with such a practice, you may not have to do as much homework as you would with other physicians' offices.

Make a Course Correction:
Consult Experts Other than the Doctor

If the doctor is unable to point caregivers in the right direction, they may sometimes find themselves at a loss about where they should look for more help. But as Dianne Turpin shared in her analogy about shopping for a new car in chapter 10, once the need for new resources arises, caregivers begin to open their eyes to find that these resources are readily available in the community. The caregivers had simply overlooked the services, because they had no need to take advantage of those offerings.

As Dianne further puts it, "We all have to become researchers, and we all have to become our own advocates." Here are some of the best ways to educate yourself as a caregiver with real-time information you can use.

Review Credible Websites and Books

If your loved one has life-limiting rheumatoid arthritis, it makes sense to start reviewing *credible* websites that can teach you about arthritis. By credible, I mean websites such as the Arthritis Foundation (www.arthritis.org) and the National Institute on Aging (www.nia.nih.gov) that have been validated by respectable agencies. These also include sites affiliated with well-respected hospitals, such as the Johns Hopkins Arthritis Center or Brigham & Women's Hospital, which are great resources.

The Internet is an incredible source of information, but caregivers must be cautious about simply looking up terms using a search engine like Google or Yahoo. If you plug in the word "Alzheimer's" in a search engine, many websites might come up that are not well-established healthcare organizations or providers. Sometimes searches will produce forums or chat rooms that can be helpful if you want to share your thoughts or ask questions of other caregivers. But when someone posts information on these sites, it may or may not be accurate.

So it's a good idea to stick to websites where the information has been vetted by a credible organization. A good rule of thumb is to stick mostly to websites that end with .org, .gov, or .edu because these websites are typically more informational and less sales oriented. Websites that end in .com are typically for-profit organizations or enterprises that may have an agenda designed to sell products and services rather than to simply educate. However, many for-profit websites do offer credible and vetted information. (I happen to believe my website, www.jenerationshealth.com, certainly falls into this category, and we have many visitors who get lots of information from our articles, blogs, and reference pages.) But generally speaking, the goal of a website that ends in .com is not typically solely to educate.

If you prefer books to articles or websites, go to your library or bookstore or download some books on arthritis for your e-reader. People sometimes forget about the library as a resource if they don't often utilize it. Librarians are great at finding information, according to Dianne Turpin. And a search of the library database or help from a librarian is always free. If you don't feel like spending your spare time reading, perhaps downloading an audio book for your iPod or borrowing a CD from the library would be better so you can listen in the car or while exercising. Don't forget that just because your library doesn't have a specific title available at your branch doesn't mean that they can't request it for you from another one. Most libraries don't charge for this service; if they do, it's minimal.

 Life Ring: Researching organizations and providers beyond the primary care physician can be a great way for secondary and tertiary caregivers to provide support to the primary caregiver.

Go to Events

Sometimes nonprofits, such as the Arthritis Foundation and the Alzheimer's Association, host conferences and educational series, fundraisers, and support group meetings. The low cost and free community educational programs they offer are frequently held at locations such as libraries and senior centers, but they also often partner with senior living communities and hospitals to host their programs. Support groups are an example of an event that nonprofits may offer in these locations. These types of events are invaluable opportunities for you to not only learn more about the condition your older loved one suffers from but also to meet other caregivers who are facing the same stressors you are. Most caregivers you meet are more than happy to tell you about their successes and mistakes, so you can benefit from their experiences. You can learn from when they went overboard and have a chance to ask them relevant questions.

In addition, assisted living communities, nursing homes, and hospitals offer seminars and other free programs that feature expert speakers. (The Jenerations Health team is proud to be on the speaking circuit for such events.) Often such events also will include a nice meal or other freebies. Remember that senior living communities frequently host these events, so you will be able to see what they have to offer you and your older loved one. This is their way of getting you to view their community, meet their staff, and eat their food. Then, if you are ever in the market for that type of service for your older loved one, you will be familiar with what they have to offer. It is also possible that the featured expert speaker might have something he or she would like to sell as well. Some expert speakers (elder law attorneys, aging life care experts, psychotherapists) may have books to sell or might suggest that you contact their office for paid services if you'd like more personalized help.

Although there may be products and services for sale, most of these events—which are common within the senior care industry—are very good, legitimate sources of community education. They can be a high-quality, inexpensive way to learn more about your older loved one's condition and find resources that can help you both. Remember, you don't have to buy or commit to anything at such events—you can simply go to obtain more education.

Talk with Staff at Assisted Living Communities or Continuing Care Retirement Communities

Consider visiting a few assisted living communities or continuing care retirement communities (CCRCs) even if you aren't immediately considering using their services (or perhaps just pop in for one of their free events, as discussed previously). Although you may not currently think you'll ever need one of these communities, circumstances for your older loved one may change, even if you can't imagine that today. Lisa Chapin Robinette, who was a former marketing director at Five Star Senior Living for many years, recommends talking to marketing directors at these places. Marketing directors—or community relations, sales counselors, etc.—are the people who take you on a tour and educate you on what the assisted living or CCRC has to offer. Often they can help you find resources you didn't know existed.

If a marketing director is experienced in senior care, she can be a tremendous resource. You can gather a great deal of information and resources particularly if you are meeting with a marketing director who is also a social worker or nurse. Social workers in the marketing role are typically adept at alerting you to other community resources that may be appropriate for your situation. So, even though they may essentially be salespeople, good, ethical salespeople are adept at listening, finding out what your older loved one wants or needs, and finding out what you want and need. They typically don't want you to consider their community unless your loved one would be a good fit.

Nurses in the marketing role are often able to explain complex medical information, speak intelligently about medications, and answer questions about medical diagnoses and procedures. They often have more time to get into detail about some of your smaller questions than your doctors might.

Senior living community staff understand that
families will shop around—even years ahead
of needing to place their older loved one—so you
needn't think you are taking advantage of their time.

Even if the marketing directors you meet with are not social workers or nurses, it is likely if they are adequately experienced in senior care that you will walk away with more information than you walked in with. Most caregivers who tour communities find it a useful exercise. Even if they only discover something they *don't want* for their loved one.

Some assisted living communities actually specialize in specific conditions. They may only accept residents with dementia or other mental health concerns. If your older loved one is diagnosed with one of these conditions, the marketing directors are typically very tuned in to other services that may be available to help you.

Senior living community staff understand that families will shop around—even years ahead of needing to place their older loved one—so you needn't think you are taking advantage of their time. Even if you spend an hour or two with the marketing director and never go back to that community, you will likely learn something and who knows—maybe you will refer other caregivers you meet to that community if you think it would be a good fit for their older loved ones.

Access Webinars or Phone Seminars

It has never been easier to access formal credible education programs from the privacy of your own home or office. The American Heart Association (www.heart.org) offers computer-accessible webinars that patients and caregivers can participate in on a number of different issues concerning heart disease. The Alzheimer's Association hosts Connected Conversations where the caregiver simply dials in to a toll-free 800 number and listens to an expert discuss a topic related to dementia. Typically there is also a period of time where participants can ask questions.

Watch Hollywood Films

Now, I'm not suggesting that caregivers get all their information about their older loved one's condition from Hollywood films. But many movies released in the past two decades offer some insight into common issues and conditions facing older adults and their caregivers. It can be a more appealing and less threatening way to learn a little more about aspects of caregiving, the normal aging process, and even some conditions that many older adults struggle with.

Some of the best films that can teach us about dementia and caregiver stress are *The Notebook*, *The Savages*, *Iris*, and *Away from Her*. One word of caution: parts of these films are not realistic. After all, movies are supposed to be entertaining. (Spoiler alert: in *Away from Her*, Fiona, a woman with Alzheimer's disease, asks to be placed in assisted living. This is definitely *not* something that generally happens! Most patients with dementia are too advanced in the progression of the illness to even weigh in on the decision.) But there is value in viewing these films because many caregivers will report seeing themselves in the portrayals. Many secondary adult children caregivers see their fathers in the James Garner character in *The Notebook*. Siblings also tend to see themselves represented in the Laura Linney and Phillip Seymour Hoffman characters from *The Savages*.

In the film *Last Vegas*, Morgan Freeman's character is being stifled by his son—a primary caregiver gone overboard. Perhaps the best most recent portrayal from the perspective of a patient struggling with young-onset Alzheimer's disease is Academy Award–winner Julianne Moore's performance in *Still Alice*. Viewing films like these can open up a new way of thinking about the caregiving process, what the older loved one is experiencing, and resources. In addition, watching films about caregiving together can be a valuable exercise for a caregiving crew. It's a great time for everyone to talk about what caregivers portrayed in the film did well or not so well.

Reading books and credible websites, attending events, accessing webinars and phone seminars, and watching Hollywood films can all provide you with insights into the aging and caregiving process and your loved one's conditions. Ideally a caregiver will do some of this research as soon as possible after she has begun the caregiving process. Unfortunately in my experience, however, most caregivers don't. They are just trying to get by with the day-to-day caregiving duties as they also manage the rest of their lives. They wait until there is some crisis before they educate themselves. While this is not ideal, it is absolutely better late than never. Learning more about caregiving and your loved one's condition is valuable at any point.

Life Jacket: I am constantly reviewing new movies, books, and websites that may help you—please check www.jenerationshealth.com for regular updates or get alerts for new reviews when you join our mailing list by emailing us at jen@cruisingthroughcaregiving.com.

TAKING NEWS CLIPS WITH A GRAIN OF SALT

While it's vitally important to educate yourself as completely as possible about your older loved one's conditions, beware of the twenty-four-hour news cycle.

The Sunday paper or a segment on a morning news show may have an expert or health reporter discussing your older loved one's condition. Caregivers often regularly read and watch these news reports. This is understandable because news reports come at us—we don't have to seek them out.

Caregivers are usually stressed and juggling competing priorities, and so it's fine to hear what the latest research has found. But you don't want to assume that every newscast or newspaper article necessarily applies to your older loved one.

Sound bites on television can have a way of sounding very urgent. But you should take news reports with a grain of salt. If you hear of a new finding that may apply to your older loved one, try to find the journal article or at least the abstract of the study that was referenced. If you still think the information may apply to your older loved one, bring it to your loved one's physician at your next appointment. But when you actually read the article or the abstract, you may find that it is not as applicable as the original news report led you to believe.

Such brief news clips are not generally great sources of education for the caregiver because the treatment featured may still be in development. The sample size of the study may be very small, and additional studies may need to be done to ensure that the results are reliable and valid. While it is great to keep abreast of new developments, typically caregivers need information that they can use and apply *now*.

Who to Radio for Help Before You Get to "Mayday!"

One of the reasons the caregiver self-education described previously is so valuable is because it makes you aware of the numerous resources out there *besides the doctor*. But if you don't have time to devote to your own caregiver self-education, here is your "cheat sheet" to the most relevant resources outside of your doctor's office. The first three I mention—Area Agencies on Aging (AAA), nonprofits, and support groups—typically offer free or low-cost help.

Your Local Area Agency on Aging

If you only contact one resource outside of your doctor's office, make it the local Area Agency on Aging—sometimes referred to as AAA. Every city, county, or cluster of counties is mandated through the Older Americans Act to establish and maintain this organization. Typically, the local government runs it, but some of these agencies are nonprofit. This organization provides services for older adults such as support groups, senior centers, Ombudsman services, information, and assistance. They can also direct you on how to report suspected abuse or neglect of an older adult in your jurisdiction. All people caring for older loved ones should become familiar with the local AAA to find out what services and programs may be relevant for their particular situation.

The AAA is an organization everyone is entitled to access. You might call simply for information and referrals. They provide a number of free and low-cost programs—such as meals and exercise classes—for both the older loved one and the caregiver to participate in. Even if money is not a concern, the local AAA is the best agency for you to phone first when you are a caregiver for an older loved one.

Most AAA staff will be able to tell you all about the resources in your community that are relevant to your caregiving situation. So if you are really short on time, you can skip the rest of this section and just call your local AAA! A database of all AAAs around the country can be found on the National Association of Area Agencies on Aging website at www.n4a.org, or on the US Department of Health and Human Services' Administration on Aging website at www.aoa.gov.

National Nonprofits with Local Chapters

There is a national nonprofit for nearly any kind of disease or condition known to humankind. The Alzheimer's Association, the Arthritis Foundation, the American Heart Association, and the American Diabetes Association have already been mentioned previously. But other helpful nonprofits for older adults and their caregivers include the American Cancer Society (www.cancer.org), the American Lung Association (www.lung.org), and the National Alliance on Mental Illness (www.nami.org). Generally, they all have local chapters in most states or cluster of states. Many even have satellite offices in smaller communities.

If your loved one has a condition that the nonprofit specializes in (as evidenced by their name), it is a very good idea at a minimum to get on their mailing list and their email update list. You also may want to "like" or "follow" them on social media. Calling and connecting with a staff person or volunteer at the organization is ideal. While the AAA is a great umbrella resource, these types of national nonprofits (especially when they have local chapters) can give you lots more specific information and describe services that are relevant to your loved one's conditions or disease(s). For people on limited budgets, there are a number of services that these nonprofits provide free of charge. They also can refer you to paid service options that are applicable to your situation.

Support Groups

I can't tell you how many times I have worked with a caregiver who claimed she wasn't a "joiner," who reluctantly went to a caregiver support group, and eventually credited that support group with saving her sanity. As Dianne Turpin suggested in chapter 4, just give it a try! One of the most valuable benefits of a support group is that the group can point out areas in which you need to make a course correction, typically before you can see it yourself. Support groups can easily be found through your local Area Agency on Aging or one of the national nonprofits with a local chapter. Many Area Agencies on Aging have general caregiver support groups, and Alzheimer's Association chapters offer dementia-specific caregiver support groups. Many hospice providers (which I discuss in chapter 14) offer grief and bereavement support groups.

Professional Practitioners

The resources that follow in the rest of this "cheat sheet" are typically private pay. Your local AAA can provide you with a list of such providers in your area, or you can search for more info within each of the categories.

Aging Life Care Experts

You may recall that in chapter 10, Maggie was referred to an aging life care expert (formerly known as a geriatric care manager). Aging life care experts are generally nurses or social workers in private practice who provide not just counseling but also all other types of coordination help. Cathy Lonas, a registered nurse and owner of Advocate 360, describes an aging life care expert as "one person that ties it all together."

While a physician is mostly looking at the older person's physical and sometimes mental or cognitive health, an aging life care expert generally provides a more comprehensive, whole-person assessment. They identify things that the older person and caregiver might need help with such as legal issues, transportation, medication management, etc. Many long-distance caregivers hire an aging life care expert to be their "eyes and ears." An aging life care expert can provide or coordinate almost any type of service to keep the older person and her caregiver happy and healthy. To find an aging life care expert, visit www .aginglifecare.org. These professionals are generally private pay, although there are some who will work with a sliding scale.

Elder Law Attorneys

Elder law attorneys specialize in issues that pertain to older adults and their families. Such issues include, among others, estate planning, veterans benefit applications, Medicaid applications, and advance directives. While many attorneys can offer these services, it is beneficial to work with lawyers who enjoy and best understand working with seniors and their families. The following websites offer more information on how to locate an elder law attorney and questions to ask when choosing one:

- Life Care Planning Law Firms Association—www.lcplfa.org

- The National Academy of Elder Law Attorneys—www.naela.org

- National Elder Law Foundation—www.nelf.org

Pharmacists

While technically you could probably hire a pharmacist to be your consultant, you usually can get their advice pro bono. Befriend a pharmacist at the drugstore where you pick up your older loved one's prescriptions. Pharmacists are experts on medication, drug interactions, and side effects, and they can offer lots of good advice typically free of charge. If you don't have a friendly helpful pharmacist at the drugstore you frequent, change pharmacies immediately! If you are getting prescriptions via mail order, you can usually make a pharmacist contact at that company.

Hospice

In chapter 14, I discuss in great detail how hospice can help you and your older loved one if there is a terminal illness. In addition to information about why hospice is such a helpful resource, chapter 14 also discusses how to find a hospice provider.

PULLING IT ALL TOGETHER

When you begin caregiving, it is crucial to develop some type of system to organize your research. In the beginning, keep everything you are given: business cards, brochures, flyers, websites, and book titles. Put them together in a notebook, folder, or drawer, or scan them into a computer file. Write down the name of the people you speak with, the date, time of day, and place where you met, etc. A resource might not make sense or seem useful today, but it could be something you desperately need in a couple of months or even a year from now.

Now you see that there are *many* other resources for you to access besides the family doctor. If you have gone overboard by being overly dependent on a primary care physician, take the opportunity to course-correct by checking out some of the organizations and professionals described in this chapter. While this is important no matter what diagnosis or conditions your older loved one is facing, it is absolutely critical when she has an irreversible dementia diagnosis, which is discussed in the next chapter.

Twelve

ADVANCED DEMENTIA CAREGIVING: CAREGIVERS MUST BE AT THE HELM

Gone Overboard: Letting Someone with Dementia Captain the Ship

You'll recall from chapter 3 that it's important to treat your older loved one as the grown-up he is, but this can be really tricky to do when your older loved one has an advanced irreversible dementia diagnosis. Sometimes in an effort to respect the older loved one and treat him as the adult he is, too much power and decision-making is left in his hands. So while people with an advanced irreversible dementia diagnosis surely are still adults, and it is important to be respectful and treat them as such, you must recognize that they have lost the reasoning skills to make decisions that are in anyone's best interest, especially their own. As a result, they can't be at the helm for all their care decisions as the disease progresses. The primary caregiver, *not the older loved one,* must be the captain of the caregiving ship.

To help you remain the captain—or crew member—of your loved one's caregiving ship, this chapter helps you with the following concepts and tasks:

- Take steps to determine whether your older loved one has an irreversible dementia diagnosis.

- Better understand why it's so important for the caregiving crew to maintain control when the older loved one has an irreversible dementia diagnosis.

- Treat your older loved one with dignity when there is an irreversible dementia diagnosis.

- Determine which of Nancy Reagan's caregiving philosophies will increase your stress and which will help you reduce it.

- Find resources to help you with dementia caregiving.

What Is Dementia?

According to the Alzheimer's Association, "dementia is a general term for a decline in mental ability severe enough to interfere with daily life." *Dementia* is simply a term that covers symptoms; it is really not a diagnosis.

Generally, people tend to think of short-term memory loss when they hear the term dementia, and that is accurate. But the term dementia can also include many other symptoms or signs, such as older loved ones getting lost in familiar places; forgetting the names of people they know well; forgetting important information; having problems with communication and familiar tasks; and suffering from disorientation, visual perception changes, impulse control problems, or poor judgment. Personality changes can also accompany these symptoms.

It's very important to understand that dementia does not happen to all older adults. *Dementia is not simply a normal part of the aging process.* Is dementia more common as we age? Yes, just as heart disease and certain types of cancer are more common as we get older. But having a heart attack or cancer is never part of the normal aging process either.

Here are some descriptions of a few older persons who could be experiencing dementia symptoms:

> **Charlotte** is an eighty-year-old woman visiting her son Henry's home. She pulls up her skirt, pulls down her underpants, squats over a potted plant in the family room, and begins to urinate. Charlotte is startled and ashamed when Henry says, "Mom, what are you doing?!"

Ben is a seventy-five-year-old man who takes a walk most evenings after dinner. One night around dusk, as he comes back to his street, he tries his key in the front door of his neighbor Frank's house instead of his own. Ben becomes angry because he thinks his key is not working. When Frank opens the front door from the inside, Ben becomes upset, because he thinks Frank has broken into *his* house. Even though Ben and Frank have been longtime neighbors and friends, Ben does not recognize Frank and thinks he is an intruder.

Alysha is a sixty-eight-year-old widowed woman who recently retired from a long career in banking. She has always prided herself on her excellent credit, her perfectly balanced checkbook, and her ability to manage her own money, which she's done ever since her husband died when their children were small. Alysha's cell phone has been turned off because she has not paid her bill. When Alysha's daughter, Catherine, investigates further, she finds that her mother has not been regularly paying any of her bills and that her checkbook has not been balanced for over six months. When Catherine asks her mother what's going on, she tells her daughter to mind her own business; she can handle her own affairs as she always has.

What symptom(s) of dementia did Charlotte, Ben, and Alysha exhibit? Write them down before you read any further.

Perhaps Charlotte could be exhibiting a visual perception problem (she may have thought she was squatting over a toilet, not a potted plant). It also could have been an impulse control issue—she had to relieve herself but couldn't wait to find a bathroom. It also could be a judgment issue—she didn't realize it was socially inappropriate to relieve herself outside of the bathroom in front of others.

Ben could be experiencing disorientation in a familiar place (his house, his neighbor's house) with a familiar person (Frank), but he also could be experiencing a visual perception problem.

Alysha is likely experiencing the symptom of not being able to complete familiar tasks or not remembering important information.

The family and friends of Charlotte, Ben, and Alysha all reacted rather typically. But Henry, Frank, and Catherine may not have necessarily recognized their older loved one's behavior as indicative of dementia symptoms because there was no short-term memory loss that is typically associated with the condition. Ideally, the caregiving family and friends of Charlotte, Ben, and Alysha will help each of them seek a diagnosis to find out what's causing their unusual behaviors.

Get a Diagnosis for Your Older Loved One

What condition or issue is causing your loved one's dementia symptoms? This is the million-dollar question, and it's unfortunately a question many caregivers never pursue. And, if they do pursue it, they don't always get a straight answer.

Start with Your Loved One's Family Doctor

Recall the three elderly people I described at the beginning of this chapter. Clearly, Charlotte, Ben, and Alysha are experiencing dementia symptoms. Yet, even if their family and friends recognize their behaviors as dementia symptoms, sometimes it is just left at that. Nobody thinks to pursue a diagnosis. In other cases I've seen, the family members may go to the family doctor (also known as an internist or a primary care physician) and describe the incident that caused them concern. A good family doctor will begin by talking to the patient (and hopefully a family member or friend who accompanies her to the doctor) to identify some examples of the memory problems or other changes that are causing concern. A medication review, verbal and written mental status tests, blood tests, and brain imaging helps the physician determine what is causing the symptoms. A good doctor will be trying to determine whether it is possible these symptoms might be reversible (depression, thyroid problem, medication side effects, etc.).

For many families and older loved ones, when the doctor pronounces that the older patient is suffering from dementia that's it: Case closed. Even some very educated people leave the doctor's office thinking, *Well, it's just dementia; at least it's not Alzheimer's.* Many people feel relieved hearing the term dementia because they assume dementia can't be nearly as bad as the dreaded Alzheimer's disease.

But a doctor telling Charlotte, Ben, or Alysha that each of them is exhibiting dementia symptoms isn't telling them a whole lot. When a doctor just says the patient has dementia but doesn't explain why, the patient and her caregiving crew aren't much closer to figuring out if the older loved one will be able to continue captaining her own ship.

When to Consult a Specialist

It is possible that the three older adults I described previously are experiencing reversible dementia symptoms that could be treated. Vitamin deficiency, a side effect of their medication, depression, or a thyroid problem can occasionally cause dementia-like symptoms. It is also possible that the person may be suffering with delirium symptoms that can look like dementia (e.g., caused by a simple urinary tract infection). It's really important for caregivers to be assertive when they ask a physician to get to the bottom of the unusual behaviors they've seen their loved ones display. Of course, if there is no reversible cause for the dementia symptoms, the patient is dealing with an irreversible progressive dementia, and caregivers need to know what type it is.

As Dr. Rabins suggested in chapter 11, it is best to start with your primary care physician. Thereafter, even though many primary care physicians are adept at understanding and diagnosing different types of dementia, it is often best for a specialist—specifically a geriatrician, geriatric psychiatrist, or neurologist who understands memory—to become involved. (Chapter 11 also discussed how to find these specialists.)

In particular, Dr. Rabins recommends that the patient experiencing dementia symptoms should see a specialist when

- They are younger than sixty years old.

- They have other medical problems in addition to the dementia symptoms.

- The caregiver sees what he or she considers unusual neurological, behavioral, or psychological symptoms.

- The primary care physician does not think she has the expertise to deal with dementia or is unable to help the family manage the symptoms.

I strongly believe that if a doctor states that it does not matter what is causing the dementia symptoms, a second opinion is in order. Some healthcare providers don't see the value in getting a precise diagnosis, because there is no curative treatment for any of the irreversible dementias. But there are some very good reasons why you want to know:

Different dementias have different prognoses. The average duration of Alzheimer's disease is eight years. Other dementias have different average trajectories.

Some dementias are believed to run in families. Therefore, it's important for blood relatives, particularly first-degree relatives, to know whether the older loved one's dementia is one that will contribute to their own healthcare risk factors.

Some medication works well for certain dementias but not as well for others. For example, when a person has Huntington's disease, the typical drugs prescribed for Alzheimer's disease like cholinesterase inhibitors (Aricept, Exelon, Razadyne) and memantine (Namenda) are not usually recommended.

The caregiving crew can learn as much as possible about the dementia their older loved one has when there is a diagnosis. The caregiving crew can be prepared for the trajectory of the disease and the challenging behaviors associated with that particular condition. They can link up with resources specific to that type of dementia. If the older loved one has Lewy Body dementia, the caregiver may want to join a Lewy Body specific support group.

The older loved one may be able to participate in clinical trials or other studies that are disease specific. For many older loved ones and their caregiving crews, participating in such studies offers an opportunity to feel like they are doing something to combat the disease. Also, for those older loved ones who have a dementia that has genetic links, they often feel good about contributing to possibly preventing this condition from happening to others they love.

Dr. Rabins says, "I do think that some doctors are unduly skeptical about, say, making a diagnosis of Alzheimer's disease, and again I think the fact that most autopsy studies show that people are eighty-five to ninety percent accurate . . . which in medicine is good." The Alzheimer's Association concurs with Dr. Rabins' opinion. Their website states, "Experts estimate a skilled physician can diagnose Alzheimer's with more than ninety percent accuracy."

If your older loved one is experiencing dementia symptoms, it's important to know what is causing them. While it's less likely to be a reversible condition, you obviously want to help your older loved one seek curative treatment if it is. As Dr. Allan Anderson says, "No one in this type of practice would want to miss calling something dementia that had a reversible, treatable cause. So if you don't do more of an investigation as to the etiology you may miss that."

If a reversible dementia is treated, typically the older loved one really can continue captaining his ship. But if the symptoms are truly being caused by an irreversible dementia like Alzheimer's disease, it is crucial for the caregiving crew to know that the older loved one should not be at the helm indefinitely. The primary caregiver and caregiving crew need to position themselves to take over captaining the ship.

TYPES OF DEMENTIA

It's a common misconception that the terms dementia and Alzheimer's disease mean the same thing. Alzheimer's is just one of the many different types of *irreversible dementia* diagnoses. Alzheimer's disease is the most common, accounting for sixty to seventy percent of all irreversible dementia conditions. An analogy that may help explain this is that there are many types of pasta but when you say the word pasta most people will first think of spaghetti. Alzheimer's disease is the spaghetti to dementia's pasta.

The remaining percentage of irreversible dementia cases are caused by conditions such as Lewy Body dementia, vascular dementia, frontotemporal dementia (FTD), Creutzfeldt-Jakob disease, Huntington's disease, and mixed dementia (meaning that there are a combination of conditions). According to the Lewy Body Dementia Association, the term "Lewy Body dementia" now includes both dementia with Lewy bodies and Parkinson's disease dementia and is currently considered the second most common type of dementia. Lewy bodies, named for Dr. Frederick H. Lewy who discovered them, are abnormal deposits responsible for extinguishing brain cells. Dr. Rabins' book *The 36-Hour Day* indicates that there are approximately seventy-five conditions that could potentially cause dementia.

~~~~~~

Earlier we heard from Dr. Rabins regarding when it is important to see a specialist. My opinion is that *anyone* who is told that he or she has a progressive, irreversible dementia should see a specialist. I routinely make this point to caregiving crews through analogies to cancer and heart disease. If your older mother had pancreatic cancer, would you think she should see an oncologist? Or would you be satisfied with the primary care physician handling the case alone? If your older husband recently suffered a heart attack, would you be comfortable having only a primary care doctor involved or would you want a good cardiologist following his case? Most caregivers would opt to consult a specialist in these situations, and I believe it is just as crucial in the case of an irreversible dementia diagnosis.

Learn as Much as You Can about Your Older Loved One's Dementia

Your older loved one who has been diagnosed with an irreversible degenerative dementia is slowly but surely losing his or her ability to reason, make decisions, and understand the consequences of those decisions. Irreversible dementia diagnoses cause the patient to eventually die from either that condition (as with Alzheimer's disease) or a complication of the disease (as with frontotemporal dementia). Because there are many causes of irreversible dementia—each with its own different prognoses and treatments—it is important to find out as much as possible about what is causing your older loved one's condition so that you can treat it most effectively and be prepared for the future.

The Alzheimer's Association's website, www.alz.org, or *The 36-Hour Day* are more in-depth resources on understanding different types of dementia and how to get a proper diagnosis. Further, there are nonprofit organizations associated with the less common irreversible dementias. They are devoted to research, fundraising, and educating the public about the particular conditions. More information can be found on these websites:

- **Association for Frontotemporal Degeneration** (www.theaftd.org): For information on frontotemporal dementia.

- **Creutzfeldt-Jakob Disease Foundation** (www.cjdfoundation.org): For information on Creutzfeldt-Jakob disease.

- **Huntington's Disease Society of America** (www.hdsa.org): For information about Huntington's disease.

- **Lewy Body Dementia Association** (www.lbda.org): For information on dementia with Lewy bodies or Parkinson's disease dementia.

- **National Stroke Association** (www.stroke.org): For information about vascular dementia.

Note: From here on in this chapter when I use the term dementia, I am referring only to a diagnosis of an irreversible dementia like Alzheimer's disease, Lewy Body dementia, or frontotemporal dementia.

Grasp and Acknowledge the Unique Challenges Involved in Dementia Caregiving

I believe caregiving for a person with dementia is one of the most challenging and stressful tasks a person can undertake. As I have discussed throughout this book, caregiving is enormously stressful no matter what conditions or illnesses your older loved one has. But a dementia diagnosis ratchets up the uncertainty and stress the caregiving crew will face.

I emphasize in chapter 3 that older adults are *adults*. They are not children or teens; they are grown-ups who have lived full lives. But because of the devastating progression of irreversible dementia, their behaviors and decision-making abilities can become increasingly childlike.

Cognitive Changes

Many caregivers respond emotionally to the cognitive changes their older loved ones are experiencing. While intellectually many caregivers understand that there is memory impairment involved with their loved one's dementia, they can still have hurt feelings when that older loved one does not recognize them. For example, Alysha sometimes calls her daughter, Catherine, by her sister's name, Claire. Intellectually Catherine understands that Alysha gets confused sometimes, but it really infuriates Catherine, particularly because Claire hardly ever helps out with Alysha. Catherine is irritated that Claire is on her mother's mind when Catherine is the one dealing with all the care issues.

Other caregivers don't ever intellectually understand that dementia messes with the short-term memory, but it does not affect it all the time. Ben's neighbor Frank has been very patient with Ben when he's tried to get into the wrong house—especially Frank's own!—because Ben's family explained the dementia diagnosis to him. But now that Frank has witnessed Ben go to the correct house at times, he believes Ben could go to the right house if Ben really focused and concentrated.

 Life Ring: Make things easier on yourself and your older loved one. Many caregivers get upset over what others would say are trivial details. But when you are already stressed-out, something small can really set you off. Colleen Walker, executive director at Brookdale Senior Living, shared a story of a caregiver who would constantly complain that her loved one would use the "good towels" when he cleaned himself up. Walker suggested the obvious: Remove the good towels from the bathroom (putting them someplace where he could not find them). Simple suggestions like this can save you a lot of unnecessary angst.

Most of the time, dementia does not follow a clear trajectory. Sometimes Alysha will call Catherine by the correct name and sometimes she will call her Claire. Sometimes Ben will go to the correct house and sometimes he will not. Think about it this way: Has your car ever made a funny noise when you started it? After a few days of this, you take it to your mechanic, and the car does not make this noise—not even once! This is the kind of thing that happens when someone has dementia. Families often lament that when the patient with dementia finally goes to the doctor to determine what is causing the symptoms, the symptoms seem to have gone by the wayside!

Even when a caregiver does understand and accept the memory problem and that it may come and go, the caregiver may still struggle with such other symptoms as language problems, poor judgment, impulse control, and visual perception problems. For example, Henry might understand and accept that Charlotte has a memory issue, but he is totally stunned that his mother would urinate in his family room.

Communication Challenges

Furthermore, communication becomes increasingly difficult when you are caring for someone who has dementia. As soon as dementia begins to wreak its havoc on the brain, the caregiver's ability to understand the older loved one diminishes, and vice versa. Particularly in the advanced stages of dementia, it is like both the caregiver and the older loved one are from different planets.

Currently, the average duration of Alzheimer's disease is eight years from the day the person begins exhibiting symptoms until the day the person passes away from the condition. (See the box that follows.) Alzheimer's disease is comprised of three stages: early, middle, and late. Let's look at communicating with a person with Alzheimer's disease through these three stages as though you are on a trip to several foreign countries.

~~~~~~

DEATH: THE SAD REALITY OF ALZHEIMER'S DISEASE AND OTHER DEMENTIAS

In coaching and training family caregivers of patients with dementia, I am alarmed at how often they don't realize that their loved one has a terminal condition. I can't count how many times a caregiver has come to me after a speaking engagement to ask, "You said people die from Alzheimer's disease—what did you mean by that?" Caregiver reactions at this point vary: some are speechless; some fill up with tears. But whether they are stunned silent or they cry, they often claim this is the first time they've heard this information.

People who have dementia die from the condition or a complication of it. Alzheimer's disease is the sixth leading cause of death in the United States. And although patients don't die from frontotemporal dementia, they typically die of pneumonia, which is a complication of it.

Maybe a doctor has discussed the fact that the dementia diagnosis their loved one has is fatal, but the caregiving family members didn't hear it because they were in shock and denial. Typically upon diagnosis, the doctor is just trying to get the patient and the caregiver through the first phase of the disease. If the person is diagnosed in the earlier stages, the doctor will probably walk them through information about the medication they will take and—I hope—will refer them to resources such as the Alzheimer's Association. But as we discuss in chapter 11, the physician won't always be familiar with community resources. Sometimes it takes caregivers a while before they start seeking more information about the disease, and so they remain unaware that the condition is terminal. They are just adjusting to the fact that their loved one is really going to keep losing more memory and seem less and less like themselves. Or maybe their doctor never mentioned that dementia is fatal.

Either way, a less stressful caregiving experience is assured when this is understood and accepted. People struggling with this concept would be well served to join a dementia support group; options can be found at the Alzheimer's Association website (www.alz.org) or on the websites for the nonprofits specializing in other dementias. Often some support group participants lend their experience to the group even though their loved ones have already passed away from dementia. Or you will likely encounter someone who at least has found a way to accept the inevitable prognosis and may be able to help you do the same.

~~~~~~

Communicating with a Person in the Early Stages of Alzheimer's Disease

Let's say as a United States citizen you are going to visit Ireland. You may get to Ireland and sure, it's greener, they talk with a funny accent, and some say they drink more Guinness than water. But you can make your way around pretty easily because the people of Ireland speak English and you are able to read the signs—those that aren't in Gaelic, that is!—when you are driving (on the wrong side of the road). Visiting Ireland is like caring for and communicating with someone in the early stages of Alzheimer's disease. It's different and there are challenges to be sure, but you can manage without a whole lot of training.

Communicating with a Person in the Middle Stages of Alzheimer's Disease

Next up on your tour is Italy, but you don't know any Italian. You are going to have a harder time than when you were in Ireland because the language is different. You will not be able to read the signs. But you don't feel completely out of sorts, especially if you studied a romance language in high school, which most of us did—you can probably pick up some of the words people are using. The food looks familiar. This is a good analogy for caring for someone in mid-stage Alzheimer's disease. It's becoming more difficult to understand your older loved one because her language abilities are being compromised. She starts to have hallucinations and delusions. She can't remember how to button her blouse. She forgets what a fork is used for.

Communicating with a Person in the Late Stages of Alzheimer's Disease

The last country you visit is Yemen. This third-world-like country comes as a complete culture shock. The people speak Arabic, much of the country is undeveloped, and women are not highly valued. This is a good analogy for caring for and communicating with someone in the late stages of Alzheimer's disease. Your older loved one seems to be in a vegetative state at times, pretty much bedbound. She is incontinent. When she needs something, she might just cry out or make a grunt.

~~~~~~

DEMENTIA CAREGIVING IS DIFFERENT FROM OTHER TYPES OF CAREGIVING

As I was taking care of my grandmother-in-law when she was dying of cancer, she could tell us when she was in pain (at least until the last few days of her life). Someone with advanced dementia is unable to communicate this effectively, and this communication breakdown begins well before end of life. When I was taking care of my grandfather when he had lymphoma, he could tell us when he wanted to be left alone. In fact, I recall my usually very gentle, loving grandfather finally saying, "Get the hell out!" to the seven or so family members in his hospital room when he wanted some peace and quiet. This gave all of us some comic relief in a very somber situation. But someone with advanced dementia is typically not going to communicate directly with the caregiver at all—not only at the end of life—but also throughout the course of the disease. The person with advanced dementia might do things like scream or make noises or try unsuccessfully to get out of bed when she is in pain. The person with advanced dementia might try to throw something at the caregiver to indicate that she wants to be left alone for a while.

Of course the tricky thing is that there might be days when the person who has dementia will be able to communicate verbally in a way the caregiver understands. This can be endlessly confusing for the caregiving crew.

~~~~~~

Should Nancy Reagan Be Your Caregiver Role Model?

Never mind your political affiliation—many of us would wish for someone like the late Nancy Reagan to be our caregiver if we had a dementia diagnosis. By all public accounts, Mrs. Reagan was as selfless a caregiver for a loved one with dementia as someone could be. Not only did she provide hands-on care for her husband, former US president Ronald Reagan, coordinating his in-home services, but she also fundraised and advocated for Alzheimer's research.

While caregiving and advocating, rather than looking exhausted and haggard, she managed to look perfectly lovely whenever she appeared in public. For many dementia caregivers she has been a role model. (For movie buffs, here's an interesting aside as an example of life imitating art: In 1957 the former first lady, then actress Nancy Davis, played nurse Lieutenant Helen Blair in the only film she appeared in with her then actor-husband Ronald Reagan, *Hellcats of the Navy*.)

Ronald Reagan, whose diagnosis of Alzheimer's disease was made public in 1994, was cared for in the privacy of his own Bel Air, California, home up until his death in 2004. The Reagans were widely reported to have physicians, nurses, housekeepers, and of course Secret Service assistance helping out in the home over that decade. (Interested readers might want to take a look at "The Long Goodbye," by J. D. Heyman and "As the Shadows Fell," by Thomas and Clift; see the references and resources list at the back of the book for more info.) Even though Mrs. Reagan was dealing with the devastating gradual loss of her beloved Ronnie, she had a stellar team of professional support. She probably didn't have to do the MET exercise included in chapter 8 to put together this team either!

During her 2001 interview with Larry King on CNN, when Mrs. Reagan was asked about the possibility of placing Mr. Reagan into some type of dementia care facility, she immediately responded, "Oh, no. Oh, no, never, never. No, no. He's going to stay at home." She also discussed not wanting to go on trips because she didn't want to leave him. The former president was also famously kept from visitors because, she believed, "I don't think Ronnie would want that. I think Ronnie would want people to remember him as he was." While a lot of us might want someone like Mrs. Reagan as our caregiver and a lot of us might think that's the right way to do it, most of what she did is just not practical for the rest of us. However, there's a lot to learn from her. Let's look at the strategies that would likely add stress to your caregiving experience and those that would reduce your stress.

Mrs. Reagan's Caregiving Strategies that May Cause You Stress

Healthcare providers often report knowing caregivers of older loved ones with dementia who attempt to emulate Mrs. Reagan's caregiving strategies. Some are consciously doing so, as they are fans of her good works advocating for dementia research and have looked to her as a caregiving role model. But more often than not, the caregiver is copying Mrs. Reagan unconsciously by subscribing to the rigorous philosophies she appeared to follow. Among those concepts are these:

- The only place for the older loved one with dementia is home.

- The caregiver should never be separated overnight from the older loved one who has dementia.

- The older loved one with dementia should be isolated from others, never go out, and never have visitors.

Let's take a look at why these strategies would be going overboard for the majority of caregivers. (Not to worry, though. I'll also show you how you can course-correct right away if you find yourself going overboard in any of these areas.)

Gone Overboard: Believing Home Is the Only Place
for Loved Ones with Dementia

As we have discussed in previous chapters, every caregiving crew must decide for themselves what is best for all involved, including the older loved one. There are many options for care. But because dementia caregiving is so very different from other types of caregiving, I believe it is particularly important to emphasize that dementia caregivers should always seriously consider the assisted living and/or nursing home route as a viable option.

It is extremely difficult to keep a person with advanced dementia at home indefinitely for many reasons. I want to look at five key reasons in more detail: the safety of the older loved one; medical care for the older loved one; socialization for the older loved one; the physical well-being of the caregiving crew; and the emotional well-being of the caregiving crew.

> **Safety for the older loved one:** Did you know that approximately sixty percent of people with a dementia diagnosis wander? Many dementia caregivers think that if at least one caregiver is home all the time it is possible to keep the older loved one home indefinitely. But even if one caregiver is always present in the home, the older loved one is still at risk. What if you step out of the room to answer the phone? To put a kettle of water on for tea? To use the bathroom? Do you have the Secret Service manning all your doors in case your older loved one wanders out of the house when you are taking a shower? I'm guessing if former president Reagan ever attempted to wander out of his home, that's who stopped him.

> **Medical care for the older loved one:** Do you have access to doctors and nurses who will come to your home to provide routine healthcare services? I'm not talking about home health aides but experts at the next level: degreed medical professionals. When Mr. Reagan fell and broke his hip, nurses were present in the home. People with dementia may fall quite a bit. They might also have other medical emergencies that the caregiving crew is

going to have to manage. For example, an older loved one with Alzheimer's disease may also have diabetes or congestive heart failure or may get the flu.

Socialization for the older loved one: Do you provide many opportunities for her to interact with others? Most caregivers really don't give this a whole lot of thought because the priority is health and safety. It is a rare caregiver who takes time to understand the principles behind activities that will improve quality of life for the older loved one with dementia. Among these are validation, exercise, music therapy, art therapy, and pet therapy. And even if caregiver(s) understand these principles, do they have time or energy to implement them? I don't know if Mr. Reagan enjoyed such services, but he was much more likely to have them than most dementia patients who reside at home. Purely based on the number of professionals involved in his care, he very well may have.

IMPROVING QUALITY OF LIFE FOR LOVED ONES WITH DEMENTIA

One of the biggest mistakes I see caregiving crews make deals with socialization of their older loved ones with dementia. Frequently persons with dementia who are kept at home spend their days sitting in front of a television, periodically dozing. While many caregivers wouldn't mind spending a day once in a while watching an episode of *Law & Order* or a *Real Housewives* marathon, lounging in front of the television day in and day out is a monotonous way to spend your life.

When the older loved one with dementia is in a nursing home or an assisted living community, caregiving crews typically aren't much more successful socializing during their visits. Well-meaning caregivers typically attempt to have a "normal" conversation with their older loved one, but they seem to forget that this person no longer has the ability to reason or to control impulses, and they often will not remember who the visitors are. This leads to boredom and frustration for both the caregiver and the older loved one.

Whether the older loved one with dementia is at home or in a community, it is essential for the caregiving crew to embrace new ways of socializing. Some television is fine, particularly if it is a show or movie that is in the patient's long-term memory (think *Gone with the Wind* or *Lawrence of Arabia* for someone in their eighties or nineties). But to truly connect and engage the patient, the caregiving crew should focus on helping the older loved one use skills that he or she still possesses.

Many older loved ones with advanced dementia, whether male or female, tend to most appreciate interaction and visits with others that are what I would call "dude-like." While certainly not true of all boys and men, the vast majority of males in our society do not necessarily need to talk to each other to enjoy each other's company. A woman often doesn't get it when her husband goes to a baseball game with a buddy, and they never talk about that buddy's impending divorce. The two men simply enjoy watching the baseball game together, and that is the way her husband is there for his buddy. Extensive conversation is not always necessary, nor is it always welcome. When trying to connect with your older loved one who has dementia, try to think of two dudes hanging out—no matter the gender of either party.

You are going to have the most satisfying experience with your older loved one when you do an activity with them rather than try to have a conversation. When a person with dementia can't speak, they still might be able to sing. Music penetrates the long-term memory, and many patients with dementia can sing along, tap their feet, or even dance to an old favorite tune. (Think the Temptations' "My Girl" or The Rolling Stones' "You Can't Always Get What You Want" for patients in their sixties or seventies.)

You might want to try some art activities. If your older loved one knitted before she was diagnosed, maybe she still can. She also may be able to paint or draw. If your older loved one enjoys animals, and you don't have a dog, take a neighbor's dog for a walk and allow her to pet Rover. Walking together, looking at the fall foliage, or enjoying a beautiful sunset, is typically going to be more satisfying for both of you than asking her how her day was.

For more tips on how to connect musically and through touch with your older loved one, consider learning more about dementia expert Naomi Feil's validation techniques from her website vfvalidation.org or reading her book *The Validation Breakthrough* coauthored with Vicki de Klerk-Rubin.

~~~~~~

Physical well-being of the caregiving crew: Do you have enough "muscle" in your caregiving crew to deal with the physically demanding work of taking care of an older loved one with advanced dementia? Recall from earlier in the chapter that we discussed how caregivers frequently understand the memory loss part of dementia, but they don't realize there are going to be other symptoms like poor judgment and impulse control problems. Many caregivers also do not understand that all dementia diagnoses eventually involve physical problems (incontinence, difficulty feeding one's self, walking, swallowing). For example, if you have arthritis, helping your older loved one to transfer in and out of bed, into a chair, etc., will likely exacerbate your symptoms.

Emotional well-being of the caregiving crew: Do you have enough people within the whole caregiving crew to keep up with the emotional challenges and reactions you'll face as your loved one declines? (If not, now is the time to go back to the MET exercise you completed in chapter 8 and revise it.)

Communication with an older loved one who has dementia can be challenging. Not only does your mom sometimes not recognize you—the caregiver—she could also have hallucinations and delusions. Maybe she accuses you of stealing her purse. Or, maybe your dad is yelling at you and you can't figure out why, even though you have tried everything—feeding him, changing the television channel, getting him a blanket. Such episodes can be emotionally traumatic for the caregiver. If only one or two caregivers are dealing on a regular basis with emotional abuse from the older loved one, they are going to burn out quickly.

Here's a quick course correction if you've gone overboard in believing that the only place for your older loved one with dementia is home: Keep all your options open.

Trying to provide in-home dementia care à la Nancy Reagan is nearly impossible for most of us. We just don't have the kind of setup she had. It's important for us to acknowledge that a nursing home or an assisted living community may be a viable and better option—both for ourselves as caregivers and for our loved ones. Many healthcare providers strongly believe that many persons with dementia experience a significantly better quality of life in such a setting if the right match is selected.

MOVING AN OLDER LOVED ONE INTO A MEMORY CARE UNIT

If the caregiving crew decides that moving the older loved one to a memory care unit at an assisted living community or a nursing home is best, the next step is deciding how to go about it. I'll tell you how it does *not* usually go: like it did in the film *Away From Her.**

---

* I want to emphasize that I'm actually a big fan of this movie and recommend it to dementia caregivers all the time. Aside from my criticism of the Julie Christie character unrealistically requesting that she be placed in a senior living community, there is a lot that dementia caregivers can relate to in this film.

The Julie Christie character who suffers with a dementia "convinces" her husband, played by Gordon Pinsent, that it's time for her to move to a senior living residence. I have never heard of such a thing happening in real life. So unless this happens to you—and I sincerely doubt it will—it's important to determine how the move will take place.

In my experience, the more stressed a caregiver is about the move, the more stressed the older loved one will be. So it's important for the caregiving crew to make peace with the concept. Often once a person with dementia moves into a memory care unit, quality of life can actually improve for the entire caregiving crew. This happens because in a good memory care unit, the staff are well trained on dementia, and activities and meals are centered around the skills the patients still possess. Once you select a memory care unit, talk to the staff about their best practices in moving residents in. Sometimes it may be couched to the patient as a temporary trial. Other times the patient might believe he is in the hospital when he is brought to his new room. Still other times it *might* be appropriate to reason with the patient if he is having a moment of clarity.

If a patient genuinely *does* understand that he is moving to a nursing home or an assisted living community, it might be appropriate for a trusted authority figure like a minister, rabbi, or doctor to have a conversation with the older loved one about it. Each move-in situation is different, and it's important to tailor your approach to your loved one's circumstances. It is nearly always going to be difficult emotionally (but frequently more so for the caregiving crew). Eventually your older loved one with dementia will adjust, but it can take days or months for that to happen. It's necessary to be patient and to collaborate with the staff to make the smoothest transition possible.

~~~~~~

If the older person is no longer decisional because of a dementia diagnosis like Alzheimer's disease, then the primary caregiver is considered the responsible party by the memory care unit.

It is also important to understand that there is a major difference between the term caregiver and other legal terms such as power of attorney or guardian as we discuss in chapter 3. Just because you are a primary caregiver it does not mean you have power of attorney or guardianship. Conversely, just because you are a power of attorney or guardian, does not mean you are necessarily even involved in the caregiving process. While it's important to clarify if you are a caregiver and to know what type you are, no legal duties automatically are assigned to somebody who functions as a caregiver.

Gone Overboard: Believing Caregivers Should Never Be Separated Overnight from Loved Ones with Dementia

The caregiving crew deserves a break. Now I know that the Reagans had what many would call a dream love story and marriage; however, it's just not healthy for the primary caregiver to hardly ever leave the house.

Think about the last time you took a vacation or a day off from work (or if you don't work outside the home, a day away from your regular routine). Doesn't taking some time away from your daily life refresh you so that you do an even better job when you return? Don't you have a newer, fresh perspective? Caregivers of older loved ones with a dementia diagnosis desperately need this break.

Here's a quick course correction if you've gone overboard in believing that you should never be separated overnight from your older loved one with dementia: Overnight breaks are okay!

Ironically, when a reluctant caregiver does leave the older loved one with dementia overnight, the patient often doesn't even realize that the primary caregiver was gone. As long as quality care is in place, it is healthy for the primary caregiver and the rest of the caregiving crew to take overnight breaks from the older loved one.

Overnight breaks are okay!

Gone Overboard: Believing Loved Ones with Dementia Should Be Isolated from Others

Many of us can certainly understand why Mrs. Reagan was protective of her husband's image. After all, he was a two-term president of the United States! But even for people in the Reagans' generation who led quieter, more ordinary lives, there may still be some lingering shame about an Alzheimer's disease diagnosis.

Let's face it: There is no shortage of situations that can be considered embarrassing when someone has dementia. Maryellen's mother, Ava, who has dementia, lives with her. When one of Maryellen's male colleagues stopped by her home to drop off some paperwork, Ava said, "I'd love to get to know him better" with a sly smile—right in front of him! Fortunately, Maryellen has cultivated a good sense of humor about the lack of inhibitions that often accompany dementia. She and her colleague were able to laugh about the incident the next day at work.

Another example is the time Dana took her father, Joel, who has dementia, out for breakfast. Joel ordered chicken parmesan, which was clearly not on the menu at 8:00 a.m. When the server tried to explain this to Joel, Joel told him that he was an ugly idiot. When Dana saw the server's eyes light up in fury, she quickly pulled out a Please Be Patient card she had received recently from the Alzheimer's Association. The size of a business card, this small preprinted note indicates that the person she is with has dementia. Dana then said, "Dad, I think we should both get the pancakes." Joel agreed, seeming to forget all about the chicken parmesan. After they ate the pancakes, Dana proceeded to leave the "ugly idiot" server a huge tip!

Here's a quick course correction if you've gone overboard in believing that your older loved one with dementia should be isolated: Don't isolate your older loved one!

While it eventually will be too difficult to take someone like Joel out for a meal, it's important for the older loved one with dementia to be around people who care for her, even if she does not know their names. It also helps family and friends to feel connected and able to offer their services as secondary and tertiary caregivers. Do the best you can to explain to your other loved ones the odd behaviors they may witness during a visit with your older loved one. Encourage them to consider learning more about your older loved one's diagnosis. And hold on to your sense of humor like Maryellen did when embarrassing situations inevitably unfold.

Mrs. Reagan's Caregiving Philosophies that May Reduce Your Stress

While I believe that some of Mrs. Reagan's strategies are not applicable for everyday folks, several of her philosophies are best practices. They include not "unloading" on all your support system members all the time, ensuring an older loved one with dementia is never left alone, and educating yourself about the disease.

Friends Can't Handle All Your Burdens

During the same Larry King interview mentioned earlier, Nancy Reagan was asked if she had supportive friends, and she said that she did. "But you know," she added, "you don't want to . . . if somebody calls you, you don't want to unload on them every time they call." Mrs. Reagan was really onto something here. While it's very important to talk about what's stressing you out as a caregiver, you don't want all your conversations and meetings with friends to be only about that. Part of the role of being a good tertiary caregiver can be to distract you from your caregiving troubles. Good friends will listen for a while, but keep in mind that many of them really don't understand unless they have done dementia caregiving specifically. And even if they have, it doesn't mean they want to talk about it all the time. If you feel the need to unload more often than not, then seriously consider joining a dementia caregiver support group or finding a good therapist.

Don't Leave Your Older Loved One Alone . . . Ever

Nancy discussed with Larry King the time when Mr. Reagan fell and broke his hip. She had been at her own eye doctor appointment when it happened. She never left him unattended, however. Secret Service and nursing staff were in the house when he fell, and they arranged for an ambulance to take him to a hospital.

 Life Ring: Falls happen. Notice that former president Reagan fell, even when surrounded by a team of professional caregivers! If your loved one is living at home, you want to make the environment as safe as possible by removing throw rugs, installing grab bars in the bathroom, and making a walker or cane as accessible as possible. But even if a person is in a nursing home or an assisted living community, falls may happen despite our best intentions.

It's startling how often caregivers will leave the older loved one with dementia alone "just for fifteen minutes" or "just while I go to the grocery store." In the blink of an eye, the older loved one could be driving, wandering to another neighborhood, turning on the stove and then leaving it unattended, and so on. Let me repeat: People with advanced dementia should *never be left completely alone*. While we've discussed at length that persons with dementia are still adults, it can be helpful to judge time alone the way you would when you're caring for a young child. A good litmus test is to ask yourself whether you'd leave a five-year-old child alone for the time frame you are considering leaving an adult with advanced dementia alone.

> *Let me repeat: People with advanced dementia*
> *should* never be left completely alone.

Educate Yourself

Mrs. Reagan learned about Alzheimer's disease and even made herself an expert in the condition. You will be a better caregiver if you understand the disease, its prognosis, and the best practices in caring for someone with the diagnosis. You will ask better questions of healthcare providers, and you will understand the kind of resources you will need. While many caregivers don't have the time or energy to become activists, Mrs. Reagan connected with others going through similar experiences through that work.

Going to the websites mentioned earlier of the nonprofits dedicated to the different types of irreversible dementia is a great way to get credible information (e.g., www.alz.org for the Alzheimer's Association). In chapter 11 we discuss the strategy of going to community events where local experts are speaking about dementia (which are typically free). Further, reading books like *The 36-Hour Day* (Mace & Rabins); *Dr. Ruth's Guide for the Alzheimer's Caregiver* (Westheimer & Lehu); and a book I mentioned earlier in this chapter, *The Validation Breakthrough* (Feil & de Klerk-Rubin) will offer not only a better understanding of dementias but also how to better communicate with your older loved one.

Make a Course Correction: Don't Let Your Older Loved One Captain the Ship

As dementia progresses, it is also crucial to not allow an affected older loved one to be responsible for too much. "There are many families who overestimate the person's abilities . . . and that then often triggers catastrophic reactions," says Dr. Rabins. The following example involving Meredith and her son, Conrad, illustrates this.

Conrad's mother, Meredith, was diagnosed with Alzheimer's disease several years ago, yet she still lives alone in her single family home. Her home is in an upper-middle-class neighborhood approximately two miles from Conrad's house, where he lives with his husband, Ian, and their sons. Conrad and Ian have been taking turns spending the night at Meredith's house because they felt she was a wander risk at night. They have two teenage boys at home; one has been having trouble with his grades recently. Conrad and Ian have not spent the night together in almost nine months, and they haven't taken a vacation in several years. When Meredith's physician suggested they strongly consider home health aides or assisted living placement, Conrad balked. "You don't understand— my mother would never allow that," he said. He emphasized that she prefers someone she knows to take care of her because when he asked her if she were open to the idea of having home health aides, she said no.

Well, that may very well be. Most people would prefer to be at home or surrounded by the people they love rather than by strangers. While it is admirable that Conrad wants to honor his mother's wishes, it is unreasonable to allow a person whose ability to reason is totally compromised to be captaining the caregiving ship. Look at the dangerous wake Meredith's boat is creating with her at the helm! The havoc created by this decision for Conrad, Ian, and their sons is unreasonable and could be avoided if the caregivers involved took the helm.

Take Back the Helm

We live in a country where it is very hard to take away someone's rights. Most of the time this is a really good thing. This freedom—the ability of individuals to make their own decisions, even bad ones—is something most of us appreciate. Even though most people don't like it when they make mistakes, wise people wind up knowing that mistakes can sometimes be necessary for us to learn from and to make better choices in the future. But as wonderful as this freedom is, it can be a real obstacle at times when we're trying to take the helm from a person with dementia. There is no specific black-and-white law that says once a person starts peeing in a potted plant or forgetting who her daughter is that she should have her rights taken away.

> *While an older loved one with dementia deserves the*
> *dignity and respect any grown-up does, caregiving*
> *crews need to adjust how much autonomy and*
> *self-determination that person can still handle.*

While an older loved one with dementia deserves the dignity and respect any grown-up does, caregiving crews need to adjust how much autonomy and self-determination that person can still handle, knowing those abilities will continue to diminish as time goes on. Your older loved one may be at the point where she is still able to decide what juice she wants, but she may no longer be able to reasonably decide whether she is able to continue driving. As director of social work for Lorien Health Systems, Joanna Frankel, MSW, LCSW-C, says a person with dementia who "forgets where the pedal is" should not be driving, and the caregiver will certainly have to intervene when this happens.

This time frame may be one of the components of caregiving that is most difficult to understand when your older loved one has dementia. There's no automatic date when someone with dementia officially can no longer make the big decisions. This is also known as losing capacity. According to the National Guardianship Association's website's terminology page (www.guardianship.org), *capacity* is defined as "legal qualification, competency, power, or fitness; the ability to understand the nature of one's acts."

It is critical to determine whether your older loved one has appointed a durable power of attorney for finance and health. The point at which this document "kicks in" varies from state to state, but the individual(s) named in these documents would become the decision-maker for the person with dementia. Guardianship, which means someone becomes legally responsible for the older loved one, is another option, but a last resort that can be costly and very time consuming to secure. Having power of attorney or guardianship are two ways to take over captaining the older loved one's ship legally if your older loved one is resistant to the decisions the primary caregiver is making. But most people with dementia do not have guardians and many have never previously appointed a power of attorney for the time when they eventually become unable to make decisions. In many cases, the caregiver is simply making decisions on behalf of the older loved one, and the person with dementia goes along with those decisions.

Taking over captaining of the caregiving ship can be a very hard concept for the caregiving crew to embrace, even if the older loved one doesn't seem to mind the decisions the caregivers are making. It can be particularly difficult if your husband was the strong patriarch of the family or your mom was the one who always took care of everyone. Caregivers often don't want to address the issue or take away more independence from the older loved one. While it is extremely uncomfortable to take over for that person, Joanna Frankel warns it can be "more dangerous to not address the issue" that is causing you concern. It is especially important for the caregiving crew to step up and start making decisions when the older loved one with dementia engages in behaviors that are unsafe and unhealthy and he does not understand the consequences of those behaviors because of the dementia.

If your older loved one does not go along with you when you are making decisions about his housing, medical care, and so forth, you may very well need to take steps to seek guardianship. Seeking the advice of an experienced elder law attorney at this time is invaluable. To find an elder law attorney in your geographic area, check out one or more of the databases listed back in chapter 11.

It is essential for caregivers at every level—primary, secondary, and tertiary—to recognize the intensity and magnitude of dementia caregiving. The most straightforward way to do this is by learning about the disease. But then you need to take it a step further: You need to emotionally wrap your head around the challenges that are to come. I believe the old Serenity Prayer written by Reinhold Niebuhr articulates this better than I ever could:

> God grant me the serenity
> to accept the things I cannot change;
> courage to change the things I can;
> and wisdom to know the difference.

To be more specific about how this applies to dementia caregiving, let me put it this way:

> Accept what you can't change (the diagnosis and the changes taking place with your older loved one).

> Have courage to change what you can (adjust your expectations and attitudes about caregiving for an older loved one with dementia) and find the courage to change your behaviors, like asking for help when you need it.

> And get, and emotionally embrace, the difference between the two.

> (Applied to dementia caregiving, this is truly wisdom.)

As we have discussed at length, dementia caregiving is a huge commitment and one of the most demanding types of caregiving you can commit to. It's important for caregiving crews to constantly revisit their commitment to the caregiving process. The next chapter helps you determine whether you want to renew or readjust your commitment to caregiving.

Thirteen

RENEWING YOUR CAREGIVING COMMITMENT

Gone Overboard: Forgetting You Chose to Be a Caregiver

As with any role in life, it's important to evaluate what's working and what's not. At work, it's important to determine from time to time if you want to remain in your current job or if looking for a new opportunity would be a better choice. The same is true of caregiving. Periodic evaluation of how things are going and if you want to continue the same course is crucial to reducing stress.

This chapter helps you with the following concepts and tasks:

- Reframe the way you look at caregiving; consider the concept that caregiving is a choice.

- Evaluate the choice you've made about caregiving thus far and understand how this can empower you.

- Determine whether you want to continue on the caregiving voyage in the same way you have been or whether you'd like to make a course correction.

The Caregiving Choice

As a childless but longtime happily married middle-aged woman, I have lost count of how many times someone has asked me why I don't have kids. People close to me—and, yes, even complete strangers!—have asked me this question. People almost always follow up by asking, "But who will take care of you when you are old?" When I am feeling generous, I just smile and say, "I have long-term care insurance," but sometimes when I am feeling a bit more forthcoming, I will respond with the truth: Having kids is no guarantee that you will have an automatic caregiver someday. There are endless examples of adult children who have nothing or very little to do with their older parents. And it's not necessarily that these adult children are bad people. Adult children opt out of caregiving for their older parents for a variety of reasons. Adult children, along with lots of adult grandchildren, nieces, nephews, spouses, friends, and family, do *not* care for their older loved ones when many of us might expect that they would or should. And, while many adult children do serve as caregivers for their older parents, having kids doesn't necessarily ensure that you will have a caregiving crew when you reach old age. There are no guarantees. And that's what I mean when I say caregiving *is a choice.*

> *When the terms "choice" and "caregiving" are used together, many caregivers react viscerally.*

Fortunately for many older adults, thousands of adult children do take on the role of caregiver every day. Back in chapter 10, we met Mark and Tracy, new parents of baby Madeline and caregivers to Mark's father, George. After his stroke, George moved into his son's home and began attending adult day care and receiving some financial support from Mark and Tracy as well. We briefly discussed that the couple, both professionals, made the *choice* to become George's caregivers.

When the terms "choice" and "caregiving" are used together, many caregivers react viscerally. Many caregivers think or even say out loud, "Caregiving, in my case, is *not* a choice. I don't want to be doing it, but I really don't have a choice here." Which of the following two statements best describes your opinion about whether Mark and Tracy had a choice in becoming George's caregivers?

I agree with it. Mark and Tracy had a choice. They did not have to become involved in George's care.

I disagree with it. Mark and Tracy did not have a choice. There was no other option.

If you disagree with it, take a few moments to consider why. Write down as many possible reasons you can think of—from guilt and obligation to altruism and love—as to why Mark and Tracy may believe they don't have a choice and are motivated to have George move in with them. Here is a list of some of the possible reasons (in no particular order) with which you may identify:

- Adult children have an obligation to take care of their parents.

- It doesn't seem like there was anyone else to take care of George.

- It would have been selfish for them to not take care of George.

- Mark and Tracy would feel guilty if they did not take care of George.

- Mark owes his father care because his father took care of him.

- Maybe Mark has no siblings or other relatives so Mark and Tracy had to become caregivers.

- Mark was a rebellious teen and believes he has to make up for that to his father now.

- Mark is worried his father would be upset with him if he didn't provide him with this level of care.

- Tracy has never felt accepted by Mark's family and thinks this would be the way to prove her worth.

- Because Mark loves his father so much, he did not feel like he had a choice.

- Mark promised his mother before she died that he would take care of George if anything happened.

- For religious, spiritual, or cultural reasons, Mark and Tracy are required to take care of George.

- Mark and Tracy would not want their friends and colleagues to think badly of them if they didn't step up and take care of George.

- Mark was so young when his mother died; he thinks he should do something now because he didn't really help out when his mother was terminally ill.

Were the reasons you wrote down similar to a number of these? If so, you're not alone: A lot of people do not believe caregiving is a choice for reasons such as these. And that's okay. If you wholeheartedly believe that caregiving is not a choice, one or more of the following qualities or characteristics probably describe you:

- You were born before 1940.

- You have a type A personality.

- You have perfectionist tendencies.

- You consider yourself to be, or have been told repeatedly that you are, a "control freak."

- You have strong religious beliefs.

- You are *not* Caucasian (you are African-American, Asian-American, Latino, American Indian, etc.).

- You come from a family where taking responsibility for the older loved ones in your family has been a tradition for generations before you.

- You experience extreme empathy for others.

If you have even one of the previously mentioned qualities or characteristics, it is likely you have a hard time seeing caregiving as a choice.

Everyone is entitled to an opinion on the concept of choosing to be a caregiver. But even if you are absolutely certain caregiving is not a choice but an obligation, please suspend your opinion while you read this chapter. It may just offer you some insight.

If you already believe that caregiving is a choice (or if I can convince you that it is!), this chapter will reinforce that belief and help you determine whether you want to continue to make that choice.

Evaluating Your Choice

Many caregivers have a belief system or narrative in their head that tells them there is no choice when an older loved one needs caregiving. But I, along with most healthcare providers, have witnessed countless examples of family members and friends who do manage to opt out of caregiving. I've worked with cases where elderly couples who have several adult children never have even one of those offspring step up as a primary or even a secondary caregiver. The older couple or widowed survivor is pretty much on her own, paying for care or managing her affairs the best she can by herself. Not only have I seen older persons who could really benefit from having a caregiver learn to manage without one; worse still, there are many cases of such older adults who are financially and/or emotionally supporting their adult children and/or grandchildren!

You probably already know this deep down, even if you are one of the readers who think Mark and Tracy had no choice. There are people in your family or friends network who are letting you down right now, not stepping up to help with caregiving. For one reason or another, they have opted out. If you are a dedicated caregiver, it may be very hard for you to comprehend this. Just as a devoted hands-on parent may have difficulty imagining how another long-distance divorced parent may only see his children annually for summer vacations, a dedicated caregiver does not understand this mind-set when it comes to caregiving.

Take a moment to think about some people you know who are not very involved in their older loved one's care. What might be some of the reasons they offer for why they cannot be part of the caregiving crew? Write down at least three reasons before you read any further.

Now have a look at some of the reasons I've heard over the years from nonparticipating family members. Do some of your reasons appear on the following list?

- They live far away and don't think there is much they can do.

- They never had a good relationship with the older person and don't want to participate.

- They don't know how to help because they are not natural at caregiving.

- They feel they have been pushed away by others on the caregiving team.

- They are very busy with their own lives and don't make time for caregiving.

- They are simply very selfish people.

- They are dependent on the older person who needs care, either financially, emotionally, or both.

- They really aren't aware that there is a caregiving need.

- They think someone else is better at caregiving than they would be.

- They assume there are programs or services out there that should meet the older person's caregiving needs.

If you are a primary caregiver, you may have a strong reaction to reading the list about why people opt out of caregiving. Thinking of those people in your family/friends network who are not helping out might make you angry or upset. While you might not like or agree with the reasons, this list demonstrates why some people *choose* not to participate in caregiving. (To better understand how to deal with these family/friends not participating, go back and reread chapter 8.)

Acknowledging that Caregiving Is a Choice May Make You Feel Better

Philosopher and theologian Thomas Aquinas once said, "A man has free choice to the extent that he is rational." I interpret this to mean that when we are rational and reasonable we have the ability to choose. If you don't currently see caregiving as a choice, is it possible that you never gave it any rational or reasonable thought? Sometimes we respond to difficult or stressful situations with knee-jerk reactions rather than considering all the possible ways to handle them.

What happens when you acknowledge that there's a choice about being a caregiver? It gives you back some of your power. It has to do with the perspective shaping how you feel. In psychology we call this a cognitive approach (the concept credited first to Albert Ellis, PhD, and then to Aaron Beck, MD). Simply put, a cognitive or cognitive behavioral approach means changing your thoughts to change the way you feel and behave. Let's examine some situations that are going on in your life, looking at them through the cognitive lens and putting them to the "choice" test.

Did you choose what you ate for dinner last night? Or did you have to eat what you ate? Maybe you ate a spinach salad for dinner. If you look at that spinach salad as something you *had to* eat because your doctor told you to lose weight, the meal may be unappealing, and you might feel annoyed and resentful. If you look at that spinach salad as something you decided to eat, however, doesn't it make you feel a little more powerful?

Or maybe you ate cheese, crackers, pepperoni, coconut shrimp, and pigs in a blanket for dinner because you were at a cocktail party. Some people might say, "I *had to* eat those items because that's really all that was available." But wasn't there a choice? You could have chosen to eat before you got to the party. You could have chosen to eat after the party. And let's face it; nobody believes your story that no crudités were served at the cocktail party! Don't you think you will feel more at peace when you shift and reframe your mind-set? Reframing your actions to *Even though there were healthier options, I chose to eat those items because they looked so darn tasty* puts you back in the captain's chair. Utilizing the cognitive approach allows you to reframe the way you perceive a situation that may feel out of your control.

Did you choose to go to work today or did you *have to*? Does it feel better when you have the attitude that you *chose* to go to work? Especially if you hate your job or dislike your boss or you have a cold, right? You could likely have called in sick, taken the day off, or just not shown up. Sure, there may be consequences to those actions, but you did have some options.

Now let's get into something more personal and emotional. Did you choose to take care of your kids today or did you *have to*? The point I want to make is that you might *feel* like you *have to* but you actually *chose to*. Unfortunately, we all know the world is full of people who have chosen to opt out of taking care of their own children.

In many ways, the commitment to be a caregiver for an older loved one is similar to the commitment to take care of your children. Of course, while children typically come with a warning of at least a few months, the older adult caregiving situations often sneak up on us.

Because we live in a world where there are many ways to prevent pregnancy if you want to, most people who have children have chosen to take responsibility for the children they bring into this world. If not, they have arranged for adoptions or even to drop off the baby via Safe Haven laws. These Safe Haven laws vary from state to state; you can drop off an infant, no questions asked, at a designated drop-off spot like a hospital or fire station. Ultimately, if you have children, you most likely have made the conscious decision that you want to care for them. But somehow this conscious thought does not necessarily come into play when caregiving arises. Many people who are caregivers have never really thought it through or asked themselves questions like these:

- How long will I be willing to care for my older loved one?

- How much time can I dedicate on a daily, weekly, or monthly basis to caregiving?

- Where will the time I spend in caregiving be "borrowed from"? Will caregiving potentially take me away from my kids, my job, or my relaxing in the evening?

- What kinds of tasks am I *not* willing to do that are associated with caregiving?

- How might caregiving impact my life in the following areas: finances; socialization; and physical, mental, or spiritual health?

- How might caregiving impact those people I love besides my older loved one? (This would include my spouse/significant other, my children, my grandchildren, etc.)

Giving yourself permission to ask these questions of yourself empowers you, which typically helps you reduce your stress. It also opens your mind to your inner feelings and possibly to a new way of approaching caregiving.

Make a Course Correction: Renew or Adjust Your Commitment

Regarding marriage, relationship author Barbara De Angelis says, "It's a choice you make—not just on your wedding day, but over and over again." This analogy applies to caregiving, too.

The day you stepped up as a caregiver, you made a decision. It may have been a decision as automatic as drinking water when you are thirsty. But it was still a decision. You have the choice now to keep on being a caregiver or to change your role.

The day you stepped up as a primary or a secondary caregiver, you made a decision. It may have been a decision as automatic as drinking water when you are thirsty. But it was still a decision. You have the choice now to keep on being a caregiver or to change your role. If, prior to committing to caregiving, you didn't ask yourself the questions listed in the preceding section, your first step in correcting your course is to revisit and answer them honestly. Because they are so important, I'm intentionally repeating the list here as a worksheet that I want you to stop and take time to fill out before you read further. You can also print a copy of this sheet by going to www.jenerationshealth.com.

....

Caregiver's Choice Worksheet

How long will I be willing to care for my older loved one?

_____

How much time can I dedicate on a daily, weekly, or monthly basis to caregiving?

_____

Where will the time I spend in caregiving be "borrowed from"? Will caregiving potentially take me away from my kids, my job, or my relaxing in the evening?

_____

What kinds of tasks am I *not* willing to do that are associated with caregiving?

_____

How might caregiving impact my life in the following areas: finances; socialization; and physical, mental, or spiritual health?

_____

How might caregiving impact those people I love besides my older loved one? (This would include my spouse/significant other, my children, my grandchildren, etc.)

_____

....

If you still aren't sure whether you are up to renewing your commitment or you want to adjust your commitment, it may be wise for you to join a support group for caregivers or to see an individual psychotherapist for some help in making your choice. Tips for finding such resources can be found in chapters 11 and 15.

Whatever you have done for your older loved one up until this point has been a gift to that person. But it is time for you to consciously determine, *to choose*, how much more of your money, energy, and time you are willing and able to offer. Making conscious choices about caregiving reduces your stress wherever you are in the caregiving process, but probably even more so when your older loved one is terminally ill, as I'll discuss in the next chapter.

Fourteen

YOUR OLDER LOVED ONE IS DYING

Gone Overboard: Denial and Using Hospice Too Late

The death of an older loved one is tough. Even when it's expected and even when you might be thinking it's for "the best." The death of an older loved one can be even tougher if you've been in denial about that person's prognosis. It will help you, your older loved one, and the rest of the caregiving crew if you better understand the death and dying process before you experience it.

This chapter helps you with the following concepts and tasks:

- Grasp that your older loved one has a terminal illness.

- Recognize signs and symptoms of the dying process.

- Tackle challenges (overboard situations) that arise when you are caring for an older loved one who is at the end of life.

- Embrace hospice by fully understanding what it offers.

- Be better able to handle the emotional experience of dealing with the death of your older loved one.

What Do You Mean My Older Loved One Is Dying?

It is not unusual for caregivers to feel completely blindsided when they realize the older loved one they have been caring for is in the process of dying. This feeling of being blindsided happens for a variety of reasons.

Many caregivers are in denial when their older loved one has a terminal illness. It may have been that the physician explained in good faith and in great detail about the older loved one's condition and prognosis but the caregiver and/or the patient really didn't grasp the news. It is possible that both were psychologically unready to digest the news when the doctor discussed it. As a result, the patient and her caregiver—or caregivers—are in denial. After all, denial is a protective mechanism that we unconsciously draw upon when we are not ready to deal with a difficult matter.

But in other cases, the physician might not have adequately addressed the reality of the older patient's illness. Yes, he or she might have stated the prognosis outright, but the patient and the caregiver did not immediately understand, because the doctor did not go into explicit detail about the fatal condition. Sometimes doctors do not state the prognosis directly, believing that when they declare that the patient has "stage IV cancer" or "Alzheimer's disease," a terminal diagnosis is clearly implied. It is also true that some doctors are simply not very good at giving bad news: They rely on support staff or nurses to do so, and somehow the severity of the prognosis is never relayed to the patient and the caregiver. Or the doctor may simply not want to give up trying to cure the older patient. In these instances, however, the older patient may not realize that the treatments he is undergoing have a minimal chance of curing his condition and may very well be reducing quality of life for the time he does have left.

Death is such a taboo subject in much of Western culture. If your older loved one has a chronic or acute condition that you suspect may be life-threatening, Heather Guerieri, RN, MSN, and executive director of Compass Regional Hospice, recommends that the patient and the caregiver write down a list of questions for the doctor. Questions such as "What is my prognosis with or without treatment?" and "Why are you suggesting this treatment? What's the benefit?" are appropriate to ask the doctor. It's especially prudent to ask these questions if you are unsure whether you are dealing with a terminal diagnosis. The patient may ask the physician directly if she is competent to do so. Otherwise, as long as the older loved one has given permission for the caregiver to speak to the doctor on her behalf, the caregiver could also pose these questions. Everyone involved should be saying, "I—we—want to know the truth."

Unfortunately, the doctor does not always go into a lot of detail with the caregiving crew about what death really looks like up close. This is an area where hospice can be invaluable—hospice staff are truly experts in the death and dying process. As we discussed in chapter 11, doctors are wonderful, but they don't know everything, and they don't always have the time to discuss things. If it's clear that your older loved one has a terminal illness, ask the doctor questions about that process so she can provide you with her insight and experience about how to best prepare. Often doctors won't take this step unless you ask. Ask what resources would help you and your older loved one through the last months. Hopefully hospice will come up during this conversation, but sadly it often does not. Many doctors still do not think of referring a patient to hospice until the very last weeks. This is unfortunate, because hospice should come much sooner. (I'll discuss this more in the "What Is Hospice, Really?" section.)

Signs and Symptoms that Death Is Imminent

A terminally ill patient can be terminally ill for months, even years. That means that he will have both good and bad days. Actually, some patients who are diagnosed with a terminal illness still work full-time jobs! But when someone is truly at the end of life (last weeks and days), there are specific signs to look out for.

Outside of healthcare professionals, most people don't know what imminent death really looks like. They may think someone is at death's door when he or she is not; conversely, they may not get it when someone is moments away from passing on. Unfortunately, a lot of us get our ideas about what death looks like from movies and television. I call this the Hollywood death that pop culture promotes. In the last scene of the film *The Notebook*, the elderly characters portrayed by Gena Rowlands and James Garner decide they are going to die together in their sleep, peacefully, and then miraculously they do. When someone has a terminal illness, and she is actively dying, however, it's notably different.

The critical signs that a terminally ill patient is close to dying may include—

- Sleeping excessively

- Chest congestion

- Restlessness (this can manifest through the patient tossing and turning, indicating through words or body language that she is uncomfortable physically)

- Withdrawal (the patient will be less engaged with others, wanting to be alone more)

- Bluish coloring of hands and feet

- Disorientation (examples of this may include not knowing if others are in the room, not remembering where she is)

- Shortness of breath

- Less need and desire for food

- Experiencing visions (as a person nears death, it is common for her to see or hear people who are not visible or audible to the rest of us)

When my grandmother-in-law was dying, it was fall. She began talking about the upcoming Thanksgiving holiday and about friends and family who had already died many years before. My mother-in-law said in shock, "She's lining up all of these dead people to invite to dinner!" When my grandfather was dying, there was a moment when he looked straight ahead and said, "It's beautiful." My husband, who was with him at the time, had no clue what Pop was seeing.

These signs can happen more frequently in the last weeks of the dying process. However, there may be days prior to the onset of this period where the patient is more active, alert, and seems like herself. While days and moments like this can be viewed as a gift, they sometimes unfortunately give caregivers false hope that the older patient is recovering. Many caregivers become excited when their loved one rallies, but others just become confused. Some caregivers assume a miracle has occurred and their older loved one will live quite a bit longer. Other caregivers become even more stressed-out (and feel guilty about it), because they were feeling relieved that they were getting to the finish line of caregiving and now wonder how much longer the older loved one will hang on.

All these feelings and thoughts are quite normal. No matter how you feel when this happens, know that this period of improvement is almost always temporary.

Overboard Situations that Arise at the End of Life

For a lot of us, facing death is *scary*. Most of us don't want to talk about it, let alone face it head-on when our elder loved one is dying. While the actual caregiving itself is tough work, the loved one's end of life presents us with psychological challenges too—one of which is our own mortality. Legal issues also come into play. If paperwork like advance directives, living wills, and wills haven't been created, still more psychological challenges, logistical issues, and caregiving crew conflicts can arise. Let's look at some of the stressful challenges—which can result in caregivers going overboard—that commonly occur when the older loved one's death is imminent.

Paperwork Is Not in Order, which Creates Drama

An *advance directive* or *living will* is a document that explains how medical decisions should be made when a patient is no longer able to express his or her wishes. According to the American Bar Association, more than half of Americans have not completed an advance directive. While an advance directive can be completed without legal assistance, I believe it is best practice to seek the advice and guidance of an elder law attorney if possible.

Advance directive documents contain questions about the circumstances under which a person would want a feeding tube, respirator, CPR, or other type of life-saving intervention when faced with a terminal condition or emergency situation. The patient's answers are a set of instructions to guide medical professionals' actions in the event the person cannot communicate due to a terminal medical condition or emergency situation. Perhaps even more important than your answers to these questions, suggests Libby Shadis, MSN, CRNP, a geriatric nurse practitioner with Personal Physician Care, is the action of simply appointing a healthcare surrogate.

Perhaps one of the reasons living wills are not completed as often as healthcare providers would like is because some people find the language and imagery the questions conjure up to be daunting. But beyond that, it is next to impossible to imagine every healthcare scenario you could potentially encounter. Shadis recommends simply identifying someone you trust who knows you well and whose decision-making abilities you respect as your healthcare agent. As part of your advance directive, you can give final-say authority to your healthcare agent; that person can then use the answers you gave as a guide for instructing doctors and other healthcare providers.

Typically, people choose a close family member or friend as their healthcare agent. When selecting the agent, it is important to consider whether this individual can stand up to scrutiny from others in the caregiving crew or family. So many well-meaning older adults assume, *My kids will just decide.* Even under the best of circumstances, when all the adult children get along well, are typically levelheaded, and truly want the best interests of the older parent carried out, there can be all sorts of reasons they don't come to consensus. What's best in one adult child's mind may be very different from what's best in another adult child's mind. Depending on the state where the older loved one resides, this conflict can hold up certain treatment or the withdrawal of treatment. And when you have a situation where all the adult children are *not* reasonable and do not have the older loved one's best interest in mind, there can be a bigger mess. Some families might have to deal with a relative who is an outlier in his or her beliefs. If there are four adult children, and all of them hold the same religious views as the mother they are caring for, they may be more likely to come to a consensus than if one of the four espouses a totally different belief system.

The caregiving crew should do everything in its power to persuade the older loved one to create an advance directive *well before a terminal illness occurs* or at least before it progresses to the very last days. How do you do this?

Here are some strategies that can keep you on a safe and steady course:

> **Create an agenda.** When you decide it's time to discuss a will, an advance directive, or a living will with your older loved one, set an agenda. Think about what your goals are for the conversation. Consider whether a public setting, such as a restaurant, would be a better location for the conversation rather than at home. If you are

talking to your mother who is still in relatively good health, changing the venue to Mom's favorite cafe rather than the kitchen in which you spent your childhood can make the discussion less intimidating.

In planning an agenda, it's important to contemplate the desired outcome of this particular conversation. Are you hoping Mom will agree by the end of the conversation to take action, or is this conversation going to be the first gentle introduction to the advance directive discussion?

Set a good example. If you want to discuss your older loved one's end-of-life plans, show them a copy of your will and advance directive. It's not just older adults or those with certain health conditions who need a will or an advance directive. Ideally, everyone over eighteen years old should have these documents. When your older loved one sees that you have your healthcare decisions in order, particularly if you are younger, it may motivate them to do the same. Perhaps people in the caregiving crew can agree to create their documents together, along with the older loved one.

Be persistent. Understand that these tough conversations may require several attempts before you get results. This can be especially frustrating if your older loved one has a number of health conditions or already has been diagnosed with a terminal illness. But be on the lookout for situations that provide natural openings for revisiting a difficult topic. A frequent catalyst for a productive change discussion is when a peer of the older person is hospitalized or becomes ill.

Empathize. While persistence is necessary with these tough conversations, empathy and patience are equally important.

Through your body language, tone of voice, and word choices, show that you understand that your older loved one may feel uncomfortable discussing some of these subjects. Many older adults may feel superstitious about completing an advance directive or a living will, feeling that if they do, they will immediately die.

Explain how it will impact the caregiving crew. Often if you share a specific example of how a caregiver might be affected if her older loved one did not have an advance directive, this can prompt your own loved one's cooperation better than just a focused conversation on why taking action would be best for the older loved one.

For instance, Roz has emphysema and has been taken care of primarily by her daughter, Debbie. Roz is married to her second husband, Ira (who is not Debbie's father), who has very little to do with Roz's care. Roz and Ira have never really had a happy marriage. Debbie is very aware of how the law works; if end-of-life decisions need to be made, Ira will be making them because he is next of kin legally. Therefore, Debbie positions her discussion with Roz about creating an advance directive as a favor that Roz could do for her, so that Debbie won't be in an awkward situation with Ira.

When you are a caregiver, you will hear many stories of families that have faced struggles over the lack of a will or an advance directive. Sharing such an example might be yet another excuse to revisit the discussion with your own loved one.

Involve others. Sometimes the person closest to the older loved one is not always the most effective communicator during these conversations. Often people who are less involved with the senior's daily life can be invaluable in emphasizing the need to discuss these tough topics. Perhaps a trusted minister or rabbi can help an older loved one understand the benefits of addressing end-of-life decisions ahead of time, while acknowledging fears about death. A respected friend of the family who works in healthcare may possess the objectivity to have a less emotional discussion with the older loved one. Or perhaps you have a brother who lives across the country that Mom tends to listen more closely to because she sees him less frequently. (By the way, this is a common phenomenon.)

Don't forget that it's not too late for others to become part of the process. Even if the only way that long-distance brother contributes is to persuade your older loved one to prepare an advance directive, that's a huge burden off your shoulders.

Although this can be a great way to utilize a secondary caregiver, such as that long-distance brother, the caregiving crew may not think of this approach because of their egos. They don't want to reach out to a sibling who has been "useless" thus far in the caregiving process. The overworked caregiving crew members are angry and frustrated with people in the family and friend network who haven't contributed. But don't forget that it's not too late for others to become part of the process. Even if the only way that long-distance brother contributes is to persuade your older loved one to prepare an advance directive, that's a huge burden off your shoulders.

Remember your older loved one is a grown-up! While you want to encourage and convince her to plan ahead for end of life, the choices she makes about legal documents and logistical matters are hers to make.

~~~~~~

ESSENTIAL END-OF-LIFE DOCUMENTS (IN PLAIN ENGLISH)

- **Advance directive:** A document indicating your healthcare wishes if you are unable to communicate with a healthcare provider.

- **Living trust:** A document that allows your will to be processed without going through probate. According to the American Bar Association's website, "Probate is the formal legal process that gives recognition to a will and appoints the executor or personal representative who will administer the estate and distribute assets to the intended beneficiaries." Many elder law and estate attorneys recommend that a living trust be created along with a will.

- **Power of attorney:** A document giving another person the ability to make decisions on your behalf. This can be done for healthcare or financial purposes.

- **Will:** A document that indicates to whom your assets will be given when you die.

~~~~~~

Caregivers Don't Like Facing Their Own Mortality

Caregivers taking care of an older loved one who is dying often begin to consider their own mortality. For many caregivers this can be very stressful. Let's take a look at how one son handled it.

Fifty-year-old Tyler is taking care of his father, Pete, who is dying. Pete, fortunately, has advance directives. Tyler's thirty-year-old daughter, Margaret, is a secondary caregiver to her grandfather. Margaret is now pestering Tyler with questions about whether *Tyler* has an advance directive. Tyler does not want to think about the prospect of his own death someday, especially right now when he is dealing with losing his father. He hates thinking about his own mortality; after all, when you are fifty, you probably have more life behind you than in front of you. And because Tyler married and had kids so early, there is still so much on his bucket list that's unaccomplished. When Margaret pushes Tyler on this advance directives issue, he thinks about all he has left to do. He always wanted to learn how to surf, for example. Is it too late? He's never visited Europe and always wanted to. Will he ever get there? Tyler thinks about all the things his father Pete wanted to do but never got to. Will that happen to Tyler?

How does Tyler make a course correction? First of all, he needs to start making changes in his life so he doesn't have regrets. He should plan on making progress toward achieving some of the dreams he's long held. He also needs to be pragmatic, reminding himself that he is a grown-up, that everyone dies, and that he owes Margaret and the rest of his family advance directives to spare them angst when he is at the end of his life.

Handling the Older Loved One Dying in Your Home

When in-home caregiving is taking place, caregiving crews often must consider the reality that the older loved one might die in one of their homes. This may happen if the older loved one currently lives in the home of one of the caregivers (typically the primary). This also may happen when the older loved one has been living independently in the community up until the last months. While many caregiving crews make the assumption that the dying older loved one would move in with the primary caregiver, that is often not the case. In many instances, a secondary caregiver may have a better setup in her home to provide in-home, end-of-life care (e.g., a first-floor bedroom). Depending on your cultural or spiritual beliefs, or simply just your age or personality, the idea of your older loved one passing away in your home may be frightening. Let's look at how a ten-year-old granddaughter dealt with the situation of her grandfather spending his last days at her home.

When Alice and her husband, Jason, were taking care of her father, Sam, in their home, their ten-year-old daughter, Katie, understood that her grandfather was dying. Because the room in which Sam resided was right next to hers, she was very anxious that Sam's spirit would always be around her if he died in their home. Alice and Jason were stunned to hear that this concerned Katie because she was always the apple of her grandfather's eye. Even though Katie loved Sam and was close to him, the idea of him dying in the room next to hers was terrifying.

Unfortunately, Alice and Jason were so exhausted and stressed from caregiving that they did not give Katie's concerns the attention they should have. When Sam died, Katie wound up having nightmares and eventually needed to go to both her minister and a child psychologist to address them. Alice and Jason very much regret not paying more attention to Katie's anxiety.

How should they have corrected their course to avoid running aground in this way? As part of the caregiving crew, Katie—and her opinions—mattered. This is not necessarily to say that Alice and Jason should have moved Sam out of their home to die, but they should have addressed their daughter's valid concerns more proactively. They could have gotten Katie to a psychotherapist to discuss her feelings, or had her join a hospice support group for kids. Perhaps it might have made sense for Sam to move to another caregiver's home until he passed. Or maybe arrangements could have been made for Katie to stay with a close friend or family member temporarily. The feelings of everyone in the caregiving crew need to be considered—even children's—and especially those who are living with the older loved one at the end of life.

Older Patients Might "Hang On" for the Caregiving Crew (or Others)

Heather Guerieri has observed that sometimes the older patient with a terminal condition tries to "hang on" for the sake of the family. The oldest patients, in particular, tend to do whatever the doctor suggests to prolong their life. For instance, the older patient who would prefer withdrawing from aggressive treatment like chemotherapy is still participating, because he perceives pressure from the caregiving crew or other loved ones to not let go. Guerieri cautions caregivers to be aware of this: "In my mind that's a horrible place to put a dying patient."

Do you think you've gone overboard in this manner and need to revisit the course you're sailing? Throughout this book, we've discussed that lower stress caregiving can only be achieved when both the older loved one's needs *and* the caregiving crew's needs are taken into consideration. I devote all of chapter 4 to this, because I think implementing this philosophy is that important. But *when to die* should be all about the needs of the older loved one and *only the older loved one.*

Lower stress caregiving can only be achieved when both the older loved one's needs and the caregiving crew's needs are taken into consideration. But when to die *should be all about the needs of the older loved one and* only the older loved one.

Guerieri believes there is a window of time (from hours to days, depending on the situation) when death can occur and that a terminally ill patient can choose this time to a certain extent. A dying patient might wait until a certain friend has visited until he passes. But it is just plain selfish when the caregiving crew or another loved one is trying to persuade the dying person to stay. I almost never use the word "selfish" when it comes to caregiving, but in this case it applies. Caregivers should try to accept the terminal diagnosis, spend as much quality time as possible with the older loved one, and make peace with the situation so the older loved one can make peace as well. When struggling with this issue, the best strategy may be for members of the caregiving crew to seek a professional mental health or spiritual counselor. Check out chapter 15 for information on how to find a psychotherapist.

Older Loved Ones Ask for Someone Outside of the Caregiving Crew

Sometimes the older loved one who is dying asks for someone who is not in the caregiving crew and, more often than not, that someone has not been around lately. Let's look at an example of how this created a challenge in one family.

Sisters Ebony and Ramona have been taking care of their father, Howard, since he was diagnosed with cancer nine months ago, and he is now failing rapidly, nearing the end of life. They have dealt with major disruptions to their family lives, marriages, and careers. Howard has been very challenging to care for and does not seem to understand how much Ebony and Ramona have sacrificed for his well-being. To add insult to injury, Howard seems focused exclusively on wanting them to contact their younger half-sister, Leyna, who has been of no help with his care up to now. Ebony and Ramona have always had some challenges in their relationship with Leyna because Howard left their mother for Leyna's mother when the two older sisters were teens.

As tired as you—the caregiver—may get of your older loved one, he or she is probably getting tired of you, too! This can hurt your feelings, but it is perfectly normal.

While it might cause hurt feelings sometimes, especially for the primary caregiver(s), the older loved one is often going to want to see people who have been less involved. Sometimes it's a matter of saying good-bye or dealing with some unfinished business. But sometimes it's simply because they just want to see other people who aren't exclusively focused on helping them go to the bathroom or go to the doctor or take their medicine. Remember this: As tired as you—the caregiver—may get of your older loved one, he or she is probably getting tired of you, too! This can hurt your feelings, but it is perfectly normal. Sometimes interacting with family and friends who don't make them feel like a sick person can lift the spirits of elderly infirm people enormously. While it's reasonable for Ebony and Ramona to feel a little hurt by Howard's wish to see Leyna, it's also very reasonable for Howard to want to see her. The two older sisters need to try to reframe their perspective on the situation.

Just how could Ebony and Ramona steer clear of this sandbar? By remembering, as we've discussed throughout this book, the importance of having as many caregivers as possible. While Leyna has not been a caregiver yet, perhaps there is a way to incorporate her (and maybe even some others) into the caregiving crew. Leyna might actually *want to be more involved* but has been hesitant to step up because of the ongoing tension with her two half-sisters.

Perhaps Ebony and Ramona could invite Leyna to join them now. Or maybe they could ask her to visit this one time and offer Howard the comfort or closure he needs. If nothing else, Leyna visiting will be something new for Howard. And if seeing Leyna lifts Howard's spirits even temporarily, or offers him some type of relief, it may even result in a more peaceful dying experience. And it's possible that their father dying could bond the sisters together in a new way if Leyna, Ebony, and Ramona are open to working together.

> *While taking care of an older loved one who is dying can be traumatic, it can also be a time when old wounds can be healed.*

When the older loved one who is dying is more at peace psychologically and has had his needs met, the caregiving experience for the crew is typically less stressful. Ebony and Ramona may want to revisit the MET exercise found in chapter 8. Instead of struggling and feeling resentful, perhaps they could reframe by looking at Leyna as a possible ally. When they complete the MET exercise and determine what to include on the Need Help With list, they should see what holes in the ship Leyna might be willing to plug. While taking care of an older loved one who is dying can be traumatic, it can also be a time when old wounds can be healed. When people who love each other realize that our time is finite, sometimes going through caregiving and death together can resolve estrangements.

When Someone New Wants to Captain the Ship

When the older loved one is deemed to be dying, dynamics can shift within the caregiving crew. Sometimes, people who have not been part of the caregiving crew up to the present step up and want to start participating. Unfortunately, these new additions may want to take over, and people who have done the majority of caregiving up until that point generally do not welcome this idea. Let's take a look at how this plays out with Eric and his mother, Ann.

Seventy-five-year-old Ann is dying of cancer. Ann's son, Eric, has not been very involved in his mother's care up until now. Ann's sisters have been her primary and secondary caregivers. Now that Ann has been pronounced terminal,

Eric has been showing up to visit Ann more and has been very critical of the way his aunts have been providing care. Although Ann's sisters had arranged for her to be at an assisted living community several years ago, before the cancer progressed, Eric is now saying he is going to move his mother into his home.

What are the possible reasons Eric is behaving this way? Write down as many as you can think of before you compare them to the list I've included here.

Did any of the following reasons make your list?

- Eric genuinely believes his aunts are not doing a good job.

- Eric feels guilty that he hasn't been involved up until this point and wants to make up for lost time.

- Eric feels like he has unfinished business with his mother, and it's hitting him that his time left with her is limited.

- Eric wants to look like the hero stepping in at the last minute to "fix" things.

- Eric knows he has not been there and feels bad that his elderly aunts have been assuming responsibilities that should have been his.

- Eric wants to save money on assisted living now that his mother is at the end of life so he can potentially inherit that money.

- Eric doesn't want others to think badly of him for not helping out when his mother is at the end of her life.

- Eric thinks—based on a moral, spiritual, or cultural belief—he should step up as his mother faces her death.

Who should be at the helm in this situation? Regardless of Eric's motivations, Ann should be able to voice her preference as to where she'd like to live and whom she wants to ask to care for her. If Ann is unable to speak for herself at this point (and the caregiving crew or other involved family members disagree among themselves), a power of attorney or an advance directive document would be invaluable. Perhaps Ann indicated in her advance directive where she'd prefer to live at the end of her life or who she would prefer to make that decision for her.

EVEN IF YOU DON'T CARE ABOUT THE MONEY, IT STILL MEANS SOMETHING

For many valid reasons, the older loved one should have an active will and/or trust as well as an advance directive. Nevertheless, many people believe this is wholly unnecessary. Maybe the older loved one does not have much in the way of assets. Or maybe the older loved one does have money, but the caregiver thinks, *I don't care about the money.*

As we all know, money is not just about money. Money often represents feelings. How would you feel if you have been your grandmother's primary caregiver for five years, and when she dies your aunt—who did not help out at all—inherits her house? Without a will or trust, the law in many states may dictate that the house would go to your aunt simply because she is the next of kin. Families become estranged and even go to war over issues like this. When the older loved one does eventually die, it is a very emotional time. And like it or not, money and assets bring up a lot of emotions for most of us. Encourage your older loved one to put her wishes about property and assets in writing as soon as possible. Again, consider seeking the services of an elder law attorney to help with this process.

What if none of these documents are in place, as happens all too often? It would benefit both Eric and his aunts to try to have a conversation that focuses on what is best for Ann. While this sounds like common sense, this may be very difficult when everyone is feeling emotional. It would be ideal if Ann's sisters could try to determine why Eric wants to change the plan now that his mother is dying. It could really be as simple as his wanting to make up for lost time. Maybe they can come up with some ideas for ways he can contribute to Ann's care without disrupting her current living situation. Or perhaps Eric can offer some good reasons why he thinks Ann should be at his home to die, and his aunts would come to understand his position. Maybe Eric has decided he will take a leave of absence from work until Ann passes away, and he'd like to spend as much time with her as possible at his home.

It is still probably not in Ann's best interest to move from the assisted living community at the end of life unless absolutely necessary, because it would be disruptive and stressful for her. But an honest, respectful conversation between Eric and his aunts is the only way to resolve the situation. But when emotions (not to mention tempers) are running high and such a conversation is not in the cards, it is a good idea to consider enlisting the help of a mediator, particularly one who specializes in senior care or older adult issues. A mediator can do wonders to help bring peace and understanding to a highly charged emotional situation in caregiving.

 Life Jacket: In selecting a mediator, it is a good idea to find someone with experience in elder care issues. A few particularly good websites to search for a good match in your area include:

- **Mediate.com**—www.mediate.com (under the drop-down menu that says "Select Type of Matter," select the word "Elder")

- **National Association for Community Mediation**—www.nafcm.org

The Older Loved One "Just Won't Die"

Sometimes the caregiving crew is adequately prepared for the older loved one to pass away . . . and she just doesn't! This is a very emotionally and logistically tricky place for a caregiving crew. Sometimes terminally ill people do rebound. An older loved one whose prognosis was to live for three more weeks is still here three months later.

In other cases, the older loved one is truly at death's door and just does not seem to be able to let go. The family and staff taking care of this person can't figure out why. Maybe this person is scared to die, because they have some unfinished business. In one case, Courtney is taking care of her brother, seventy-seven-year-old Hank, who is dying from emphysema. Hank is hanging on because he is waiting to make peace with his forty-five-year-old son, Leonard, who is an addict. Hank feels guilty because several years ago, upon discovering Leonard stealing from the family, Hank cut him out of their lives. Hank has insisted Courtney and others in the family reach out to Leonard and ask him to visit. They left nearly a dozen messages for Leonard, but he has not returned any of the calls. Courtney suspects Leonard is out on a bender or perhaps even in jail again.

While it may have been reasonable for Hank to banish Leonard in a tough love effort, it is still common for someone in Hank's position to feel guilt. Courtney and the other caregivers tried to reassure Hank that he did the right thing and to prepare him for the eventuality that Leonard may not come. Ultimately, the only thing that seemed to give Hank some peace was a visit from his rabbi. Even though Hank was not completely settled in his unfinished business with Leonard, the caregiving crew made every effort to see that Hank passed as peacefully as possible by reassuring him and reaching out for spiritual counsel.

When Should the Caregiving Crew Embrace Hospice?

Once you know whether you and your loved one are dealing with a terminal illness, it is important to become as educated as possible about any special illness-related considerations that might accompany the death process. Dr. Rabins cautions that caregivers of people dying from Alzheimer's disease must be prepared that their older loved one will be very physically dependent during the later stage of the disease and up until death. These patients typically are incontinent and require assistance with bathing, dressing, and even need to be fed. Your loved one's doctor can usually help you understand what is typical at end of life, but as I discussed in chapter 11, you don't want to rely exclusively on the doctor for resources and help at this time.

When the doctor believes your older loved one has approximately six months longer to live, it is time to embrace hospice. Hopefully, that doctor will recommend some hospice organizations to consider, but if she doesn't, Guerieri recommends simply calling a hospice provider for some information about their program and, perhaps, about an assessment of your older loved one. Request a home visit and allow them to tell you about their services. You may call one provider and not feel that it is the right match. You can always try another, because most jurisdictions have multiple hospice provider options. To find a hospice provider in your area, check out the National Hospice and Palliative Care Organization's database at http://www.nhpco.org/find-hospice.

> *When the doctor believes your older loved*
> *one has approximately six months longer*
> *to live, it is time to embrace hospice.*

What Is Hospice, Really?

Hospice is possibly the most widely misunderstood healthcare service of our time. First, let's clarify what hospice is *not*. Hospice is absolutely *not* euthanasia. It is *not* assisted suicide. It is *not* a way to hasten death.

While hospice is medical care, its goal is not to cure a terminal illness. According to the Hospice Foundation of America (www.hospicefoundation.org), "Hospice offers *medical* care toward a different goal: maintaining or improving quality of life for someone whose illness, disease, or condition is unlikely to be cured." Hospice offers supportive palliative care (comfort care) to a patient whose life expectancy is approximately six months.

Just because patients meet the arbitrary six-month prognosis criterion for hospice certainly does not mean they will definitely die within six months. Many hospice patients "graduate," meaning they begin feeling better and no longer meet the six-month criterion. While they are still considered terminally ill and are not cured, they simply no longer need hospice. Occasionally a hospice patient will rebound and go back to whatever life was before they entered hospice care. They can then reenter hospice when they are more symptomatic.

Guerieri says families often say they wish they had known about hospice sooner. And why wouldn't they? Hospice offers nursing care, physician oversight in conjunction with the patient's doctor, help with personal care for the patient, a social worker, volunteer visits, and spiritual support if desired. In a 2013, a *New York Times* article by Susan Seliger titled "Preparing for a Loved One to Die at Home," Dr. Stacie K. Levine, a geriatrician and palliative care expert, was quoted as saying, "I have been doing this for over a decade and I find my patients who choose hospice sooner at home may live a little longer."

In addition, hospice offers up to thirteen months of grief support to the family after the patient passes away.

Despite those positive results, physicians often do not bring up the topic of hospice. Some think it will upset the patient or caregiver. Other physicians just don't want to give up trying curative treatments. Unfortunately, still other doctors simply don't understand the benefits that hospice can offer or have bought into some of the myths about it. Guerieri says two of the most common myths about hospice are that it is only for cancer patients or that patients go into it with only a few days to live.

A VARIETY OF HOSPICE SERVICES

The vast majority of hospice is home based. In this way, hospice services can be received wherever the patient lives. Some of the most familiar varieties of home-based hospice include the following:

- The most common option is in-home hospice. Most hospice services are provided at the private home.

- Hospice is provided at the assisted living community or nursing home where the older patient resides.

- Hospice can also occasionally be offered at a residential or inpatient facility such as—

  - In-patient hospice care centers (medical model for active symptom management)

- Residential hospice houses (more of a home away from home); this option is most often utilized if a caregiver is completely exhausted and needs a break

~~~~~~

Why Does Hospice Get a Bad Rap?

"My mom isn't bad enough for hospice."

"Hospice just wants to drug you up."

"I've heard that hospice makes you die faster."

These are just a few real-life objections I've heard from family caregivers on why they are reluctant to use hospice. Unfortunately, these objections are in no way based in reality.

As I previously mentioned, some people think hospice is associated with assisted suicide or euthanasia, which is absolutely incorrect.

Others believe embracing hospice signifies giving up. True, the patient will no longer receive treatment that is focused on curing the terminal illness, but the patient is entering a different type of care. The patient is not giving up; rather, to borrow a term from Facebook COO Sheryl Sandberg, he or she is "leaning in" to a different philosophy of care.

Some people think hospice means you have to go live somewhere else. And while there are special hospice facilities (see "A Variety of Hospice Services" earlier), by far, most hospice services take place in the private home.

Guerieri says many families are uncomfortable with the standard hospice practice of using morphine to treat pain. She has seen situations where the nurse gets blamed for "killing" the patient, because the family believes the patient died *because* of pain medicine. Actually, many healthcare providers have stories about older patients who have said they won't accept morphine, because they don't want to become drug addicts. Guerieri often has to reassure patients and families that there is no risk of becoming an addict if the person has pain for the morphine to "attach to." Yes, if there is no pain and you take morphine or another potentially addictive drug, you can develop an addiction. But when there is pain at the end of life, the morphine is simply relieving that pain.

Finally, when people hear the term hospice, they think the person is going to die right away. This false belief may come from the fact that many patients begin using hospice way too late, when they are imminently dying.

Make a Course Correction: Apply What You've Learned

I hope you are reading this book, this chapter, before your older loved one is in the later stage of an illness or actively dying. If so, you can apply what you've learned by asking the right questions, making every effort to persuade your older loved one to prepare the proper legal documents, and interviewing hospice providers when the time comes.

But even for people who are reading this as their older loved one is actively dying, it's not too late. The following tips help you make a course correction if you've found yourself going overboard on any of the issues discussed in this chapter:

- **Find out as much as you can about your older loved one's illness.** Determine approximately how long your older loved one has to live and whether there are any special considerations related to dying from her particular diagnosis. But know this: no doctor has a crystal ball; when you are given an approximate time frame for how long that person will live, it is an estimate only.

- **Ask your doctor, aging life care expert, and/or elder law attorney for a referral to some hospice providers you can interview.** Or go to this database and plug in your zip code to find options in your area—http:// www.nhpco.org/find-hospice. Ask the hospice providers you speak with to come to your home to explain their services and to provide an assessment. Ultimately you will need a doctor to prescribe hospice but you can certainly do the research before you get the "order."

- **If your older loved one does not have a will or an advance directive, be on the lookout for a time when he is lucid enough to complete the necessary form(s).** Even if everyone in the caregiving crew and/or family is on the same page today, it does not mean that will always be the case. You never know what kind of reaction different family members or caregiving crew members will have when the person draws close to death or dies.

Caregivers sometimes don't accept that their older loved one has a terminal diagnosis. Many caregivers do not properly understand what's involved, and many even fear it. They also frequently do not embrace the concept of hospice when the older loved one is terminal until the loved one has only days to live. In spite of the reservations caregivers may have, hospice is a tremendously underutilized resource that helps people with terminal illness and their families.

Understanding the terminal diagnosis and using hospice almost always makes the death and dying experience less overwhelming for the caregivers and can also significantly enhance the quality of life up until the end for the patient.

Can you ever truly be prepared for the death of someone you love? Probably not completely. But by implementing the strategies in this chapter, you will likely fare better than most caregivers. And speaking of faring better than most caregivers, wouldn't it be great if you could set up *your future caregiving crew* for success? Let's take a look in the next chapter at how you can do just that.

Fifteen

BEYOND CAREGIVING

Avoid Going Overboard: Set Up Your Future Caregiving Crew for Success by Taking Care of Yourself Now

Have you ever silently (or even not so silently) lamented things your older loved one could have done to make the caregiving experience easier for everyone? How she could have made her aging process better for herself and, in turn, more manageable for the caregiving crew? If only she had written down her advance directives. If only she hadn't smoked. Perhaps you have been so overwhelmed with your caregiving duties that you've never given much thought to *if only* scenarios before now. Actually, there's a lot that we can control ahead of time that determines how well our own aging experience will go and the impact it will have on our future caregivers. This chapter offers tips that help you with the following action items:

- Improve *your* overall aging experience.

- Delay needing a caregiver yourself some day.

- Minimize the burden you place on future caregivers.

- Have fewer regrets and avoid the pain of "despair" rather than "ego integrity" (more on that later).

Caregiving Impacts Everyone

"There are only four kinds of people in the world—those who have been caregivers, those who are currently caregivers, those who will be caregivers, and those who will need caregivers."

As former first lady Rosalynn Carter famously articulated so well, caregiving eventually touches everyone's life whether they are expecting it to or not. Most readers of this book are living proof, because like many caregivers, you never expected to take on the job and did not anticipate the reality of what life would be like as a caregiver.

According to the US Department of Health and Human Services' Administration on Aging, there are currently nearly 45 million US citizens older than 65 (about 14 percent of the population). By 2040, nearly 22 percent of Americans will be over 65. Better healthcare and medical technology has made living longer the norm. As hard as it may be to imagine, you are probably going to live to old age—and that means most likely you will need help of some kind at some point from a caregiver yourself.

Throughout *Cruising through Caregiving*, we've repeatedly mentioned that no caregiver is perfect. But wouldn't it be great to help *your future caregiver(s)* get closer to perfection by applying insights you've garnered from your own experience as a primary or secondary (or even tertiary) caregiver? Maybe if *you* do some preplanning for your aging experience, there will be fewer sandbars for your future caregiving crew to hit. Maybe an understanding of what you have been through will keep them from going overboard. Now, I'm not suggesting you write a memoir of your caregiving experience as a handbook for others to follow specifically; your future caregiver probably would not appreciate that at all. What I am suggesting, though, is for you to seriously consider what caused you the most stress, how you reduced that stress, and how you may prepare now so that a less stressful caregiving experience will be a reality for your future caregiver.

First, think about who your future caregiver(s) are likely to be. This may be hard to imagine, especially if you have young children. But consider those children (or nieces, nephews, siblings, friends) and how you feel about all of them. Think about your love for them, and allow that to motivate you to do some future planning now. I had a recent conversation with Vincenzo who was caring for his mother, Carmela. Because Carmela was so resistant to preparing advance directives or having any conversations about her wishes, Vincenzo was left guessing when end-of-life decisions needed to be made. Vincenzo said he never wants to put his kids in that heart-wrenching situation. Soon after Carmela died, Vincenzo and his wife finally put together their advance directives and gave a copy to each of their adult children.

Like many caregivers, you never expected to
take on the job and did not anticipate the reality
of what life would be like as a caregiver.

Next, consider what your caregiving experience has taught you so far. This is a bit of a loaded question, because if today is your third day of caregiving, the answer is likely to be extremely different from the answer you'd give if it were your third year of caregiving. And your answer is likely to be significantly different if you are reflecting on this question three years after the older loved one you'd been caring for has died.

But if you seriously consider what you learned from your caregiving experience at different points, you may be very likely to save your future caregivers from some of the challenges and stressors you experienced. You will also almost surely enhance your eventual experience as a care recipient.

So take notes while you are caregiving. Or if you are no longer caregiving, take some time to think back on it. Make a list of the sandbars you hit that you would not want your future caregiver to also experience. How did hitting those sandbars negatively impact you, the rest of the caregiving crew, and your older loved one? Take this list and consider whether some of the advice offered in this chapter might have helped you out if your older loved one had followed it. When caregivers make these lists, major areas they wish their loved ones had handled differently commonly include taking better care of themselves, doing better financial planning, and planning better for the end of life. Let's look at each of these three principal areas in greater detail.

Take Care of Yourself Now

Just as there is no perfect caregiver, nobody can do everything perfectly to prepare for getting older. But when you plan as much as possible for your aging process and the possibility that you may someday need a caregiver, it can positively impact your future quality of life—and that of your future caregivers. While some parts of your aging process are out of your control, like your genetics and family history, much of your aging experience is very much in your hands. Do the best you can to take good care of yourself now.

Many of us know what to do to be our healthiest physically, mentally, and financially, but we do not follow all the best practices all the time. I call these best practices the boring advice nobody wants to hear. When healthcare providers, elder law attorneys, or financial advisors discuss these best practices, many of us want to crawl under a chair or roll our eyes, because they involve lifestyle changes or choices that we know would be good for us but that we are not necessarily practicing regularly. We may not be practicing them because they are time consuming, overwhelming, or we just don't know how to go about implementing them.

These best practices for good physical health include maintaining good nutrition, exercising regularly, getting enough sleep, and valuing preventive care (expressed by going to regular dental and doctor checkups). Best practices for good mental and cognitive health include keeping intellectually and socially engaged and getting help from others when needed. Even though you have probably heard these before, I believe revisiting them is worth it, because they really are our best shot at the healthiest and happiest aging process possible. For many of us, pulling them all together on a daily basis is far from easy (for me, too!). Let's see if I can help make it easier to attain these best practices in taking better care of yourself. If you can embrace and integrate even some of them into your life, both you and your future caregiver will benefit.

Best Practices for Physical Health

According to the World Health Organization's Constitution (1946), "Good health is a state of complete physical, social and mental well-being, and not merely the absence of disease or infirmity."

How do we achieve this? Let's start with the boring advice about physical health. I know you know this stuff, and some of you may be working on it already. Or some of you might find the subject so daunting you've given up trying to make it part of your life. But try to consider how you might improve upon one or more areas of these best practices. If you're not motivated to do it for yourself, perhaps your motivation could be trying to tidy up some of your physical health habits as a gift to your future caregiver(s).

Nutrition

Countless studies have demonstrated that practicing good nutrition can reduce the likelihood of many diseases, including certain types of cancers, type 2 diabetes, and heart disease. Interestingly enough, Alzheimer's disease is strongly linked to heart disease, so preventing or managing heart disease may reduce one's risk for Alzheimer's disease.

Nutrition is a tough one for many of us, especially in our American culture where food is readily available and less healthy food can seem more convenient and appealing. But there is tons of research that indicates eating moderate food portions; eating plenty of fruits, vegetables, lean protein, and whole grains; and drinking alcoholic and caffeinated beverages in moderation can protect us against many unwanted diseases. Not only can good nutrition be protective, it also can put us in a better position for fighting a health challenge if we are diagnosed with disease.

Exercise

According to the Centers for Disease Control and Prevention (CDC), just 150 minutes per week of moderate exercise is recommended for adults. While it may sound like quite a bit, this is only two and a half hours per week! While many people may set the goal of walking or running a half hour for five days per week, it turns out you don't have to be so regimented. Even ten minutes at a time counts. Some brisk walking for ten minutes, fifteen times per week, can meet this goal.

If you have taken care of an older loved one who was sedentary, you know firsthand the added burden this creates for the caregiver. Lack of exercise is associated with increased risk of some cancers, cardiovascular disease, and other conditions. And remember what we talked about in the nutrition section. Because cardiovascular disease is associated with Alzheimer's disease, getting regular exercise may contribute to reducing that risk as well.

If you are not already regularly exercising or if you are a sporadic exerciser, all the experts say it's important to find something you enjoy. Swimming, tai chi, yoga, walking, lifting weights, joining a running club, zumba—the options seem to be endless. There are even workouts that you can stream to your television or computer if you have a basic Netflix or Amazon Prime membership, and there are also free offerings on YouTube. With all these options, there is almost always something that can make exercise palatable for each of us. Some people who thought they hated exercise have actually found it entertaining due to all the music and video options that can enhance it. Many people these days are also highly motivated by wristband fitness tracker technology like Jawbone UP or Fitbit. These wristbands track your steps daily, and you can even sync them up with friends or family to keep track of each other, compete, or just give kudos when someone meets or exceeds a goal. Using this technology can even become a way to connect over common goals with loved ones who don't live close by.

~~~~~~

MAINTAIN A HEALTHY WEIGHT

Keep in mind that even if you have a healthy weight but are not eating a high-nutrient diet and exercising to maintain it, your health can suffer. I have worked with countless older adults whose weights are in a perfectly healthy range, but because they neglect nutrition or exercise, their overall health suffers. Alternatively, you can eat very healthfully and exercise regularly and still not maintain a healthy weight. The goal for all of us (and it's certainly easier said than done for many of us, myself included!) should be to do all three!

Maintaining a healthy weight has a lot to do with eating the right amount of food (calories) that your body needs, but nutrition, exercise, and sleep (which I'll discuss next) each play a part. Furthermore, preventive care can play a big part in maintaining a healthy weight. If you are struggling with weight issues, a good primary care physician can help motivate you with new ideas or make suggestions about weight loss or exercise programs that may be appropriate for you. Good preventive care can also help detect underlying conditions or medication side effects that may be interfering with achieving or maintaining a healthy weight.

~~~~~~

Sleep

As we age, one of our top complaints is that we are not sleeping as well as we once did. Insomnia occurs more often. Most sleep experts will tell you that seven to nine hours is what most adults, including older adults, require to function optimally. But many older adults fail to get the sleep they need. The National Sleep Foundation indicates that the lack of optimal sleep can lead to a variety of health issues, including obesity, heart disease (linked to Alzheimer's), and diabetes.

Common sense tells us that if we are tired, we might turn to high-fat, high-calorie food and excessive caffeine for energy. We're also less likely to go to that party or book club event or to play golf if we are tired—opting for lazing on the couch and watching television instead. As you'll see further on in the best practices for mental health, sleep is interrelated with many other healthy habits; the lack of it can lead us to do less well in some of these other areas.

~~~~~~

QUIT SMOKING

While I am not a smoker, I do feel quite a bit of empathy for people who still smoke. What started out many decades ago as a very "cool" or "hip" habit has turned you into persona non grata. You even used to be able to smoke in hospitals or on airplanes, and now you can barely smoke outside anymore. While we all know that smoking is terrible for you and people around you, it doesn't make it any easier for people who are truly addicted to smoking to quit. But quitting is worth persevering, and you should quit as many times as it takes. Even reducing the number of cigarettes you smoke can have a positive impact on your health.

~~~~~~

Preventive Care

Important preventive care includes regular visits to your primary care physician, dentist, and any necessary specialists. As you well know, caregivers commonly cancel and reschedule preventive care appointments for themselves while never considering doing the same for the older loved one they are caring for. But to make caregiving easier for your future caregiver and also make aging better for yourself, preventive care is essential.

A good primary care physician will keep an eye on your weight, nutrition, and sleep habits, and besides checking your blood work, he can listen to your concerns and make appropriate referrals for specialists and mental health providers when necessary. Perhaps you took care of an older loved one who let a condition get out of control because she hadn't sought preventive care. Make preventive healthcare a priority for your health not just so your caregiver has an easier time or your aging process goes better. Preventive care will also help you feel better *now*.

~~~~~~

THE BEST PREVENTIVE CARE: LOWER YOUR STRESS LEVELS

One of the worst ways to stress yourself out is by trying to be perfect in the best practices we know we should be (but are not always) following in nutrition, exercise, sleep, finances, planning ahead, and all the other stuff addressed in this chapter. When you make yourself crazy through feeling guilty, ashamed, or bad about yourself, you are inevitably going to experience a stress reaction. Simply do the best you can in these areas. If you've identified a weakness or an area to improve, work on it but don't constantly beat yourself up if you are struggling.

The principal goal of this book is to reduce the stress you feel while caregiving. The data are clear: too much stress can take years off our lives. But caregiving for an older loved one is not the only stressor you may face. Stress is potentially everywhere. It can exist when you are involved in any of the following activities:

- Babysitting your grandkids

- Having an argument with a friend

- Traveling (even if it's taking a trip you are excited about)

- Dealing with unexpected bills

- Handling change to a routine

- Coping with the death of a friend, family member, neighbor, or coworker

- Running late to an appointment or meeting

- Facing new challenges at work

- Overcrowding your schedule

What are some ways you can work to reduce the stress in your life? Is it through planning better systems and habits? Is it arriving fifteen minutes early to appointments? Is it by giving yourself time to grieve if you are experiencing loss? Is it by seeking counseling? Is it by developing new healthy ways to cope with stress like exercise, spending more time with friends, or saying no to babysitting your grandkids *every* Saturday night?

Reducing your stress level will go a long way toward improving every single aspect of your mental, cognitive, and physical health.

Best Practices for Mental and Cognitive Health

Best practices for physical health are obvious, and I bet every reader has heard them all before. But these mental and cognitive health practices may be less familiar to you. Although our culture has made major advances in understanding the importance of good mental health, there can still be stigma attached to mental health conversations. Some people may think if they aren't depressed they really don't need to read this section but this section is important for everyone.

Be Intellectually Engaged

The Alzheimer's Association recommends staying intellectually active and curious as we age. While doing crossword puzzles, learning new things, and remaining cognitively engaged is not linked to reducing Alzheimer's disease, it may delay the appearance of symptoms if one is predisposed. Further, staying cognitively active may minimize the normal aging declines we all experience.

Remaining cognitively engaged can take many forms. Learning something new is always a great way to accomplish this: Read a book, take a class, or take some type of lessons (golf, piano, etc.). Another way is by continuing to work— whether part-time or full-time, or volunteering. While some people remain in the workforce strictly for the paycheck, there are many who continue because of a passion for their field or vocation. Maybe you want to remain cognitively engaged by continuing to work but you never did like your job. Your retirement years may be a time when exploring a second or third career is a great option.

Be Social

Isolating yourself has been demonstrated to be negative for overall health. Can you honestly say you engage with other people as much as you should? If so, great! But if not, how can you be a bit more social? One of the reasons so many people struggle when they retire is because they don't have as much human contact as they used to. Perhaps you are a homebody, and you don't love parties. That's fine, but can you meet a friend weekly for lunch or a game of tennis? If you aren't a talker, consider going to a concert where you can listen to the performance in the company of others, but you don't have to talk too much to the other attendees.

Maintain Old Relationships, but Cultivate New Ones, Too

You may be thinking, I have adult children and grandchildren and they take up a lot of my time. Or between work friends, neighbors, and my old college buddies I keep in touch with, I have more friends than I can count. It's very possible that you have a strong network of friends and family, but it is never too late to develop new relationships.

Were you surprised by who did not help out with your older loved one's care? Were there people who helped out that you didn't really know about before your older loved one got sick? Maybe Mom's friend from church you'd only heard mentioned in passing visited each week, while Mom's sister never showed up. People are often surprised by who is or is not available to help out when there is a crisis or a caregiving situation arises. It is never too late to make new friends. This is not to suggest that you widen your social circle simply so you can call on these new friends to be your caregivers someday. But, as we get older, people in our inner circle do pass away and may have care needs of their own.

You probably also know that some people are not meant to be in your life forever. Most people have at least one story of a friend or family member they used to be close with, but who they haven't talked to in ages. Or maybe there was a falling out. The point is, you may think you have more than enough people in your social network, but it is never too late to add new relationships to your life. It is always nice to develop new friendships just to have more like-minded folks to spend time with. Further, there is no shortage of studies that indicate having friendships can protect us from detrimental physical and mental health conditions as well.

Invest Time and Effort in Financial Planning

The best practices for good financial health include saving and investing for retirement and sharing some financial information with future caregivers. Maybe you are one of the rare caregivers whose older loved one had significant financial resources, and you didn't have to concern yourself with how to pay for the items and services she needed. If you are, fantastic! Let's plan on you doing the same for your future caregivers! But more likely you are one of those caregivers whose older loved one did not have enough money to pay for necessary services and items. Hopefully this inspired you to prepare better so you and your future caregivers are not in that position. Some of the best ways to do this include properly saving and investing for retirement years, and letting your most likely future caregiver(s) know what your financial picture looks like.

Unless you are extremely wealthy, it is important to be really mindful of what your likely life expectancy is. How long does your money need to last? What type of lifestyle do you want to live? One of the major problems that many older adults are currently experiencing is that they have outlived their assets, or their retirement plan includes Social Security and that's it. This is one of the reasons an earlier chapter discussed how important it is to really consider whether it makes sense to prematurely quit your job to be a caregiver. Many caregivers who prematurely leave the workforce wind up having less money for their own retirement. If you were in a situation where you had to financially support or even just augment your older loved one's lifestyle and/or healthcare needs, then you especially understand that it would be better to try to not put your future caregiver in that situation. It may be wise to consult with a financial planner about a solid plan if you have not already. If you already have, it is a good idea to update it regularly.

Do you need to get long-term care insurance? Many people think they will never qualify for long-term care insurance, but most middle-aged and many older adults do still qualify. While it may be expensive, it may be worth at least getting a quote to see if it makes sense for you. Like any insurance, you hope you will never need it, but it sure can make the caregiving experience much better for your future caregivers if they don't have to be concerned about money.

Finally, let your future caregiver(s) in on what your financial picture looks like. Again, as with mental health issues, those born prior to 1940 are typically extremely private about their money. They tend to be reluctant to discuss finances, whether their situation is good or bad. Perhaps you are caring for an older loved one who falls into this category, and you experienced firsthand the frustration of not knowing what the budget was for certain services she needed. While you don't need to reveal everything to your adult children or other loved ones, letting them know approximately how much money you have and how to access it (where you've stored account passwords, for instance) will ensure a less stressful caregiving experience for them. And, while you can certainly allow trusted future caregivers access to your money when needed, be sure to identify who has your financial power of attorney in the event you are unable to make decisions. This is typically best handled through working with an elder law attorney (the "Professional Practitioners" section in chapter 11 covers where to find one in your area).

Plan Better for Your End of Life

The best practices for end-of-life issues include preparing a will/trust and an advance healthcare directive. So, enough with the excuses. Create your will and advance directive or living will now. If you have experienced caring for an older loved one who did not have these, you know what a mess it creates when people do not make their wishes known. I believe the absolute greatest gift you can give your future caregiver is this. It is a gift of certainty to know without question what your wishes are and what you do and don't want.

Although you can prepare these yourself, many people feel most comfortable securing the assistance of an elder law attorney. Here are some questions to consider when preparing your advance directive or living will:

- Are there any people you want to protect yourself from?

- Is there anybody you don't want to be part of your caregiving crew?

- Is there anybody you absolutely don't want having any say in your caregiving if you were to become incapacitated?

- What kind of death do you want?

- How do you feel about feeding tubes, ventilators, and artificial hydration?

- Would you want to be kept alive if you were likely to just sit or lie in a hospital room or a nursing home indefinitely, unable to talk or participate in your usual activities?

- Have you consulted a spiritual advisor to help you complete the advance
  directive? (This is an important question because often people want to
  complete their advance directives according to what their religion says,
  but they have not researched fully their religion's stance on issues. If your
  religion is important to you, it's important to have a thorough understanding of what the doctrine says about feeding tubes, ventilators, artificial
  hydration, etc.)

While most people find it difficult to answer these personal and uncomfortable questions, you should nevertheless attempt to answer them honestly
and thoroughly. To help you put this in perspective, if you think these questions
are difficult for you to answer, how do you think your future caregiver(s) will
feel about having to answer them? Again, if your older loved one did not
prepare advance directives or a living will, you probably know the answer to
this one already.

Aim for Ego Integrity

Let's pull together everything we've talked about so far with a closer look at ego
integrity versus despair.

Many decades ago, psychologist Erik Erikson identified a psychological stage
he called "Wisdom, Ego Integrity vs. Despair" for people in older adulthood. This
theory suggests that as we age we all engage in what Erikson calls "a life review."
A life review essentially means you look at how your life has unfolded. How
many regrets do you have? How happy are you? If you look back on your life and
feel pretty good about it, you are likely in "ego integrity" which Erikson says leads
to wisdom. Sure, you might have some regrets, but you feel mostly positive about
how you have spent your time thus far.

If you look back on your life and feel mostly disappointed and regretful, you are
likely in "despair." This is not a pleasant place for your mind to be. Often it leads
to sadness and bitterness and can even trigger depression. Erikson also theorized
that older adults in despair have a harder time accepting their own mortality.

Pretty much everyone has done a life review at one point or another. From
the teenager who decides her grades need to be better to get into a good college

to the middle-aged man who chooses a new career, many of us are assessing and reassessing how our life is going. Often we do this when we make the dreaded New Year's resolutions list. Many of us also do this when we celebrate a landmark birthday like thirty, forty, or fifty, etc.

When you engage in a life review at the New Year or on a landmark birthday, it is common to feel as if you have plenty of time to complete whatever you set your mind to. Maybe you want to lose weight, buy a beach house, spend more time with family, or change your life in some other way. But when we do a life review at age sixty or later, there's often a shift. Look, if you are reading this, you can likely expect to live until you are at least eighty. Even doing a life review at fifty, you may think, *Well, at least I have another thirty or even thirty-plus years left to execute my new plan.* But when you are sixty or older, it starts to hit you: *Whoa, I may not have much time left. I am too old to have a baby. I am too old to change careers. I am too old to find a good relationship. I am too old to learn how to play piano.*

Despair can kick in.

Life Ring: If you are feeling despair when you do a life review, remember there are many, many wonderful examples of older adults who have reinvented their lives when others may have deemed it "too late." Look at actor and social activist George Takei—best known for his role in *Star Trek.* Over the past decade, while in his seventies, he took on the announcer role on *The Howard Stern Show*; brought his show, *Allegiance,* to Broadway; and became a social media juggernaut. Some might say he is experiencing his best years in his seventies.

I had the pleasure of meeting him briefly when my company, Jenerations Health Education, was one of the cosponsors of a speech he gave at a National Speakers Association convention. Check out the media section of my website, www.jenerationshealth.com, to read a series of articles on what older adults can learn from George Takei.

Think for a moment about the older loved one you have cared for. For most caregivers it's pretty easy to see which side the older loved one leaned toward. If you are still not sure, perhaps the case described in the following box will help you, because it illustrates how two people with nearly identical lives can find themselves at opposite ends of the integrity-despair spectrum after reviewing their lives.

SIMILAR LIVES, DIFFERENT PERSPECTIVES

Born within months of each other, Maura and Bridget are cousins. They grew up in the same middle-class neighborhood in Philadelphia and have lived in Philadelphia their entire lives, near their extended family members. They both recently turned seventy-five and are looking back on their lives.

Both women married young, in their early twenties. Both women were stay-at-home mothers, and each raised two children. Their husbands earned roughly the same amount of money. The difference between them is the lens through which they view their lives.

Maura always hoped to leave Philadelphia. When she was a young wife, she hoped she and her family would move outside the city, perhaps to the prestigious Main Line area or somewhere in Bucks County. She had always wanted to become a teacher. But she never felt like it was a real possibility for her, because no women in her family had ever attended college. She also had always dreamed of purchasing a summer house at the nearby New Jersey shore town of North Wildwood. Maura envisioned that she, her husband, children, grandchildren, and future generations would gather at this beach house for long weekends each summer. Maura also always wanted to visit Europe. Unfortunately for Maura, none of these things have yet happened. Maura complains pretty often about what she does not have.

Bridget enjoys living in Philadelphia and always has. She liked being a homemaker and mother and loved the camaraderie of raising her children near her siblings and cousins. She loves that she, her husband, children, and grandchildren go away to the nearby Pocono Mountains annually to spend time together. Although she, too, wished for a vacation home (in the mountains, not at the beach), she does not think often about the fact that they never bought one. While Bridget would never suggest her life has gone perfectly, she is pretty satisfied overall. She occasionally thinks it must be nice to have more money and to own a vacation house in the mountains, but she rarely brings it up.

If the late Erik Erickson were to meet with Maura and Bridget, obviously he'd deem Maura in despair and Bridget in ego integrity. It's all about their perspectives. If you didn't already, you probably know now which camp the older loved one you cared for fell into. If you were performing a life review today, which camp would you fall into?

~~~~~~

Strive for ego integrity rather than despair. Perhaps optimism and gratitude don't come so naturally to you. Consider working on this. Some ways to get closer to ego integrity may include keeping a gratitude journal, meditating, or entering into psychotherapy. Studies suggest that you can become more optimistic; it's not too late if you have a pessimistic nature. Your future caregiver will feel less burdened if you are grateful and optimistic—in ego integrity rather than despair. Your aging process will also go better. And, should you feel like you are in despair, get help.

Get Help for Mental Health Conditions Early and Often

This special section would not be complete without addressing the very real fact that many of us are trying to cope with life despite having a chronic or an acute mental health condition. So, even though the best practices for maintaining good mental and cognitive health outlined earlier may help you, if you suspect you are struggling with a true clinical mental health condition, it's vital to seek professional help.

Thousands of mental health conditions are catalogued by the American Psychiatric Association in the *Diagnostic and Statistical Manual of Mental Disorders* (commonly known as *DSM-5*). This section is only going to touch on two of the most common conditions for caregivers: anxiety disorders and clinical depression:

> **Anxiety and worry.** Conditions involving anxious thoughts, worry, and panic are among the most common conditions caregivers face. These are known, according to the *DSM-5*, as anxiety disorders, obsessive-compulsive and related disorders, and trauma and stress-related disorders. Many people who struggle with anxiety have dealt with it since adolescence or young adulthood. Typically, many of these disorders are chronic conditions that can be treated but are often triggered during times of stress. Many people who suffer with an anxiety disorder don't always acknowledge it as such, referring to it instead as "my nerves" or "I'm a worrier."

> **Clinical depression.** Clinical depression includes symptoms like sadness, change in eating or sleep habits, low energy, and not enjoying activities one used to like. According to the Anxiety and Depression Association of America, depression can sometimes even include physical symptoms like headaches. And for older adults, depression can sometimes include memory loss and confusion.

If you are taking care of an older loved one with an anxiety disorder or depression, it is very possible the patient struggles with acknowledging that a problem exists. Those born prior to 1940 are especially prone to feeling shame about a mental health condition. It is also quite possible that the older loved one refused treatment, or if she did accept treatment, there was tremendous reluctance.

While there is still some stigma associated with going to counseling or taking psychotropic medication, there is a lot less these days. If you think about it, you probably personally know at least a few people who have openly talked about going to marriage counseling, that their kids or grandkids have seen the school psychologist, and that another friend is taking Prozac or Xanax. While I have mixed feelings about the fact that pharmaceutical companies have taken to directly marketing to patients via television commercials, I believe there is some good coming out of that practice. Viewers may look at a commercial and think, *Those symptoms sound like me* and decide to talk to their doctor about it.

To have a better aging experience and to make things easier on your future caregiver, try to address any mental health conditions early. If you took care of an older loved one who refused to address a mental health condition, you know this better than anyone! Especially with anxiety and depression, medication is not always indicated. Long-term counseling is not usually necessary either. There are also many holistic ways to treat milder symptoms of anxiety and depression, including yoga, meditation, exercise, and acupuncture, just to name a few. So get help when you need it. Not only will this improve your quality of life now—and your aging experience—your future caregiver will also surely appreciate it.

~~~~~~

FIND A GOOD MENTAL HEALTH PROVIDER

How do you find a quality psychotherapist or counselor? Discussing a referral to a mental health provider with your primary care doctor is often the best first step. Also, if you do know a friend or family member who talks openly about seeing a therapist, consider asking that person for the name of the provider. You can also usually perform an online search on your insurance provider's website for counselors near you. If you are struggling with anxiety or depressive symptoms specifically, you may want to search the Anxiety and Depression Association of

America's database at http://treatment.adaa.org/ to find a registered
member who has experience treating those conditions.

~~~~~~

Learn from when *You* Went Overboard: Set Yourself and Your Future Caregivers Up for Success

One of the best ways I know for you to give your future caregivers a jump on
success is to create a lifestyle care plan. This is a way to inform your future
caregivers in great detail about your wishes concerning your lifestyle if you are
unable to speak or communicate in some other manner.

A private company, Advance Care Plan, offers a lifestyle care plan service.
They provide a template where you can create some rules and suggestions for
your future caregivers to follow. Once you pay a fee for the service, you can
create this document online and periodically update it with all the information
you may not be able to tell a caregiver in the future. This is not a will or an
advance directive. It goes above and beyond those legal documents.

When might something like this come in handy? Well, those of you who
have taken care of an older loved one with advanced dementia may already be
thinking how useful something like this would have been when Mom's doctor
recommended a low-sugar diet. If Mom had written in a lifestyle care plan,
"Let me eat whatever I want, even if there are health consequences," it would
have been clear what her wishes were. This document would have saved your
caregiving crew from wondering, *Should we just let her eat cookies for dinner
because that's all she seems to enjoy lately?*

A lifestyle care plan could also be invaluable if someone has had a stroke, is
non-communicative at the end of life, and in countless other scenarios.

In my lifestyle care plan, I would include a detailed instruction such as "I
always want a glass of water within reach." This is such a simple, easy request,
but I doubt it would even occur to my own husband to make sure this happened
if I were not able to communicate. One patient I worked with said she was going
to use this document to remind her future caregivers that she absolutely couldn't
stand the smell of strong perfume or cologne. These are the types of preferences
you may have trouble articulating after a surgery or if you have a dementia

diagnosis. These are the types of things you can think about now and have in writing to accompany your medical and legal documents.

If you don't want to spend the money on a service like www.advancecare plan.com, consider keeping a notebook now for your future caregiver. Just make sure it's legible, and store it with your medical and legal documents. And make sure your attorney and/or next of kin knows exactly where to find all these items. Start today!

Let people know now what you want in your future. Talk about it often. My husband and I currently plan to live in a continuing care retirement community (CCRC) someday. We also talk about how we would never want to be on a feeding tube or respirator if there would be no reasonable hope for a quality of life recovery. We would not want that to be the way to extend our lives if we had a terminal illness or suffered a stroke. During the final months of my grandmother's life, my family (eleven of us total) had a conference call regularly to discuss what was going on with my grandmother's health and how we were going to handle her care. One of these conference calls focused on the need to speak with her about updating advance directives. During this call, many family members admitted that they didn't have living wills or advance directives. One of my aunts used the occasion to tell everyone that if she is a "vegetable" she wants "the plug pulled." While this wasn't the most politically correct way of articulating her wishes, we all got her meaning.

I hope you will never need a caregiver. But statistically speaking, you probably will. To reduce stress for your future caregivers, let the people who care about you know where your documents are. Discuss what your wishes are now. Without obsessing, embrace as many healthy habits as you can. Be part of the paradigm change in our culture where people tell their loved ones what they do and don't want if they are unable to speak for themselves. Do your part so your future caregiver and your whole caregiving crew will have the least stressful caregiving experience possible.

CONCLUSION

Thank you for reading this book and thank you for being a caregiver to someone you love. I hope you have gotten ideas and inspiration about how to save money, energy, and time while caregiving to reduce stress for yourself and your caregiving crew.

I'd love to hear how you have begun reducing your stress in caregiving! If you'd like to connect with me to share your comments or to ask a question, please reach out in one of these ways:

- jen@cruisingthroughcaregiving.com

- www.cruisingthroughcaregiving.com

- https://www.facebook.com/jenerationshealth/

- https://www.linkedin.com/company/jenerations-health-education-inc-

- Twitter @fitzpatrickjen

Please check out www.jenerationshealth.com for more free articles, movie and book reviews, and other resources that may be able to help you continue to reduce your stress.

I truly hope this book has helped you cruise through caregiving as smoothly as possible.

ACKNOWLEDGMENTS

Thank you to my husband, Sean FitzPatrick. You are the greatest blessing of my life. I am grateful every day for your love, support, and complete acceptance of me. Thanks for never saying that starting a business or writing a book was crazy!

I am grateful for all my friends, family, and colleagues who always asked how the book was coming and didn't give me too much grief when I told them I was "still working on it."

Greenleaf Book Group assigned me the best possible match for an editor, Linda O'Doughda. Her insights and suggestions were invaluable. Thanks also to the whole team at Greenleaf Book Group for your professionalism, support, and belief in this book.

Thank you to all the busy professionals in the world of caregiving who agreed to be interviewed for this book or to give helpful advice about its contents, including: Allan Anderson, MD; Jane Anthony, LBSW; Cheryl Burris, RN; Madelyn Campbell, MSW, LCSW; Evan Farr, JD, CELA; Mary Faith Ferretto, MSW, LCSW-C; Joanna Frankel, MSW, LCSW-C; Mary Fridley, RN, BC; Sherry Gilde; Stephanie Goldstein, LBSW; Heather Guerieri, RN, MSN; Kevin Knapp; Christine Levy; Cathy Lonas, RN, BSN, MSBA; Denise Manifold, MA; Louise Montgomery, ADC/MC CDP; Ann Morrison, RN, PhD; Marie O'Shea; Taylor Penvose; Peter Rabins, MD, MPH; Lisa Chapin Robinette, CSA; Libby Shadis, MSN, CRNP; Dianne Turpin, MBA, M.Ed.; Colleen Walker, CTRS; Noelle Wilson; and Gail Yerkie, RN, BSN.

Thank you to the very special team at Jenerations Health Education: Cathy Brock, MA; Mary Fridley, RN, BC; Lesa Lee, LCSW-C; Barb Miller; Ann Morrison, RN, PhD; and Darlene Snow. You have my most sincere gratitude for all that you do. Thank you to all of our wonderful clients and audiences—we would not exist without you. Thank you to the staff and members of the National Speakers Association who gave so much instrumental advice either personally or through their down-to-earth presentations on the subject of authorship and publishing a book—especially Dianna Booher, Bill Cates, Ron Culberson, Valerie Grubb, Vicki Hess, Shep Hyken, and Rory Vaden.

Last, but most important, I thank God for all my many blessings, including finding my passion so early in life and for giving me the opportunity to serve older adults and their families.

Appendix

MEET THE EXPERTS

Allan Anderson, MD, is the vice president of dementia care practice at Integrace and is the medical director for the Samuel and Alexia Bratton Memory Clinic at Bayleigh Chase. Dr. Anderson is also an assistant professor in the Department of Psychiatry at Johns Hopkins University and a past president of the American Association for Geriatric Psychiatry (AAGP).

Cheryl Burris, RN, is the owner of Senior Living Geriatric Care Management Services. Burris has over twenty years' experience working with older adults and their families.

Madelyn Campbell, MSW, LCSW, is a senior social worker at a large Philadelphia-area continuing care retirement community (CCRC). She received her masters of social work degree from Bryn Mawr College.

Evan Farr, JD, CELA, is a certified elder law attorney and author of three best-selling books, including *The Nursing Home Survival Guide.* Farr has been named by SuperLawyers.com as among the top five percent of elder law and estate planning attorneys in Virginia every year since 2007, and in the Washington, DC, metro area every year since 2008.

Mary Faith Ferretto, MSW, LCSW-C, is an aging life care expert and the president of Ferretto Elder Care Consulting.

Joanna Frankel, MSW, LCSW-C, received her masters of social work from the University of Maryland. She currently works as the director of social work for Lorien Health Systems.

Sherry Gilde is a sales counselor with Five Star Senior Living at the Somerford Place of Annapolis community. She has twenty years' experience working with older adults and caregivers.

Stephanie Goldstein, LBSW, is the director of social services at a Genesis HealthCare facility. She has worked in the areas of dementia management, nursing home social work, and assisted living marketing for over fifteen years.

Heather Guerieri, RN, MSN, is the executive director of Compass Regional Hospice. She received her undergraduate degree in nursing at Salisbury University and her masters in nursing at Towson University.

Kevin Knapp is the owner of a New Jersey franchise of Right at Home, an in-home senior care company based out of Omaha, Nebraska.

Christine Levy has over fifteen years' experience working with older adults. She has worked in several Midwest and East Coast assisted living and long-term care communities in the marketing and sales departments.

Cathy Lonas, RN, BSN, MSBA, owner of Advocate 360 (an aging life care/geriatric care management company) in the Washington, DC, area, has over twenty years' experience working with older adults and their families. She earned her bachelor of science in nursing from Johns Hopkins University and her master's degree in marketing and gerontology from Virginia Technical University. Although Lonas held her master's degree prior to becoming a registered nurse, she intentionally sought work as a nursing assistant for a full year to learn as much as possible about what really goes on in a nursing home on the night shift.

Denise Manifold, MA, earned a master's degree in health promotion from the University of Delaware and has worked in the senior living industry for over fifteen years. Manifold has spent the majority of her career in senior living sales and sales management and is currently a regional vice president of sales with Brightview Senior Living.

Louise Montgomery, ADC/MC CDP, is the director of recreation and engagement, assisted living, for Bayleigh Chase.

Ann Morrison, RN, PhD, is a former Johns Hopkins School of Medicine faculty member and director of their Alzheimer's Treatment and Memory Center Caregiver Family Program. She is currently an associate speaker with Jenerations Health Education.

Marie O'Shea received her bachelor's degree from Towson University and has been working in the field of dementia care for over twenty years. O'Shea is currently a community sales director with Brightview Senior Living.

Taylor Penvose has a bachelor's degree in gerontology and has worked for more than fifteen years in dementia care. Penvose is currently a marketing director with Arden Courts, a company specializing in senior living memory care.

Peter Rabins, MD, MPH, is coauthor of the renowned book *The 36-Hour Day*. He earned his medical degree from Tulane University and is a former professor of psychiatry and behavioral sciences at Johns Hopkins University.

Lisa Chapin Robinette, CSA, is a certified senior advisor. Robinette previously worked in senior living marketing and for P.A.C.E., a Program for All-Inclusive Care for the Elderly. She earned her bachelor's degree from the University of Nevada, Reno.

Libby Shadis, MSN, CRNP, is a geriatric nurse practitioner with over fifteen years' experience working with older adults and their families. She currently practices with Personal Physician Care.

Dianne Turpin, MBA, M.Ed, is retired. Turpin worked for twenty-plus years with two Area Agencies on Aging.

Colleen Walker, CTRS, has over twenty years of senior care experience in administration, management, and therapeutic recreation. She is currently an executive director with Brookdale Senior Living.

Noelle Wilson has over twenty years of experience in senior living and has been both a marketing director and executive director at Arden Courts, a company specializing in senior living memory care.

Gail Yerkie, RN, BSN, is the director of Kent County Medical Adult Day Care Center.

REFERENCES AND RESOURCES

References

Administration on Aging, US Department of Health and Human Services, Administration for Community Living. Accessed March 1, 2016. "Aging Statistics." http://www.aoa.acl.gov/aging_statistics/index.aspx.

Administration on Aging, US Department of Health and Human Services, National Center on Elder Abuse. Accessed February 14, 2016. "Types of Abuse." http://www.ncea.aoa.gov/FAQ/Type_Abuse/index.aspx#self.

Alzheimer's Association, Alzheimer's and Dementia Caregiver Center. Accessed February 12, 2016. "Wandering and Getting Lost." https://www.alz.org/care/alzheimers-dementia-wandering.asp.

American Psychiatric Association. 2013. *Diagnostic and Statistical Manual of Mental Disorders (DSM-5)*, 5th ed. American Psychiatric Publishing.

Barker, Robert L. 2003. *The Social Work Dictionary.* NASW Press.

Bennetts, Leslie. 2007. *The Feminine Mistake: Are We Giving Up Too Much?* Hachette Books.

Berglund, Erik, Per Lytsy, and Ragnar Westerling. July 29, 2015. "Health and Wellbeing in Informal Caregivers and Non-Caregivers: A Comparative Cross-Sectional Study of the Swedish General Population." *Health and Quality of Life Outcomes* 13: 109. doi: 10.1186/s12955-015-0309-2.

Caposella, Cappy, and Shelia Warnock. 2004. *Share the Care: How to Organize a Group to Care for Someone Who Is Seriously Ill.* Touchstone.

Centers for Disease Control and Prevention, Division of Nutrition, Physical Activity, and Obesity. Last updated June 4, 2015. "Physical Activity Is Essential to Healthy Aging." http://www.cdc.gov/physicalactivity/basics/older_adults/index.htm.

Farr, Evan. 2012. *The Nursing Home Survival Guide*. Quality Legal Publications.

Feil, Naomi, and Vicki de Klerk-Rubin. 2012. *The Validation Breakthrough*, 3rd ed. Health Professions Press.

Heyman, J. D. December 15, 2003. "The Long Goodbye." *People* 60(24). http://www.people.com/people/archive/article/0,,20148963,00.html.

Hooyman, Nancy, and H. Asuman S. Kiyak. 2010. *Social Gerontology: A Multidisciplinary Perspective*, 9th ed. Pearson.

Hospice Foundation of America. 2014. "What Is Hospice?" http://hospicefoundation.org/End-of-Life-Support-and-Resources/Coping-with-Terminal-Illness/Hospice-Services.

Kroenke et al. May 2012. "Social Networks, Social Support and Burden in Relationships, and Mortality after Breast Cancer Diagnosis." *Breast Cancer Research and Treatment* 133(1): 375–385. doi: 10.1007/s10549-012-2253-8.

Lebow, Grace, and Barbara Kane. 1999. *Coping with Your Difficult Older Parent*. William Morris Paperbacks.

Litzelman et al. June 2014. "Role of Global Stress in the Health-Related Quality of Life of Caregivers: Evidence from the Survey of the Health of Wisconsin." *Quality of Life Research* 23(5): 1569–1578. doi: 10.1007/s11136-013-0598-z.

Mace, Nancy L., and Peter V. Rabins. 2011. *The 36-Hour Day*. Johns Hopkins University Press.

Maust, D. T., H. C. Kales, and F. C. Blow. July 2015. "Mental Health Care Delivered to Younger and Older Adults by Office-Based Physicians Nationally." *Journal of the American Geriatrics Society* 63(7): 1364–1372. doi: 10.1111/jgs.13494.

McLeod, Beth Witrogen. 1999. *Caregiving: The Spiritual Journey of Love, Loss and Renewal*. Wiley.

Morris, Virginia. 2014. *How to Care for Aging Parents*, 3rd ed. Workman Publishing Company.

National Guardianship Association. http://www.guardianship.org/pdf/ Terminology.pdf.

Parker, Kim, and Eileen Patten, "The Sandwich Generation: Rising Financial Burdens for Middle-Aged Americans," *Social & Demographic Trends*, Pew Research Center, January 30, 2013, http://www.pewsocialtrends .org/2013/01/30/the-sandwich-generation/.

Perkins et al. July 2013. "Caregiving Strain and All-Cause Mortality: Evidence from the REGARDS study." *The Journals of Gerontology*, Series B 68(4): 504– 512. doi: 10.1093/geronb/gbs084.

Rhodes, Linda. 2012. *The Essential Guide to Caring for Aging Parents*. Penguin Group.

Roth et al. November 2013. "Family Caregiving and All-Cause Mortality: Findings from a Population-Based Propensity-Matched Analysis." *American Journal of Epidemiology* 178(10): 1571–1578. doi: 10.1093/aje/kwt225.

Seeman et al. July 2011. "Histories of Social Engagement and Adult Cognition: Midlife in the U.S. Study." *The Journals of Gerontology Series B: Psychological Sciences and Social Sciences* 66B (Suppl 1): i141–i152. doi: 10.1093/geronb/ gbq091.

Seliger, Susan. January 14, 2013."Preparing for a Loved One to Die at Home." *The New York Times*. New Old Age blog. http://newoldage.blogs.nytimes. com/2013/01/14/preparing-for-a-loved-one-to-die-at-home/?_r=0.

Sheehy, Gail. 2011. *Passages in Caregiving*. William Morrow Paperbacks.

Tao, A., and Jeffrey S. Janofsky. "Capacity, Competency, and Guardianship." *Johns Hopkins Psychiatry Guide*.

Teo et al. October 2015. "Does Mode of Contact with Different Types of Social Relationships Predict Depression Among Older Adults? Evidence from a Nationally Representative Survey." *Journal of the American Geriatrics Society* 63(10): 2014–2022. doi: 10.1111/jgs.13667.

Thomas, Evan, and Eleanor Clift. June 21, 2004. "As the Shadows Fell. The Story of Ronald Reagan's Last Decade Is at Once Grim and Tender. The Personal History of How Nancy Coped with his Alzheimer's." *Newsweek.* http://www.newsweek.com/shadows-fell-128609.

Thomas, G. et al. May 2015. "Informal Carers' Health-Related Quality of Life and Patient Experience in Primary Care: Evidence from 195,364 Carers in England Responding to a National Survey." *BMC Family Practice* 16:62. doi: 10.1186/s12875-015-0277-y.

Westheimer, Ruth K., with Pierre A. Lehu. 2012. *Dr. Ruth's Guide for the Alzheimer's Caregiver.* Quill Driver Books.

World Health Organization. 1946. "Constitution of WHO: Principles." http://www.who.int/about/mission/en/.

Resources

Administration for Community Living, US Department of Health and Human Services—www.aoa.gov

Aging Life Care Association (formerly National Association of Professional Geriatric Care Managers)—www.aginglifecare.org

Alzheimer's Association—www.alz.org

American Academy of Neurology—https://patients.aan.com/findaneurologist/

American Association for Geriatric Psychiatry—http://www.aagponline.org

American Cancer Society—www.cancer.org

American Diabetes Association—www.diabetes.org

American Geriatrics Society's Health in Aging Foundation— http://www
.healthinaging.org/find-a-geriatrics-healthcare-professional/

American Heart Association—www.heart.org

American Lung Association—www.lung.org

Anxiety and Depression Association of America—http://treatment.adaa.org/

Area Agency on Aging. See National Association of Area Agencies on Aging.

Argentum (formerly Assisted Living Federation of American; database of
assisted living communities)—www.alfa.org

Arthritis Foundation—www.arthritis.org

The Association for Frontotemporal Degeneration—www.theaftd.org

Continuing Care Retirement Communities (CCRCs) database—www.ccrcs.com

Creutzfeldt-Jakob Disease Foundation—www.cjdfoundation.org

Eldercare locator, Department of Health and Human Services (to find nearby
services for older adults and their families by topic)—www.eldercare.gov

Family Caregiver Alliance National Center on Caregiving—www.caregiver.org

Family Medical Leave Act, United States Department of Labor—www.dol.gov
/whd/fmla/

Geriatric Mental Health Foundation—www.gmhfonline.org

Hospice Foundation of America—www.hospicefoundation.org

Huntington's Disease Society of America—www.hdsa.org

IRS (Internal Revenue Service; tax info for caregivers)—https://www.irs.gov
/Help-&-Resources/Tools-&-FAQs/FAQs-for-Individuals/Frequently-Asked
-Tax-Questions-&-Answers/IRS-Procedures/For-Caregivers

Lewy Body Dementia Association—www.lbda.org

Life Care Planning Law Firms Association—www.lcplfa.org

Mediate.com, Everything Mediation (database of mediators)—www.mediate.com

Medicare (and a database of nursing homes)—www.medicare.gov

National Academy of Elder Law Attorneys—www.naela.org

National Adult Day Services Association—www.nadsa.org

National Adult Protective Services Association—www.napsa-now.org

National Alliance on Mental Illness—www.nami.org

National Association for Home Care & Hospice—www.nahc.org

National Association of Area Agencies on Aging (to find an Area Agency on Aging)—www.n4a.org

National Center on Elder Abuse, Department of Health & Human Services' Administration on Aging—www.ncea.aoa.gov

National Elder Law Foundation—www.nelf.org

National Hospice and Palliative Care Organization—www.nhpco.org/find-hospice

National Institute on Aging, US Department of Health and Human Services—www.nia.nih.gov

National Sleep Foundation—www.sleepfoundation.org

National Stroke Association—www.stroke.org

State Health Insurance Assistance Programs—www.shiptacenter.org

World Health Organization—www.who.int/en/

INDEX

O

ABOUT THE AUTHOR

Jennifer L. FitzPatrick, MSW, CSP (Certified Speaking Professional), is a gerontologist with over twenty years' experience in working with older adults and older generations. She started her career in a nursing home at age sixteen and is the founder of Jenerations Health Education, a full-service training company.

Through Jenerations Health Education, Jennifer assists organizations across all industries to increase profits and employee productivity by promoting support for working caregivers and improving communication between different generations. She helps healthcare organizations tailor services and programs to meet the needs of the ever-expanding aging patient population. Jennifer and her team also offer Care Coaching services to individual caregivers.

Jennifer holds a master's degree in social work from the University of Maryland and recently earned the Certified Speaking Professional (CSP) designation through the National Speakers Association. The CSP is held by only approximately seven hundred professional speakers worldwide.

Jennifer is an education consultant with the Alzheimer's Association of Greater Maryland and has also has taught gerontology at the college level since 2001. Her current academic appointments include teaching as an adjunct instructor with Johns Hopkins University's Certificate on Aging program. She is passionate about helping students transition into careers serving older adults and their caregivers.